ALAN DUNN'S
ULTIMATE COLLECTION
of CAKE DECORATING

ALAN DUNN'S

ULTIMATE COLLECTION
of CAKE DECORATING

NEW
HOLLAND

CONTENTS

CAKES

Introduction

My interest in cake decorating was fuelled at an early age – my grandfather was a baker and although he had retired by the time I had taken a real interest, the seeds had already been planted. But it was only later on in my teens that I started developing ideas and designs for what I think of as proper celebration cakes.

In December 1986 I decorated my very first Christmas cake – this was not a particularly impressive design and the royal iced coating was so badly executed that it was almost impossible to cut through – but it spurred me on to seek cake decorating books from both the school and public libraries. A few months later I discovered some magical books – they contained beautifully designed and executed sugarpaste-coated cakes decorated with sugar flowers. It was then that I realised cake decorating was going to play a major part in my life. The next opportunity I had to design a celebration cake was for Mother's Day. I decorated the cake with simple hand-modelled sugarpaste roses – this endeavour was much more successful than the previous year's Christmas cake attempt and really marked the starting point for my interest and passion for making sugar flowers. The next cake I worked on was for my grandparents' diamond anniversary – a bell-shaped cake with hand-moulded roses. It was around this time that I attended my first sugar flower class and joined The British Sugarcraft Guild. It was through these classes and monthly guild branch meetings that I realised that sugar flowers could be taken to another level.

This book is a celebration of cakes, flowers, fruit, vegetables and the odd nut too! Flowers and cakes have proved to be a successful combination for centuries and for me too they are a real motivation to strive to create interesting floral designs for any occasion. For years I have included berries, fruits and nuts into my work and for the first time I am now creating vegetables, which are proving to be a really fun addition.

Here, I have tried to create designs that are ideal as impressive centrepieces for most of the major celebrations in life. Many of the cake themes are interchangeable to make them appropriate for other occasions, and hopefully the variety of designs will help you to create an individual style of your own too!

Alan Dunn

EQUIPMENT AND MATERIALS

There is a huge array of sugarcraft equipment and materials commercially available. Here, a variety of items that I consider to be very useful are listed.

EQUIPMENT

Non-stick board

This is an essential addition to the flower-maker's workbox. Avoid white boards as they strain the eyes too much. Some boards can be very shiny, making it difficult to frill the petals against them. If this is the case, simply roughen up the surface using some fine glass paper prior to use or turn over the board and use the back, which is often less shiny. I always apply a thin layer of white vegetable fat rubbed into the surface of the board, then remove most of the excess with dry kitchen paper – this stops the paste sticking to the board and also makes you check each time to see if it is clean from food colour.

Rolling pins

It's good to have a selection of non-stick rolling pins in various sizes. They are essential for rolling out flowerpaste, sugarpaste and almond paste successfully.

Foam pads

Foam pads are ideal to place petals and leaves on while you soften the edges – especially if you have hot hands that tend to dissolve the petals as you are working them. Prior to buying this product, check that it has a good surface as some have a rough-textured surface that will tear the edges of

your petals or leave marks on them. I either prefer the large blue pad called a Billy's block or the yellow celpad.

Wires and floristry tape

I buy mostly white paper-covered wires, preferring to colour or tape over as I work. The quality varies between brands. The most consistent in quality are the Japanese Sunrise wires. These are available from 35-gauge (very fine but rare) to 18-gauge (thicker). Floristry tape is used in the construction of stems and bouquets. They contain a glue that is released when the tape is stretched. I use mainly nile green, brown and white tape from the Lion Brand tape company.

Tape shredder

This tool contains three razor blades to cut floristry tape into quarter-widths. I have a couple of tape shredders and have removed two blades from one of them so that it cuts the tape into half-widths. It is often best to use a tiny amount of cold cream rubbed onto the blades with a cotton bud and also a little onto the lid that presses against the blades – this will help the tape run smoothly against the blades as it can often stick to an excess of glue left behind from the tape. It is also wise to remove any excess build-up of glue from the blades

using fine-nose pliers and also to replace the blades regularly. Handle with care at all times.

Paintbrushes and dusting brushes

Good-quality, synthetic brushes or synthetic-blend brushes from the art shop are best for flower-making. I use mainly short, flat, not too soft bristle brushes for applying layers of food colour dusts to flowers and leaves. It is best to keep brushes for certain colours so that it takes away the need to wash them quite so regularly. I use finer sable or synthetic-blend brushes for painting fine lines or detail spots onto petals.

Petal, flower and leaf cutters and veiners

There is a huge selection of petal, flower and leaf cutters available from cake decorating shops, both in metal and plastic. Petal and leaf moulds/veiners are made from food-grade silicone rubber. They are very useful for creating natural petal and leaf texturing for sugar work. The moulds have been made using mostly real plant material, giving the finished sugar flower a realistic finish. Like the flower cutters, there is an impressive selection of commercial veiners to choose from.

Posy picks

These are made from food-grade plastic and come in various sizes. They are used to hold the handle of a spray or bouquet of flowers into the cake. The food-grade plastic protects the cake of contamination from the wires and floristry tape used in the construction of floral sprays. Never push wires directly into a cake.

Stamens and thread

There is a huge selection of commercial stamens available from cake decorating shops. I use mainly fine white and seed-head stamens, which I can then colour using powder colours. Fine cotton thread is best for stamens. I use lace-making Brock 120 white thread, although some thicker threads may also be useful for larger

flowers. An emery board is great for fluffing up the tips of the thread to forms anthers.

Glue

Non-toxic glue sticks can be bought from stationery or art shops and are great for fixing ribbon to the cake drum's edge. Always make sure that the glue does not come into direct contact with the cake. I use

Homemade leaf/petal veiners

There are several craft products available that can be used to make moulds for leaves, petals, fruit, nuts, etc… It is important to try to find a food-grade product. Silicone plastique is a good medium to use with a quick-drying time. When making a mould of a petal or leaf it is important to choose items with prominent veins. Note that most flowers and foliage produce stronger veins as they age. To make a mould:

1 Silicone plastique can be purchased as a kit. Mix the two compounds together thoroughly. The white material is the base and the blue is the catalyst – once mixed you will have about 10 to 20 minutes' working time before the mixed medium sets – this often depends on the room temperature at the time. Flatten the product onto a sheet of plastic wrap or a plastic food bag: this is important as the product tends to stick to everything in its sight.

2 Press the back of your chosen leaf or petal into the silicone putty, taking care to press the surface evenly to avoid air bubbles, which will create a fault in the veiner. When the compound has set, simply peel off the leaf or petal. Trim away any excess silicone from around the mould using a pair of scissors.

3 Next, very lightly grease the leaf veiner with cold cream cleanser – be careful not to block up the veins with the cream as this will ruin the final result. Mix up another amount of the two compounds and press firmly on top of the first half of the leaf veiner, again taking care to press evenly. When the second half has set, pull the two sides apart: you now have a double-sided leaf veiner!

a hi-tack non-toxic craft glue to attach stamens to the end of wires. I feel that no harm is being done sticking inedible items together with other inedible items. However, the glue should not come into direct contact with the sugar petals as it will dissolve them.

Scissors, pliers and wire cutters

Fine embroidery and curved scissors are very useful for cutting fine petals, thread and ribbons too. Larger florist's scissors are useful for cutting wires and ribbon. Small, fine-nose pliers are another essential. Good-quality pliers from electrical supply shops are best – they are expensive but well worth the investment. Electrical wire cutters are useful for cutting heavier wires.

Plain-edge cutting wheel (PME) and scalpel

This is rather like a small double-sided pizza wheel. It is great for cutting out quick petals and leaves, and also for adding division lines to buds. A scalpel is essential for marking veins, adding texture and cutting out petal shapes too.

Tweezers

It is important to use fine, angled tweezers without ridges (or teeth). They are useful for pinching ridges on petals and holding very fine petals and stamens. They are also very handy when arranging flowers to push smaller items into difficult, tight areas of an arrangement or spray.

Metal ball tools (CC/Celcakes)

I use mostly metal ball tools to work the edges of petals and leaves. These are heavier than plastic ball tools, which means that less effort is needed to soften the paste. I mostly work the tool using a rubbing or rolling action against the paste, positioning it half on the petal/leaf edge and half on my hand or foam pad that the petal is resting against. It can also be used to 'cup' or hollow out petals to form interesting shapes.

Dresden/veining tool (J or PME)

The fine end of this tool is great for adding central veins to petals or leaves, and the broader end can be used for working the edges of a leaf to give a serrated effect or a 'double-frilled' effect on the edges of petals. Simply press the tool against the paste repeatedly to create a tight frilled effect or pull the tool against the paste on a non-stick board to create serrations. The fine end of the tool can also be used to cut into the edge of the paste to cut and flick finer serrated-edged leaves. I use a black tool by Jem for finer, smaller leaves and flowers, and the larger yellow PME tool for larger flowers.

Ceramic tools (HP/Holly Products)

A smooth ceramic tool is used for curling the edges of petals and hollowing out throats of small flowers, as well as serving the purpose of a mini rolling pin. Another of the ceramic tools, known as the silk veining tool, is wonderful for creating delicate veins and frills to petal edges.

Celsticks (CC/Celcakes)

Celsticks come in four sizes and are ideal for rolling out small petals and leaves and to create thick ridges. The pointed end of the tool is great for opening up the centre of 'hat'-type flowers. The rounded end can be used in the same way as a ball tool, to soften edges and hollow out petals.

Kitchen paper ring formers

These are great for holding and supporting petals to create a cupped shape as they dry allowing the paste/petal to breathe, which speeds up the drying process (plastic formers tend to slow down the drying process). To make, cut a strip of kitchen paper, twist it back onto itself and then tie it in a loop, or for larger petals, cut a sheet of kitchen paper diagonally across, twist and tie.

MATERIALS
Egg white

You will need fresh egg white to stick petals together and to sometimes alter the consistency of the paste if it is too dry. Many cake decorators avoid the use of fresh egg white because of salmonella scares. I continue to use Lion brand eggs and always work with a fresh egg white each time I make flowers. There are commercially available edible glues which can be used instead of egg white but I find that these tend to dissolve the sugar slightly before allowing it to dry, resulting in weak petals.

White vegetable fat

I use this to grease non-stick boards and then wipe of it off with dry kitchen paper. This does two things: it conditions the board, helping prevent the flowerpaste sticking to it, and it also removes excess food colour that might have been left from the previous flower-making session. You can also add a tiny amount of white fat to the paste if it is very sticky. However, you must not add too much as it will make the paste short and slow down the drying process. You must also be careful not to leave too much fat on the board as greasy patches will show up on the petals when you apply the dry dusting colours.

Cornflour bag

An essential if you have hot hands like mine! Cornflour is a lifesaver when the flowerpaste is sticky. It is best to make a cornflour bag using disposable nappy liners; these can be bought from most large chemists. Fold a couple of layers of nappy liners together and add a good tablespoon of cornflour on top. Tie the nappy liner together into a bag using ribbon or an elastic band. This bag is then used to lightly dust the paste prior to rolling it out and also on petals/leaves before they are placed into a veiner.

Petal dusts

These are my favourite forms of food colour. These food colour dusts contain a gum which helps them to adhere to the petal or leaf. They are wonderful for creating very soft and also very intense colouring to finished flowers. The dusts can be mixed together to form different colours or brushed on in layers which I find creates more interest and depth to the finished flower or leaf. White petal dust can be added to soften the colours (some cake decorators add cornflour but I find this weakens the gum content of the dust, often causing a streaky effect to the petal). If you are trying to create bold, strong colours it is best to dust the surface of the flowerpaste while it is still fairly pliable or at the leather-hard stage. A paint can also be made by adding clear alcohol (isopropyl) to the dust. This is good for adding spots and finer details. Another of my favourite uses of this dust is to add it to melted cocoa butter to make a paint that is ideal for painting designs onto the surface of a cake. Petal dusts can be used in small amounts to colour flowerpaste to create interesting and subtle base colours.

Paste food colours

I use only a small selection of paste food colours. I prefer to work with a white or a very pale base colour and then create stronger finished colours using powder food colours. I add paste colours into sugarpaste to cover the cakes but even then I am not a huge fan of strongly coloured cake coverings. It is best to mix up a small ball of sugarpaste with some paste food colour and then add this ball to the larger amount of paste – this will avoid you adding too much colour to the entire amount of sugarpaste. There's nothing worse than a screaming yellow cake!

Liquid colours

These are generally used to colour royal icing as they alter the consistency of flowerpaste, sugarpaste and almond paste but they can also be great to paint with. I use a small selection of liquid colours to paint fine spots and fine lines to petals. I mostly use cyclamen and poinsettia red liquid colours for flower-making.

Craft dusts

These are inedible and only intended for items that are not going to be eaten. Craft dusts are much stronger and much more light-fast than food colour dusts. Care must be taken as they do tend to migrate the moment you take the lid off the pot. Dust in an enclosed space as once these colours get into the air they have a habit of landing where you don't want them to. To prevent spotty cakes, it is best to keep the cake in a box while you are dusting the flowers, whether it is with these or petal dusts.

Edible glaze spray

There are several ways to glaze leaves. Recently I have been using an edible spray varnish made by Fabilo. This glaze can be used lightly for most leaves or sprayed in layers for shiny leaves and berries. Spray in a well-ventilated area, perhaps wearing a filter mask. Spraying leaves is much quicker than the method below which I also use from time to time.

Confectioner's varnish

Confectioner's varnish can be used neat to create a high glaze on berries and foliage. I mostly dilute the glaze with isopropyl alcohol (often sold as dipping solution or glaze cleaner in cake decorating shops). This lessens the shine, giving a more natural effect for most foliage and some petals. I mix the two liquids together in a clean jam jar with a lid. Do not shake as this produces air bubbles. Leaves can be dipped straight into the glaze, shaking off the excess before hanging to dry or placing onto kitchen paper to blot off any excess. The glaze can also be painted onto the leaf but I find the bristles of the brush pull off some of the dust colour, giving a streaky

effect. You need to watch the leaves as a build-up of glaze can give a streaky shiny finish which is not desirable. I use various strengths of glaze:

¾ **glaze** (1 part isopropyl alcohol to 3 parts confectioner's varnish) gives a high glaze but takes away the very plastic finish often left by full, undiluted confectioner's varnish.

½ **glaze** (equal proportions of the two). This is used to give a natural shine for many types of foliage, including ivy and rose leaves.

¼ **glaze** (3 parts isopropyl alcohol to 1 part confectioner's varnish). This is used for leaves and sometimes petals that don't require a shine but just need something stronger than just steaming to set the colour and remove the dusty finish.

When the varnish has dried, you might like to use a scalpel to scratch or etch through the glaze into the surface of the flowerpaste to create fine white veins on the likes of ivy leaves.

RECIPES

Here are the recipes that will help you along your way with the projects in this book.
There are recipes for modelling pastes, royal icing and two wonderful fruitcakes too.

FRUITCAKE

Double the quantities for a three-tier wedding cake and line another small tin just
in case there is some cake mixture left over. This recipe will fill a 30 cm (12 in)
round cake tin, plus a little extra for a smaller cake. Even if I only need a 20 cm
(8 in) oval cake I still make up this full quantity and bake extra cakes with the
remaining mixture – it is hardly worth turning the oven on just for one small cake.
The variety and amount of each dried fruit can be changed to suit your own taste.

INGREDIENTS

1 kg (2 lb 3 oz/8 cups) raisins

1 kg (2 lb 3 oz/8 cups) sultanas

500 g (1 lb 2 oz/4 cups) dried figs, chopped

500 g (1 lb 2 oz/4 cups) prunes, chopped

250 g (9 oz/2 cups) natural colour
glacé cherries, halved

125 g (4½ oz/1 cup) dried apricots, chopped

125 g (4½ oz/1 cup) dried or
glacé pineapple, chopped

Grated zest and juice of 1 orange

200 ml (7 fl oz/½ cup) brandy (the odd dash of
Cointreau or cherry brandy can be good too)

500 g (1 lb 2 oz/2 cups) unsalted butter,
at room temperature

250 g (9 oz/2 cups) light muscovado sugar

250 g (9 oz/2 cups) dark muscovado sugar

4 tsp apricot jam

8 tsp golden syrup

1 tsp each of ground ginger, allspice,
nutmeg, cloves and cinnamon

½ tsp mace

500 g (1 lb 2 oz/4 cups) plain flour

250 g (9 oz/1½ cups) ground almonds

10 large free-range eggs, at room temperature

1 Use a large pair of scissors to halve and chop the various fruit that require it from the list. Add or subtract the fruit accordingly to suit your taste, but make sure the weight remains the same. Mix the dried fruit, orange zest and juice, and alcohol together in a plastic container with a lid. Seal the container and leave to soak for about a week if time allows. Otherwise overnight will do.

2 Preheat the oven to 140°C/275°F (gas 1). Cream the butter in a large bowl until soft. Gradually add the two types of sugar and beat the together. Stir in the apricot jam, golden syrup and spices (including the mace).

3 Sieve the flour into a separate bowl and stir in the almonds.

4 Beat the eggs together and add slowly to the butter/sugar mixture, alternating it with the flour/almond mix. Do not add the eggs too quickly as the mixture might curdle.

5 Before you add the fruit, set aside a small amount of un-fruited batter – this will be used on top of the fruited batter to stop the fruit catching on the top in the oven. Mix the soaked fruit into the remaining larger amount of batter. Grease and line the tin(s) with non-stick parchment paper. Fill the tin with batter to the required depth – I usually aim for about two-thirds the depth of the tin. Apply a thin layer of the un-fruited batter on top and smooth over. Bake for 4 to 6 hours, depending on the size of the cake. It is important to smell when the cake is ready – some ovens cook faster than others. The cake should shrink slightly from the sides of the tin, be firm to the touch and smell wonderful. If in doubt test with a skewer – if it comes out clean the cake is ready.

6 Allow the cake to cool slightly in the tin, add a couple of extra dashes of alcohol, and leave to cool further in the tin. Store wrapped in non-stick parchment paper and plastic wrap. Allow to mature for as long as you have – a few days to a few months works well.

SUNSHINE FRUITCAKE

This is a wonderful option for those who prefer a lighter cake. The white chocolate gives a very pleasant aftertaste.

INGREDIENTS

150 g (5½ oz/1¼ cups) glacé cherries (multi-coloured ones look great), halved, washed and allowed to dry

100 g (3½ oz/1 cup) ground almonds

100 g (3½ oz/½ cup) each of dried ready-to-eat pineapple, mango, peach, apricot and pear

1 medium Bramley apple, grated

50 g (2 oz/2 squares) grated white chocolate

75 g (2½ oz/¾ cup) dried cranberries

3 Tbsp brandy (cherry brandy or Calvados work well too!) (optional)

225 g (8 oz/1 cup) unsalted butter, at room temperature

225 g (8 oz/1 cup) caster sugar

1 tsp salt

4 large free-range eggs

250 g (9 oz/2 cups) plain flour mixed with ¼ level tsp baking powder

1 tsp vanilla essence

1 Preheat the oven to 180°C/350°F (gas 4). Line a 20 cm (8 in) round cake tin with greaseproof paper.

2 Toss the glacé cherries in the ground almonds and set aside. Chop the remaining exotic fruits and then toss them with the grated apple and white chocolate, dried cranberries and brandy. Leave for an hour or so.

3 In a separate bowl, beat the butter, sugar and salt together until pale and fluffy. Beat in the eggs, one at a time, alternating with a tablespoon of flour and beating well between each addition. Add and stir in the remaining flour and vanilla essence. Then add the exotic fruit mixture and the cherries with the ground almonds and stir well to incorporate the fruit.

4 Spoon the mixture into the prepared cake tin. Level the top and bake at 180°C/350°F (gas 4) for the first 30 minutes, turning the heat down to 150°C/300°F (gas 3) for the remaining cooking time (2 to 2½ hours total baking time). Cover the cake with foil if you feel the cake is catching or turn the oven down a little. Leave the cake to cool in the tin before turning out.

ROYAL ICING

This recipe is ideal for small amounts of royal icing required to create brush embroidery, lace, embroidery and other piped techniques.

INGREDIENTS

1 medium free-range egg white, at room temperature

225 g (8 oz/1¾ cups) icing sugar, sifted

1 Wash the mixer bowl and the beater with a concentrated detergent and then scald with boiling water to remove any traces of grease and leftover detergent. Dry thoroughly.

2 Place the egg white into the mixer bowl and the majority of the icing sugar and mix the two together with a metal spoon.

3 Fix the bowl and beater to the machine and beat on the lowest speed until the icing has reached full peak – this takes about 8 minutes. You may need to add a little extra sugar if the mixture is too soft.

COLD PORCELAIN

This is an inedible air-drying craft paste that can be used in almost exactly the same way as flowerpaste. The bonus with this paste is that the flowers made from it are much stronger and less prone to breakages. However, because it is inedible, anything made from this paste cannot come into direct contact with a cake's surface, so flowers made from cold porcelain need to be placed in a vase, container, candle-holder or Perspex plaque. I tend to treat flowers made with this paste pretty much as I would fresh or silk flowers. There are several commercial cold porcelain pastes available but you can make your own – the recipe below is the one that I prefer. I use measuring spoons and measuring cups to measure out the ingredients.

INGREDIENTS

2½ Tbsp baby oil

115 ml (4 fl oz/½ cup) non-toxic hi-tack craft glue (Impex)

115 ml (4 fl oz/½ cup) white PVA wood glue (Liberon Super wood glue or Elmers)

125 g (4½ oz/1 cup) cornflour

Permanent white artist's gouache paint

1 Work in a well-ventilated area when making this paste. Wear a filter mask if you suffer from asthma. Measure the baby oil and the two glues together in a non-stick saucepan to form an emulsion. Stir the cornflour into the mixture. It will go lumpy at this stage but this is normal!

2 Place the pan over a medium heat and stir the paste with a heavy-duty plastic or wooden spoon. The paste will gradually come away from the base and sides of the pan to form a ball around the spoon. Scrape any uncooked paste from

the spoon and add it to the mix. The cooking time will vary – usually around 10 minutes – between gas, electric and ceramic hobs, but the general rule is the lower the heat and the slower you mix the paste, the smoother the resulting paste will be. I'm impatient so I tend to turn up the heat a little to cook faster. Keep on stirring the paste to cook it evenly. You will need to split the paste and press the inner parts of the ball against the heat of the pan to cook it too – be careful not to overcook.

3 Turn the paste onto a non-stick board and knead until smooth. The paste is quite hot at this stage. The kneading should help distribute some heat through the paste to cook any undercooked areas. If the paste is very sticky then you will need to put it back in the pan to cook longer. It is better if it is slightly undercooked as you can always add heat later – if the paste is overcooked then it is almost impossible to work with.

4 Wrap in plastic wrap and leave to cool – moisture will build up on the surface of the paste that, if left, will encourage mould growth, so it is important to re-knead the paste when cool and then re-wrap. Place in a plastic food bag and then in an airtight container, and store at room temperature. This paste has been known to work well two years after it was made if stored like this.

5 Prior to making flowers you will need to add a smidge of permanent white gouache paint. The paste looks white but by its very nature dries clear, giving a translucence to the finished flower. Adding the paint makes the finish more opaque. Handling the paste is quite similar to working with sugar except I use cold cream cleanser instead of white vegetable fat, and glue or anti-bacterial wipes/water to moisten the petals to stick them. Cornflour is used as for handling flowerpaste. The paste shrinks a little as it dries – this is because of the glue. This can be disconcerting to begin with but you will gradually get used to it and it can be an advantage when making miniature flowers.

FLOWERPASTE

I always buy ready-made commercial flowerpaste (APOC) as it tends to be more consistent than homemade pastes. The following recipe is the one I used prior to discovering the joys of ready-made flowerpaste! Gum tragacanth gives the paste stretch and strength too.

INGREDIENTS

5 tsp cold water
2 tsp powdered gelatine
500 g (1 lb 2 oz/3 cups) icing sugar, sifted
3 tsp gum tragacanth
2 tsp liquid glucose
3 tsp white vegetable fat,
plus 1 extra tsp to add later
1 large fresh egg white

1 Mix the cold water and gelatine together in a small bowl and leave to stand for 30 minutes. Sift the icing sugar and gum tragacanth together into the bowl of a heavy-duty mixer and fit to the machine.

2 Place the bowl with the gelatine mixture over a saucepan of hot water and stir until the gelatine has dissolved. Warm a teaspoon in hot water and then measure out the liquid glucose – the heat of the spoon should help to ease the glucose on its way. Add the glucose and 3 teaspoons of white fat to the gelatine mixture, and continue to heat until all the ingredients have dissolved and are thoroughly mixed together.

3 Add the dissolved gelatine mixture to the icing sugar/gum tragacanth with the egg white. Beat at the mixer's lowest speed, then gradually increase the speed to maximum until the paste is white and stringy.

4 Remove the paste from the bowl, knead into a smooth ball and cover with the remaining teaspoon of white fat – this helps to prevent the paste forming a dry crust that can leave hard bits in the paste at the rolling out stage. Place in a plastic food bag and store in an airtight container. Allow the paste to rest and mature for 12 hours before use.

5 The paste should be well-kneaded before you start to roll it out or model it into a flower shape, otherwise it has a tendency to dry out and crack around the edges. This is an air-drying paste so when you are not using it make sure it is well wrapped in a plastic bag. If you have cut out lots of petals, cover them over with a plastic bag.

TECHNIQUES

These are some of the essential techniques that you will use time and time again when creating floral celebration cakes.

COATING A CAKE WITH ALMOND PASTE

I adore the flavour and texture of almond paste. A layer of natural-coloured white almond paste gives a smooth, round-edged base on which to apply a layer of sugarpaste, creating a more professional finish and excellent eating quality too! It is important that the work surface is free of flour or cornflour, as if any gets trapped between the almond paste and the sugarpaste it can cause fermentation, encouraging air bubbles. It is best, but not always essential, to leave the almond paste-coated cake to dry out and firm up for a few days prior to icing.

1 Before applying any form of coating, the cake must be level. To do this, carefully cut off the top of the cake if it has formed a dome during baking. Then turn the cake upside down so that the flat bottom becomes the top. Fill any large indentations with almond paste if required. Place the cake onto a thin cake board the same size as the cake so that it is easier to move. You might also prefer to add a strip of almond paste around the base of the cake to seal it and the cake board tightly together.

2 Warm some apricot jam and a dash of water, brandy or Cointreau, and then sieve to make an apricot glaze that can be painted onto the surface of the cake. This will help to stick the almond paste to the cake and help seal it to keep it fresh. Apricot glaze is used as the colour is not too dark and the flavour tends not to fight with the taste of the cake or almond paste. You may also be able to buy ready-sieved apricot glaze in a jar – which also benefits from a dash of alcohol.

3 You will need a long, non-stick rolling pin large enough to roll out almond paste to cover at least a 30 cm (12 in) cake. Plastic smoothers are also essential to create a professional finish: a curved smoother for the top of the cake and a square-edged one for the sides. Rolling out almond paste to an even thickness can be tricky, and a novice cake decorator might find a pair of marzipan spacers useful to roll against. Depending which way they are placed, they can produce thick or thin sheets of almond paste/sugarpaste. It is best to store the paste in a warm place prior to kneading to help soften it slightly – otherwise it can be quite hard to work with. Knead the paste on a clean, dry surface to make it pliable.

4 Lightly dust the work surface with icing sugar. Place the almond paste on top and if needed position the spacers on either side of the paste. Roll the paste out lengthways using the non-stick rolling pin. Turn it sideways and reposition the spacers on either side again. Continue to roll out the paste until it is large enough to cover the cake. A measuring tape, string or even using the length of the rolling pin to gauge the exact size of the cake top and its sides can be useful. It is always best to allow slightly more than you think you will need, especially for awkward-shaped cakes or anything with corners to it.

5 Using a round-edged plastic smoother, polish and smooth out the surface of the almond paste. Start gently, gradually increasing the pressure to even out any slightly uneven areas of the paste.

6 Place the rolling pin on top of the almond paste and use it to help lift the paste over the cake. Remove the rolling pin and ease the almond paste into place. Smooth the surface of the cake to exclude any air bubbles. Tuck the paste to fit the sides. If you are working on a cake with corners, then concentrate on these first of all.

7 Use the curved-edge smoother to polish the top of the cake. Use strong, firm hand movements to 'iron out' any imperfections. Use the edge of the straight-edged smoother to cut and flick away the excess paste from the base of the cake. Finally, use the straight-edged smoother to iron out the sides of the cake using a fair amount of pressure. Place the cake onto a sheet of greaseproof paper and, if time allows, leave to firm up overnight or for a few days prior to coating with sugarpaste.

COATING A CAKE AND CAKE DRUM WITH SUGARPASTE

Plastic sugarpaste smoothers are essential when covering a cake with sugarpaste. The round-edged smoother is good for working on the top of the cake and the straight-edged smoother is good for working on the sides, giving a sharper edge at the base. Covering a cake with sugarpaste is a fairly straightforward process – however, practice is needed to achieve very neat results. If you are colouring the sugarpaste it is best to use paste food colour or to thicken liquid colours with icing sugar. It is safer to colour a small amount of sugarpaste and then knead this into the larger amount of paste to control the depth of colour rather than create a paste that is too brightly coloured.

1 Knead the sugarpaste on a clean, dry sugar- and flour-free surface until smooth and pliable. Take care not to knead in too many air bubbles. When fully kneaded, lightly dust the work surface with sieved icing sugar and place the sugarpaste on top, with any cracks against the work surface. Roll out, smooth and polish the paste as described for the almond paste coating.

2 Moisten the surface of the almond paste with clear alcohol (Cointreau, kirsch or white rum can all be used). Use a sponge to apply the alcohol as this gives a more even covering. Any dry areas will encourage air bubbles to be trapped between the almond paste and the sugarpaste. The alcohol helps to stick the sugarpaste to the almond paste and also acts as an antibacterial agent.

3 Pick up the sugarpaste onto the rolling pin and lower it over the cake, taking care to position the paste so that it will cover the sides evenly. Remove the rolling pin. Use your hands and then the round-edged smoother to create a smooth finish and eliminate air bubbles. Next, lift and ease the paste against the sides of the cake. If the cake has corners or points, deal with these first as they often crack or tear. Be careful not to stretch the sugarpaste too much as you work. Trim the excess paste from the base of the cake using a flat knife or the edge of a straight-edged smoother. Use the same smoother to iron out the sides of the cake. Use a pin to prick any air bubbles/pockets that might appear (brightly coloured glass head pins are best for this job so that you can easily spot them when not in use) and then smooth over with the sugarpaste smoothers. Continue to use the curved-edge smoother on the top of the cake and the straight-edged smoother on the sides to create a good, even finish. The edges of the coating or any difficult points or curved areas can be given extra attention with a pad of sugarpaste pressed into your palm and used to polish the paste.

4 To coat a cake drum, roll out the sugarpaste and carefully place it over a drum moistened with clear alcohol. Smooth over with the round-edged smoother and then trim off the excess with a flat knife. Smooth the cut edge with a smoother to neaten it. Next, polish with a pad of sugarpaste pressed into your palm.

5 Soften a small amount of sugarpaste with clear alcohol (Cointreau, kirsch or white rum) and place at the centre of the cake drum. Carefully lower the cake which should be on a cake board of the same size over the top. Gently press down the top of the cake with the round-edged smoother to bond the cake and the drum together. Use the straight-edged smoother to blend and create a good join between the cake and the drum. Smooth over any areas that need extra attention with the sugarpaste pad technique.

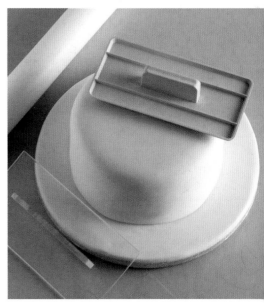

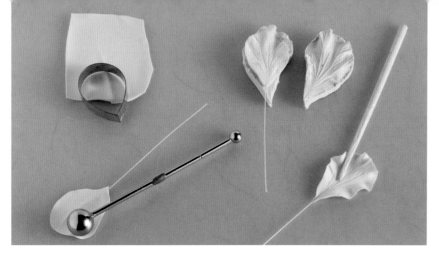

WIRING PETALS AND LEAVES

This is my favourite method of constructing flowers. It gives the flowers much more movement and extra strength too, resulting in fewer breakages.

1 Knead a piece of flowerpaste and form roughly into the shape of the petal or leaf you are making. Press it down against a non-stick board to flatten it slightly. Use a celstick or rolling pin to roll the flowerpaste, leaving a ridge for the wire. Try to create a tapered ridge, angling the pin slightly so that the ridge is thicker at the base of the petal/leaf. The thickness and length of the ridge will depend on the size of the petal/leaf you are making. There are also boards available commercially which have grooves in them that create a similar ridged effect when the paste is rolled over them. These can be great for smaller petals and leaves but I find they produce too fine a ridge for many of the larger flowers that I make.

2 Cut out the petal/leaf shape using a cutter, scalpel or plain-edge cutting wheel, leaving the ridge to run down the centre. If you are using a cutter, lift up the shape and place it onto a very light dusting of cornflour and then press firmly with the cutter and scrub it slightly against the paste and the board so that the shape remains slightly stuck in the cutter. This will enable you to quickly rub the edge of the cutter to create a cleaner-cut edge, removing any fuzzy bits!

3 Moisten the wire very slightly – too much will result in the paper coming off the wire and also slow down the drying process of the petal on the wire. Hold the ridge firmly between your finger and thumb, and hold the wire in the other hand very close to the end of the wire that is being inserted into the shape. Push the wire in gradually so that it supports a third to half the length. Use a ball tool to soften and thin the edge of the shape using a rolling action, working the tool half on your hand/foam pad and half on the edge of the paste.

4 Place the petal/leaf into a double-sided petal/leaf veiner and press the two sides firmly against the shape to texture it.

5 A frilled edge can be added using a cocktail stick or a ceramic veining tool, working at intervals to encourage a natural frilled effect.

GLAZING

Glazing can help give a leaf or petal a more realistic appearance. Care must be taken not to glaze flowers too heavily as this can make them look unnatural.

STEAMING

Using powder colours on sugar flowers often leaves a slightly dry-looking finished flower; this can be changed to create a slightly more waxy appearance and also help to set the colour to stop it leaving marks on the surface of the coated cake. Hold each flower in the steam from a boiling kettle for a few seconds, or until the surface turns slightly shiny. Take care not to scald yourself and also not to get the sugar too wet as it will dissolve fairly fast. Allow the flower to dry before wiring into a spray. If you are trying to create a velvety finish to something like a red rose, then the steaming process can be used and then re-dust the flower – you will find that this will hold onto more dust, giving the desired effect.

EDIBLE GOLD AND SILVER LEAF

I love using sheets of gold 23-carat and silver leaf to embellish side designs on cakes.
However, the sheets are very fine and tend to tear and fly very easily. Using the following
method creates a more convenient way to control this delightful trickster!

1 Roll out some well-kneaded
flowerpaste very thinly using a non-
stick rolling pin. Lift up the paste and place
the sticky side that was against the non-stick
board carefully over a whole single sheet
of gold/silver leaf. Smooth the flowerpaste
from behind onto the leaf to adhere the
two together. Turn the flowerpaste over to
reveal the coated side. Trim off the excess
uncoated paste from the edges. Leave to set
for about 20 minutes to give a more paper-
like finish and then cut out shapes using a
paper punch or flower/leaf cutters. Keep
any leftover pieces of the gilded paste to
use at a later stage – these dried pieces of
paste can be broken into small shards and
used to create an alternative decorative
effect combined with painted images,
added to piped embroidery designs
or even combined with dragées.

2 A crackle effect can also be achieved
by resting the gold/silver leaf-coated
flowerpaste a little and then re-rolling to
reveal the colour of the flowerpaste beneath
– this can be particularly effective using
purple, red or black flowerpaste as a
backing for gold or silver leaf.

3 For a jewelled, textured effect, sprinkle
some coloured sugar crystal sprinkles
on top of the freshly bonded gold/silver leaf
flowerpaste and then quickly roll this into
the surface using a non-stick rolling pin to
embed the crystals into the paste.

FLOWERS

Fringed nigella

I came across this unusual fringed form of nigella recently –
it was quite a surprise as nigella, or 'love in a mist' as it is
often called, is generally a much smaller delicate blue flower!
There are some green versions of this flower too.

MATERIALS

33-, 30- and 28-gauge white wires
Pale green cold porcelain (p 14–5)
Nile green floristry tape
Vine, daffodil, sunflower, plum, coral,
white and foliage petal dusts
White seed-head stamens
Hi-tack non-toxic craft glue
White flowerpaste

EQUIPMENT

Wire cutters
Dusting brushes
Non-stick board
Stargazer B petal veiner (SKGI)
Fine curved scissors
Plain-edge cutting wheel
Ball tool
Dresden tool

STAMEN CENTRE

1 Cut several short lengths of 33-gauge white wire. Blend a small
ball of pale green cold porcelain onto
the end to create a fine, tapered carrot
shape. This is to represent each section
of the ovary at the centre of the flower.
Pinch a slight ridge down one side at the
base. Repeat to make 5 to 8 sections.
As the cold porcelain begins to firm up
you should be able to curl and twist
each section prior to taping together
with quarter-width nile green floristry
tape. I use cold porcelain for the centre
as it enables the stamens to be glued
easily around it to create a neat join.

2 Dust the centre with vine green
petal dust. Next, take small sets
of white seed-head stamens (3 to 5 in
a set) and glue each set together at
the centre with non-toxic craft glue.
Flatten and work the glue from the
centre towards either end of the stamens.
Repeat with the other groups, trying not
to apply too much glue as this will cause
bulk and also take much longer to dry.
Once the glue has set, cut the stamens
in half and then trim away the excess
using sharp scissors to leave only a short
length to each group with a fine line of
glue holding them together.

3 Apply a little more glue to the
base of each short stamen group
and attach around the base of the ovary
sections. Squeeze the base of the
stamens into place. Leave to set. Dust the
filaments (the length) with vine petal dust
and the tips with a mixture of daffodil
and sunflower.

FRINGED PETALS

4 These vary in size and are a little
random in their make-up too which
is good for the flower-maker! Cut several
lengths of 33-, 30- or 28-gauge white
wire, depending on the size of petal you
are working on. Blend a ball of well-kneaded white flowerpaste onto the wire
to create a long, tapered petal shape.
Keep the base broad and the tip fine.
Flatten the shape against the non-stick
board using the flat side of the stargazer
B petal veiner. You might need to trim
the edges slightly to neaten them up with
fine scissors or a plain-edge cutting
wheel.

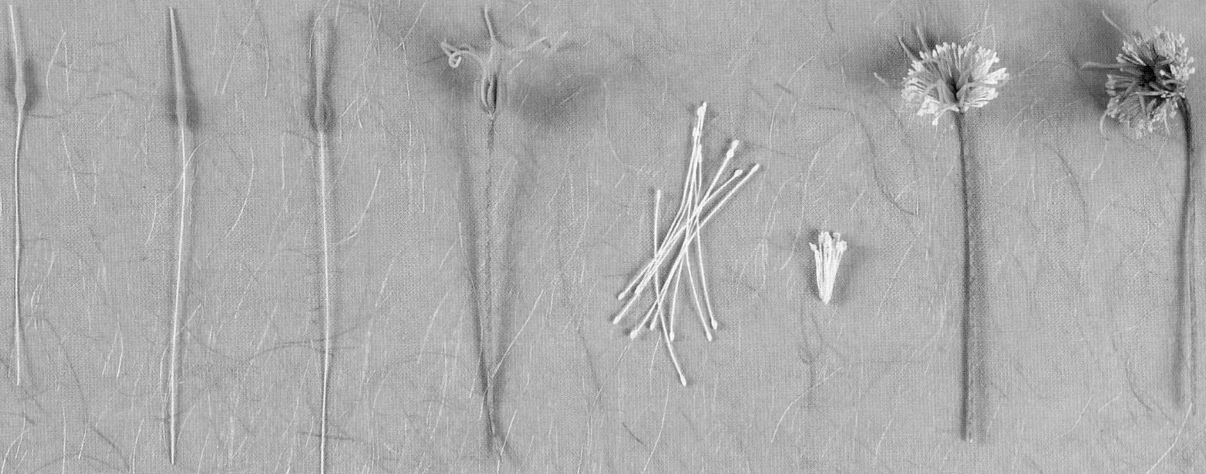

5 Soften the edge of the petal with the ball tool and then texture using the double-sided stargazer B petal veiner.

6 Use fine curved scissors to make a long cut on either edge of the petal to create a tri-lobed shaped petal. Open up the sections and then add finer shorter snips to the edges of the three sections.

7 Next, place the petal against the non-stick board and press each of the fringed sections with the broad end of the Dresden tool to thin them out slightly.

8 Pinch the petal from the base to the tip to create a central vein. Repeat to make numerous petals, curving them slightly to give the flower more movement.

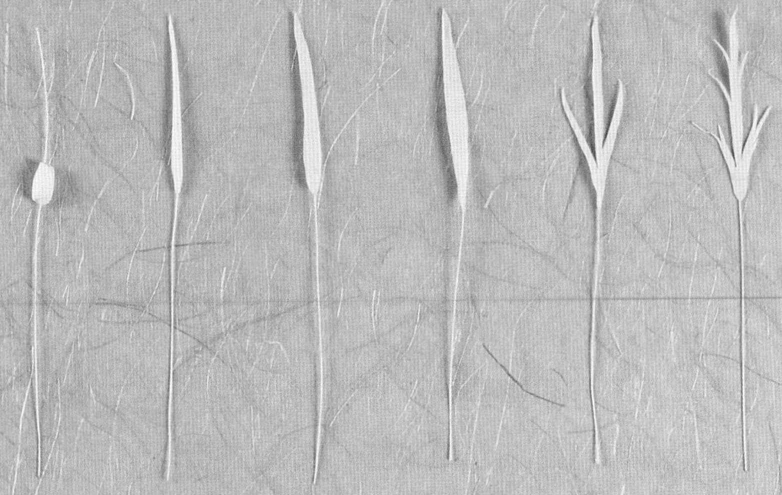

COLOURING AND ASSEMBLY

9 The petals can be dusted before or after assembly with a mixture of plum, coral and white petal dusts, concentrating most of the colour at the base of each petal. Tinge the edges with vine green and small amounts of foliage green too. Tape the petals around the centre using quarter-width nile green floristry tape.

LEAVES

10 These are very fine and look good made from fine 33-gauge white wires and twisted nile green floristry tape. Add groups of leaves directly behind the flower. Dust them with foliage and vine green.

Sweet violet

The sweet violet, with its heady fragrance, has been used to symbolise love for thousands of years. It is also the flower of Aphrodite, the goddess of love. In years gone by, violets were strewn on the floors of cottages and churches to conceal the musty smell of damp and to sweeten the air. Although there are cutters available for making violets, I actually prefer to use the method that was first taught to me 20-odd years ago: simply using a pair of scissors to cut the varying sizes of petal and then pinching and pulling each petal between finger and thumb to create the desired petal shape. This method, commonly known as the pulled flower method, can be used to make many types of filler flowers.

MATERIALS

White and holly/ivy flowerpaste
Cornflour bag (p 11)
26-gauge white wire
Nile green floristry tape
Fresh egg white
African violet, deep purple, daffodil, white, sunflower, vine green, foliage and aubergine petal dusts
Black paste food colour
Isopropyl alcohol
Edible spray varnish

EQUIPMENT

Smooth ceramic tool
Scissors
Fine-nose pliers
Non-stick rolling pin
Heart-shaped cutters
Dresden tool
Ball tool
Violet leaf veiner (SKGI)
Dimpled foam
Dusting brushes
Fine paintbrush
Calyx cutter (R15 OP) (optional)

FLOWERS

1 Form a ball of well-kneaded white flowerpaste into a cone shape. Open up and thin out the broad end using the pointed end of the smooth ceramic tool – you might need a light dusting of cornflour to prevent the paste sticking to the tool.

2 Next, divide the shape into five unequal-sized petals using a pair of scissors. You are aiming to end up with one larger lip petal with two small petals on either side of it, plus two medium-sized petals together at the top of the flower.

3 Spread the petals apart and then carefully pinch each into a pointed shape between your finger and thumb. The next stage is to 'pull' each petal between your finger and thumb: hold the petal firmly across the top with your thumb uppermost and your forefinger supporting the underside of the petal. Rub your finger against the petal but keep your thumb steady. This will flatten the petal and enlarge it. Repeat the process on all the petals.

4 Rest the flower over your forefinger and gently broaden and thin each petal using the ceramic tool.

5 Pinch the underside of the large petal to create a central vein and a curve to the petal. Pull and curl the two small side petals down towards the large petal and curl the two medium petals backwards. Correct the back of the flower into a fine pointed shape.

LEAVES

7 Roll out some holly/ivy flowerpaste, leaving a thick ridge for the wire. Cut out the leaf shape using a heart-shaped cutter. Insert a wire moistened with fresh egg white into about half the length of the thick ridge. The gauge will depend on the size of the leaf.

8 Use the Dresden tool to pull out serrations on the edge of the leaf at intervals. Soften the edge with the ball tool and then texture using the violet leaf veiner. Pinch the leaf from behind to accentuate the central vein and give an angle at the indent of the heart shape. Allow to firm up on dimpled foam for a little while before dusting.

10 Use a fine paintbrush and black paste food colour diluted with isopropyl alcohol to paint a series of fine lines on the base petal.

11 Curve the stem of the flower using fine-nose pliers. Add a couple of fine pointed floristry tape bracts part way down the stem. Add a calyx if required – here I have simply dusted a mixture of vine green and foliage petal dusts where the stem joins the back of the flower.

COLOURING AND ASSEMBLY

6 Tape over a 26-gauge white wire with quarter-width nile green floristry tape. Bend a hook in the end using fine-nose pliers, moisten with fresh egg white and then pull the wire through the centre and out behind the two medium petals. Try to embed the hook into the thickness around the centre to secure and support the shape. Add a stamen if desired. Allow to firm up a little before colouring.

9 Dust the flower with African violet petal dust. Leave a pale white area at the centre of the broad petal. Define the edge with a little deep purple. Add a yellow highlight in the broad petal with a mixture of daffodil and white petal dusts. Add a tiny amount of sunflower petal dust at the very centre of the flower using a fine paintbrush.

12 Dust the leaves with foliage and vine green petal dusts. Add the odd tinge of aubergine. Spray lightly with edible spray varnish.

Hearts entangled

Here is one of my favourite succulents – often known as hearts entangled or string of hearts (*Ceropegia woodii*). The variety used here has patterned leaves but other varieties have plain green leaves too if you are feeling a bit lazy! I have created only the foliage – the curious tiny flowers are like parachutes that trap insects, encouraging pollination.

LEAVES

1 The leaves could be made with small heart cutters – however, I find this makes them look a little mass-produced and so I prefer to make them using a pulled/freehand method. Cut lots of short lengths of 33- or 30-gauge white wire, depending on the size of leaf you are making. If you can buy 36- or 35-gauge wire, then that is even better for the smallest leaves.

2 Take a small ball of well-kneaded pale green flowerpaste and form it into a cone shape. Insert a wire moistened with fresh egg white into the broad end of the cone and then place against the non-stick board. Use your fingers to press and squeeze the flowerpaste against the board to form a very naïve heat shape. If you are worried about leaving your fingerprints, then you might prefer to place a plastic food bag over the top prior to forming the shape.

3 Next, hollow out the underside of the leaf using the small ball tool, working on both sides to encourage more of a heart shape. Pinch the leaf

from behind to create a very gentle central vein. Repeat to make lots of leaves, pairing them as you work.

ASSEMBLY AND COLOURING

4 I prefer to tape the leaves onto a long stem prior to colouring but you might prefer to work the other way. Tape two tiny leaves onto the end of a 28-gauge white wire using quarter-width nile green floristry tape. Continue to add the leaves in pairs down the stem, gradually increasing in size as you work. Add extra wire if needed to support the length.

5 Dust the back of each leaf with a mixture of plum and aubergine petal dusts. Catch the upper edges here and there too, and also the trailing stems benefit from a light dusting. Use a mixture of foliage and white to dust the upper surface of the leaves. Dilute some foliage with isopropyl alcohol and paint darker green splodges onto the surface of each leaf. Leave to dry and then add some diluted spots of white bridal satin too. Spray with edible spray varnish or steam to set the colour, trying not to make the leaves too shiny.

MATERIALS
33-, 30- and 28-gauge white wires
Pale green flowerpaste
Fresh egg white
Plastic food bag
Nile green floristry tape
Plum, aubergine, foliage, white and white bridal satin petal dusts
Isopropyl alcohol
Edible spray varnish

EQUIPMENT
Wire cutters
Non-stick board
Small ball tool
Dusting brushes
Fine paintbrush

Blue sun orchid

It can be quite difficult finding attractive blue flowers to use on cakes. This version of the blue sun orchid was designed and made by my friend Sathya. I needed a blue flower for a man's cake so she kindly donated this species!

MATERIALS
30- and 28-gauge white wires
White flowerpaste
Fresh egg white
Nile green floristry tape
African violet, deep purple, plum, white, daffodil, sunflower and vine petal dusts
Isopropyl alcohol

EQUIPMENT
Ceramic tool (HP)
Fine scissors
Non-stick rolling pin
Spathoglottis orchid cutter set (TT825-826)
Cupped Christmas rose petal veiner (SKGI)
Dresden tool
Dusting brushes
Fine paintbrush

COLUMN

1 Insert a 30-gauge white wire into a small ball of white flowerpaste. Thin down the base of the ball to create a slender teardrop shape. Hollow out the underside of the column using the rounded end of the ceramic tool. Texture the top tip of the column by snipping it with fine scissors. Indent at the centre using the pointed end of the ceramic tool. Curve slightly.

OUTER PETALS AND SEPALS

2 All five outer petals are made in the same way with the same size cutter. Roll out some white flowerpaste thinly, leaving a thick ridge for the wire. Cut out the petal shape using the larger cutter from the spathoglottis orchid set.

3 Insert a 28-gauge white wire moistened with fresh egg white into the thick ridge to support about half the length. Soften the edge and then vein using the cupped Christmas rose petal veiner.

4 Pinch the base of the petal through to the tip to create a central vein, then curve backwards. Repeat to make six petals/sepals.

ASSEMBLY AND COLOURING

5 Using quarter-width nile green floristry tape, tape one petal underneath the column to represent the lip and then two at the side to represent the wing petals. Add the remaining three petals evenly spaced behind them to represent the dorsal and lateral sepals.

6 Work a ball of white flowerpaste behind the petals to cover about 2.5 cm (1 in) of the wire to create a fleshier feel to the back of the flower. Work the paste into the base of the petals using the broad end of the Dresden tool.

7 Dust the flower with a mixture of African violet, deep purple, plum and white petal dusts. Add stronger colouring to the edges of each petal. Dust the centre of the textured section on the column with a mixture of daffodil and sunflower petal dusts. Dust the neck of the flower with vine green petal dust.

8 Dilute some African violet and deep purple petal dusts with isopropyl alcohol and paint some fine spotted detail to the lip and wing petals.

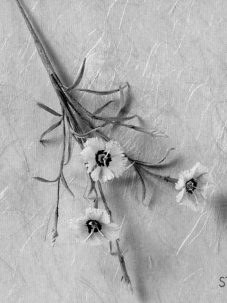

Dianthus

Often known as Pinks, there are about 300 species of dianthus from Europe, Asia, Africa and North America. The single dianthus illustrated here is quite simple to make and is a very pretty filler flower; it also works well in bunches on its own.

MATERIALS

White seed-head stamens
Hi-tack non-toxic craft glue
33-, 28- and 26-gauge white wires
Pale pink and pale holly/ivy flowerpaste
Fresh egg white
Plum, white, foliage and aubergine petal dusts
Cyclamen liquid food colour
Clear alcohol (Cointreau or kirsch)
Nile green floristry tape

EQUIPMENT

Fine scissors
Non-stick board
Celstick
Dianthus cutter (TT459)
Dresden tool
Fine calyx cutter (optional)
Leaf/petal veiner
Plain-edge cutting wheel
Dusting brushes
Fine paintbrush

STAMENS

1 Take one white seed-head stamen and fold it in half. Cut the tips off both ends. Fold it in half and cut at the bend using fine scissors. Glue them back together with a tiny amount of non-toxic craft glue. Flatten them and leave to set. Apply a tiny amount of extra glue and then attach to the end of a half-length 26-gauge white wire. Squeeze the two together firmly, holding to about the count of ten. Repeat to make as many sets of stamen required. Allow to dry. Trim the stamens a little and then curl their tips using the sides of a small pair of scissors to run against them.

FLOWER

2 Form a ball of well-kneaded pale pink flowerpaste into a long cone shape. Pinch the broad end of the cone into a 'wizard's hat' shape. Place the brim of the hat against the non-stick board and roll out the base using the celstick to thin it out and create a tight waistline around the thicker area of the shape.

3 Place the dianthus cutter over the thick area of the shape and cut out the flower, scrubbing the cutter against the board to create a good cut edge. Remove the shape from the cutter and place back against the board.

4 Use the celstick to broaden and thin each petal, leaving the central part of each petal slightly thicker. Next, use the broad end of the Dresden tool to thin the top edge of each petal, pulling the paste against the board, which will both thin and give a slightly frilled edge.

5 Pick up the flower and open up the centre using the pointed end of the celstick. Next, use fine scissors to snip into the edges of the petals to create the fringed edge.

6 Moisten the base of the stamens with fresh egg white and thread through the centre of the flower, leaving the tips of the curled stamens slightly proud of the top of the flower. Work the back of the flower between your finger and thumb to thin it down into a slender neck. Trim off any excess. Pinch the base of each petal from behind to create a little movement in the petals. Flick the edges to create more movement in the fringed edges. Go back and add extra snips if needed.

CALYX

7 This can be cut out using a fine calyx cutter or, for a quick finish, the paste behind the flower can be snipped with fine scissors to create the five sepals. Add two snips at the very base of the calyx to create the characteristic scale shape.

BUD

8 Insert a half-length of 28-gauge white wire into the base of a cone-shaped piece of pale pink flowerpaste. Thin down the shape to create a slender bud shape. Pinch three flanges from the tip of the bud to represent the outer three petals. Keep pinching to thin out each petal and then twist the petals back onto themselves to create a spiralled petal formation. Snip the calyx as described for the flower.

LEAVES

9 Cut short lengths of 33-gauge white wire. Attach a small ball of pale holly/ivy flowerpaste onto the end of the wire and blend it onto the wire to create a fine, slender leaf shape. Place the shape against the non-stick board and flatten it using the flat/plain side of any of your leaf/petal veiners. Trim the leaf if needed using scissors or the plain-edge cutting wheel. Soften the edges and then pinch a central vein from the base to the tip. Curve slightly. Repeat to make numerous leaves, bearing in mind that the leaves always occur in pairs.

COLOURING AND ASSEMBLY

10 Dust the flower petals and buds with plum petal dust. Add a touch of white to calm down the pink if required. The backs of the petals and the buds are a much paler pink than the upper surface of the petals.

11 Use a fine paintbrush and cyclamen liquid food colour to add detailed markings at the base of each petal to create a decorative eye. Use a touch of white petal dust diluted with clear alcohol at the very centre of the flower.

12 Dust the leaves and the calyces with a light mixture of foliage and white petal dusts mixed together. Add tinges of aubergine at the tips of the leaves and base of the calyx if desired.

13 Tape the leaves in pairs onto each flower and bud stem using quarter-width nile green floristry tape. Dust the stems to match the calyx and leaves.

Rose

Roses (*Rosa*) are the most requested flower for bridal work and for cake decorators too!
There are several methods for creating roses – the method described here
is the style that I prefer and use most often.

EQUIPMENT

Fine-nose pliers
Non-stick rolling pin
Rose petal cutter set (TT549, 550, 551)
Foam pad
Metal ball tool (CC)
Very large rose petal veiner (SKGI)
Cornflour bag (p 11)
Plastic food bag
Smooth ceramic tool or cocktail stick
Kitchen paper ring former (p 11)
Dusting brushes
Non-stick board
Curved scissors
Grooved board
Rose leaf cutter (Jem)
Large briar rose leaf veiner (SKGI)
Set of three black rose leaf cutters (Jem))

MATERIALS

30-, 28-, 26-, and 18-gauge white wires
Nile green floristry tape
White and holly/ivy flowerpaste
Fresh egg white
Vine, edelweiss, daffodil, sunflower, moss, foliage,
forest, aubergine, plum and ruby petal dusts
Edible spray varnish or half glaze (p 12)

ROSE CONE CENTRE

1 Tape over a half to three-quarter length of 18-gauge white wire with half-width nile green floristry tape. Bend a large open hook in the end using fine-nose pliers. Form a ball of well-kneaded white flowerpaste into a cone shape to measure about two-thirds the length of the smallest rose petal cutter you are planning to use. Moisten the hook with fresh egg white and insert into the rounded base of the cone. Push the hook into most of the length of the cone. Pinch the base of the flowerpaste onto the wire to secure the two together. Reshape the point of the cone if required – I tend to form a sharp point with a more rounded base. Allow to dry for as long as possible.

2 Colour a large amount of white flowerpaste to the required colour; here I have used vine green petal dust to give a soft off-white base colour. I usually colour the paste paler than I want the finished rose to be.

FIRST AND SECOND LAYERS

3 Roll out some of the coloured flowerpaste fairly thinly using a non-stick rolling pin. Cut out four petals using the smaller of the two rose petal cutters you are planning to use. Place the petals on the foam pad and soften the edges using the metal ball tool – work half on the edge of the petal and half on the pad using a rolling action with the tool. Try not to frill the edges; at this stage you are only taking away the raw cut edge of the petal. Vein each of the petals in turn using the double-sided very large rose petal veiner – dust with a little cornflour if needed to prevent sticking, especially if your veiner is being used for the first time. For smaller roses it is not always essential to vein the petals but the larger flowers benefit from it greatly.

4 Place the first petal against the dried cone using a little fresh egg white to help stick it in place. It needs to be positioned quite high against the cone so that you have enough of the petal to curl tightly to form a spiral effect around the cone. It is important that this cone is not visible from the overview of the finished rose. Do not worry about covering the cone near the base – there are plenty more petals to follow that will do that job. I tend to curl the petal in from the left-hand side. Leave the right-hand edge of the petal slightly open so that the next petal can be tucked underneath it.

5 Moisten the remaining three petals with fresh egg white and start the second layer by tucking a petal underneath the first petal on the cone. Stick down the edge of the first petal over the new petal. Place the next petal over the join created and then turn the rose to add the third petal. I tend to keep these petals open to start with so that I can get the positioning correct before tightening them around the cone to form a spiral shape. Leave one of the petals open slightly to take the first petal of the next layer. Some roses have slightly pinched petals – this can be done as you add each layer by pinching the top edge to create a slight point. This number of petals can be used to make small rosebuds but the cone base should be made slightly smaller so that the petals cover the whole of it.

THIRD, FOURTH AND FIFTH LAYERS

6 Roll out some more coloured flowerpaste and cut out nine petals using the same size cutter as before. Soften the edges and vein the petals as before. Cover the petals with a plastic food bag to stop them drying out – otherwise it is a case of cutting out and working on only three petals at a time.

Tuck the first petal underneath the open petal from the previous layer of the rosebud and continue to add the other petals as described above, attaching them in layers of three petals at a time. It is important to keep positioning petals over joins in the previous layer and not to line up petals directly behind each other. Gradually start to loosen the petals slightly as you work on the fourth and fifth layers. Pinch and curl the edges slightly more as you attach the fifth layer.

SIXTH LAYER

7 Roll out some more coloured flowerpaste and cut out three petals using the slightly larger rose petal cutter. Soften and vein as before. This time, start to hollow out the centre of each petal using a large ball tool or by simply rubbing the petal with your thumb.

31

8 Moisten the base of each petal with fresh egg white, creating a 'V' shape. Attach to the rose as before, trying to place each petal over a join in the previous layer. Pinch either side of the petal at the base as you attach them so that it retains the cupped shape and allows the rose to breathe. Curl back the edges using the smooth ceramic tool, a cocktail stick or just your fingers to create more movement in the petal edges. I tend to curl either edge of the petal to create a more pointed petal shape. At this stage you have made what is termed a 'half rose'.

FINAL LAYER

9 I prefer to wire the petals individually for the final layer of the rose; this gives more movement and also a much stronger finished flower. Roll out some coloured flowerpaste, leaving a subtle ridge down the centre. Cut out the petal using the same size cutter as for the previous layer. Hook and moisten the end of a 26-gauge white wire. Insert it into the very base of the ridge. Soften the edges and vein as described previously. You will need cornflour dusting onto either the petal or the veiner

at this stage to prevent the flowerpaste sticking to the veiner. Press the veiner firmly to create stronger veins. Remove from the veiner and hollow out the centre using your thumb and also start to curl back the edges. Allow the petal to dry slightly in a kitchen paper ring former. Repeat to make about eight to ten petals; the number varies with each rose that I make. As the petals are beginning to firm up, you can keep going back to add extra curls to the edges if required.

ASSEMBLY AND COLOURING

10 I prefer to tape the individually wired petals around the half rose and then dust the rose as a whole – I balance the colour better this way. You might prefer to dust and then tape. It is best if the petals are not quite dry at this stage so that you can reshape and manipulate them. Tape the first wired petal over a join in the petals of the half rose using half-width nile green floristry tape. The next petal is placed onto the opposite side of the rose and then I continue adding the petals to cover gaps and joins in the previous layer. As before, try not to place petals in line with petals of the layer underneath.

11 Mix together edelweiss, vine, daffodil and sunflower petal dusts. Probe the flower with a brush loaded with this mix to add a 'glow' at the base of each petal on the back and front. I tend to be heavier with this colour on the back of the petals. The rose pictured has been dusted lightly with a very light mixture of vine, moss and edelweiss petal dusts.

CALYX

12 As the outer petals of the rose have been individually wired I find it is best to wire each sepal of the calyx too. This gives a stronger finish but also allows the flower-maker to represent a calyx with very long, slender sepals. A quicker calyx may be added using a rose calyx cutter if time or patience won't allow a wired calyx. Cut five lengths of 28-gauge white wire. Work a ball of holly/ivy flowerpaste onto the wire creating a long, tapered carrot shape. Place the shape against the non-stick board and flatten using the flat side of one of the double-sided veiners. If the shape looks distorted, simply trim into shape with a pair of scissors.

13 Place the flattened shape onto the foam pad or the palm of your hand, and soften and hollow out the length using the metal ball tool. Pinch the sepal from the base to the tip. Cut fine 'hairs' into the edge of the sepal using curved scissors. Repeat to make five sepals. I tend to leave one sepal without hairs – although remember there are some varieties of rose that have no hairs to their calyces at all.

14 Dust each sepal on the outer surface with a mixture of foliage and forest green. Add tinges of aubergine mixed with plum or ruby petal dust. Use the same brush used for the green mixture and dust lightly on the inner surface of each sepal with edelweiss petal dust. Lightly glaze the back of each sepal with edible spray varnish or half glaze.

15 Tape the five sepals to the base of the rose, positioning a sepal over a join. Add a ball of flowerpaste for the ovary and pinch and squeeze it into a neat shape. Some florists' roses have almost no ovary – they have been bred out to prolong the life of the cut flower. Dust and glaze to match the sepals.

LEAVES

16 I don't often use rose leaves as foliage in bridal bouquets, however, they are essential for arrangements. Rose leaves on commercial florists' roses tend to grow in sets of three or five. I generally make one large, two medium and two small for each set. Roll out some holly/ivy flowerpaste, leaving a thick ridge for the wire (a grooved board can speed up this process greatly). Cut out the leaves using the rose leaf cutters. I like the shape of the black rose leaf set of cutters, however, these do not allow you to roll the paste too thickly as they are shallow and the paste often sticks to them. You just need to ignore this and carry on working. Insert a 30-, 28- or 26-gauge white wire moistened with fresh egg white into the leaf, depending on its size. I usually insert the wire about half way into the ridge.

17 Soften the edge of the leaf and vein using the large briar rose leaf veiner. Pinch from behind the leaf to accentuate the central vein and give more movement to the leaf. Repeat to make leaves of various sizes. Tape over a little of each wire stem with quarter-width nile green floristry tape. Tape the leaves into sets of three or five, starting with the largest leaf and two medium-size leaves, one on either side. Finally, add the two smaller leaves at the base.

18 Dust the edges with aubergine and plum or ruby petal dusts mixed together. Use this colour on the upper stems too. Dust the upper surface of the leaf in layers lightly with forest green and more heavily with foliage and vine green. Dust the backs with edelweiss using the brush used for the greens. Spray with edible spray varnish.

Full-blown rose

Using this style of rose on a cake adds an instant informal edge to any design. Open roses are much easier to make than standard, styled roses and having each petal individually wired gives more movement too.

MATERIALS

26-, 28- and 30-gauge white wires
White, pale green, holly/ivy and pink flowerpaste
Small seed-head stamens
Hi-tack non-toxic craft glue (Impex)
Vine green, white, daffodil, sunflower, plum, ruby, nutkin brown, aubergine, foliage and forest petal dusts
Nile green floristry tape
Edible spray varnish (Fabilo)

EQUIPMENT

Wire cutters
Fine-nose pliers
Sharp scissors
Tweezers
Dusting brushes
Rolling pin
Non-stick board
Heart-shaped rose petal cutter set (AD)
    or see templates on page 254
Sharp scalpel (optional)
Christmas rose petal veiner (SKGI)
Ball tool
Kitchen paper
Foam pad
Sharp curved scissors
Grooved board
Rose leaf cutters (J)
Large briar rose leaf veiner (SKGI)

STAMENS

1 Cut a half-length of 26-gauge white wire. Bend a small open loop in one end using fine-nose pliers. Bend the loop back against the main length of wire. Hold the hook at the centre with pliers and bend it to form a 'ski' stick. Attach a small amount of pale green paste onto the hook. (I tend to use cold porcelain for this stage, but it's up to you.)

2 Cut some short lengths of seed-head stamens and quickly insert into the soft paste. Allow to dry.

3 You will need a third to half a bunch of stamens to complete the centre for the flower – this will depend upon the size of the flower you are making. Divide the stamens into smaller groups. Line up their tips so that they are evenly positioned. Bond each group together at the centre using hi-tack non-toxic craft glue. Squeeze the glue into the strands of the stamens and flatten them as you work. Leave a short length of stamen at either end unglued. Allow to dry for a few minutes.

4 Cut the stamens in half and trim away the excess to leave short lengths. Attach these small groups around the dried centre using a very small amount of hi-tack non-toxic craft glue. Leave to dry. Curl the stamens using tweezers to create a more relaxed, natural-looking set of stamens.

5 Dust the stamen centre and the length of the stamens with vine green petal dust. Mix together sunflower and daffodil petal dusts and colour the tips of the stamens. Add tinges of nutkin brown and aubergine to the tips if desired.

PETALS

6 I use several sizes of cutter to complete one rose. The number is not an exact measure although I use no fewer than 15 petals for this style of rose and usually try to make 5 petals of each size. Roll out some pink flowerpaste leaving a thick ridge for the wire. Cut out the petal using one of the heart-shaped rose petal cutters or use the template on page 254.

7 Insert a moistened wire (the gauge will depend upon the size of the petal). Soften the edge of the petal and then vein using a Christmas rose petal veiner.

8 Hollow out the centre of the petal using a ball tool. Curl back the edges of the petal and leave to firm up slightly in a kitchen-paper ring former. Repeat to make the required number of petals.

COLOURING

9 Mix together white, daffodil, sunflower and a touch of vine green petal dusts and dust a patch of colour at the base of each petal on both sides. Next, dust the petals quite heavily with plum petal dust. Rub the dust onto the petals to create an intense colour. Add some aubergine to the edges of each petal. The back of each petal should be slightly paler.

ASSEMBLY

10 Tape a few of the small petals tightly around the stamens using half-width nile green floristry tape. Continue to add the other petals, gradually increasing the petal size as you build up the flower. It helps if the paste is still slightly pliable at this stage so that you can 'snuggle' the petals together to create a more realistic rose.

CALYX

11 Cut five lengths of 30-gauge white wire. Work a ball of pale green flowerpaste onto the wire creating a long tapered carrot shape. Place the shape against the board and flatten using the flat side of one of the double-sided veiners. If the shape looks distorted simply trim into shape with a pair of sharp scissors.

12 Place the flattened shape onto a foam pad or the palm of your hand and soften and hollow out the length using the ball tool. Pinch the sepal from the base to the tip. Cut fine 'hairs' into the edge of the sepal using a pair of sharp curved scissors. Repeat to make five sepals.
I tend to leave one sepal without hairs – although remember there are some varieties of rose that have no hairs to their calyces at all.

13 Dust each sepal on the outer surface with a mixture of foliage and forest green. Add tinges of aubergine mixed with plum or ruby petal dust. Use the same brush used for the green mixture and dust lightly on the inner surface of each sepal with white petal dust. Lightly glaze the back of each sepal with edible spray varnish.

14 Tape the five sepals to the base of the rose, positioning a sepal over a join. Add a ball of paste for the ovary and pinch and squeeze it into a neat shape.

LEAVES

15 Roll out some holly/ivy flowerpaste, leaving a thick ridge for the wire (a grooved board can speed up this process greatly). Cut out the leaves using the rose leaf cutters. (You will find that the black rose leaf set does not allow for very thick leaves – these tend to stick in the cutter.) Insert a moistened 26-, 28- or 30-gauge wire into the leaf depending on its size.

16 Soften the edge of the leaf and vein using the large briar rose leaf veiner. Pinch from behind the leaf to accentuate the central vein and give more movement to the leaf. Repeat to make leaves of various sizes. Tape over a little of each wire stem with quarter-width nile green tape. Tape the leaves into sets of three or five, starting with the largest leaf and two medium-sized leaves, one on either side. Finally add the two smaller leaves at the base.

17 Dust the edges with aubergine and plum or ruby dusts mixed together. Use this colour on the upper stems too. Dust the upper surface of the leaf in light layers with forest green and more heavily with foliage and vine green. Dust the backs with white petal dust using the brush used for the green colours. Spray with edible spray varnish.

Egyptian fan orchid

This is based on an orchid called bulbophyllum. I have added a twist of artistic licence to make this flower a bit more user friendly. I like the fan shapes that these collective orchids make and so have nicknamed it the Egyptian fan orchid. They are very useful for adding a touch of drama to a spray or arrangement.

MATERIALS

White flowerpaste
22- and 33-gauge wire
White and nile green floristry tape
Plum, African violet and aubergine petal dusts
Isopropyl alcohol, to dilute plum petal dust

EQUIPMENT

Rolling pin
Non-stick board
Single daisy petal cutter
Sharp scalpel (optional)
Stargazer B petal veiner (SKGI)
Plain-edge cutting wheel
Fine-nose pliers
Sharp fine scissors
Dusting brushes
Stencil brush/new toothbrush

LATERAL SEPALS

1 These are fused together into one large, almost split, daisy-like petal. Roll out some white paste leaving a thick ridge at the centre. Cut out the petal shape using a large daisy petal cutter. Cut into the thick ridge using a sharp scalpel or fine scissors.

2 Insert a 33-gauge wire into each of the two split thick areas. This can be a bit tricky to deal with at first. Soften the edges and then vein using the stargazer B petal veiner. Add extra veins using the plain-edge cutting wheel. Twist the wired sections back onto themselves and tape the two wires together using quarter-width white floristry tape. Use fine scissors to make a small V-shaped cut at the tip of the petal. Leave to dry.

3 Dust with a mixture of plum and African violet petal dusts. Add tinges of aubergine at the base.

COLUMN, LABELLUM AND LATERAL PETALS

4 Attach a tiny cone of paste to the end of a 33-gauge wire. Hollow out the underside and leave to dry.

5 Make the labellum and lateral petals from tiny teardrop-shaped pieces of paste. Flatten them and pinch onto the column.

DORSAL

6 Make in the same way as the labellum and lateral petals, but it is much larger and curves over the rest of the smaller petals.

7 Dust the whole of this section with aubergine. Tape onto the base of the daisy-shaped petal.

8 Repeat to make several orchids and tape them in a fan formation onto a 22-gauge wire using half-width nile green floristry tape.

9 Add tiny spots of colour by loading a stencil brush/new toothbrush with diluted plum petal dust. Flick colour all over the orchids.

Eyelash orchid

This orchid is made using freehand techniques. It is based on one of the South American Epidendrum orchids, with a touch of artistic licence added to speed up the flower-making process!

MATERIALS
26-, 28- and 33-gauge white wires
White and pale green
   flowerpaste
Fresh egg white
Nile green floristry tape
White, vine green,
   plum, foliage and
   aubergine petal dusts
Edible spray varnish (Fabilo)

EQUIPMENT
Wire cutters
Non-stick board
Stargazer B petal veiner (SKGI)
Sharp scissors
Dresden tool (JEM)
Fine curved scissors
Plain-edge cutting wheel (PME)
Sharp scalpel

OUTER PETALS

1 Cut some 33-gauge wire into thirds. Roll a small ball of well-kneaded white flowerpaste and insert a dry wire into it. Work the paste down the wire firmly between your finger and thumb to create a fine elongated carrot shape. The size of the orchid varies so it does not matter too much about the exact length just as long as you are fairly consistent with all five petals.

2 Smooth the length of the petal between your palms and then place against a non-stick board. Flatten the petal using the flat side of the petal veiner.

3 Pick up the flattened petal shape from the board and if the edges are uneven simply trim them with a sharp pair of scissors. Place the petal into the stargazer B veiner and squeeze both sides of the veiner to firmly texture the petal.

4 Pinch the petal from the base to the tip to emphasize the central vein. Curve the petal. Repeat to make five.

LABELLUM

5 Repeat the above process to create the lip. Use slightly more paste to create a longer petal shape. Try to leave a broader section at the base of the petal. Flatten and vein using the stargazer B veiner.

6 Place the lip onto the board and work the broad section at the base of the petal using the broad end of the dresden tool. This thins out the section to create a frilly effect. Cut into the section with a fine pair of curved scissors to create the fringed 'eyelash' effect required. Pinch and curve the length of the lip.

COLUMN

7 Roll a small sausage of white flowerpaste and attach at the base of the lip using a tiny amount of fresh egg white. Quickly open up the broader tip of the column using the broad end of the dresden tool. As you do this support the back of the column between your finger and thumb – this also helps to create a 'backbone' ridge to the shape.

ASSEMBLY

8 Tape two of the outer petals onto either side of the lip petal using quarter-width tape. Add the three remaining petals behind these two to complete the shape. If the paste is still pliable at this stage it will enable you to reshape and position the petals to create a more relaxed flower.

9 Dust the outer petals with a light mixture of vine green and white petal dust. Tinge the edges with aubergine and plum mixed together.

10 There is a long back to this orchid which is optional. Simply add a sausage of white flowerpaste onto the back and work it around the wire to neaten the join in the back of the petals. Draw a few fine lines down the length of the back using the plain edge-cutting wheel. Dust as for the outer petals.

LEAVES

11 Roll out some green flowerpaste leaving a thick ridge for the wire. Cut out a freehand leaf shape. Insert a 28- or 26-gauge wire depending upon the size of the leaf. Soften the edge and then texture using the stargazer B petal veiner.

12 Pinch the leaf to accentuate a central vein. Curve and allow to firm up a little before dusting.

13 Dust with layers of foliage and vine green petal dusts. Add an aubergine tinge to the edge of the leaf. Spray lightly with edible spray varnish.

Radish

I adore radishes and have been wanting to make them in sugar or cold porcelain for several years now, so here at last, is my version of this beautiful vegetable. There are about three species of radish (*Raphanus*) originating in Europe and western Asia. The cultivated varieties provide a wonderful range of colours, shapes and sizes.

MATERIALS
26- and 28-gauge white wires
Pale green and white flowerpaste
Fresh egg white
Foliage, vine, kiko, racy red, plum, ruby and aubergine petal dusts
Nile green floristry tape
Fine fibre from a sweetcorn, fine lace maker's thread, or sisal (optional)
Hi-tack non-toxic craft glue (optional)
Edible spray varnish

EQUIPMENT
Fresh radish leaves
Silicone plastique
Scissors or wire cutters
Rose petal cutters (TT)
Non-stick board
Dresden tool
Radish leaf veiner set (homemade or Aldaval)
Dusting brushes

LEAVES

I made my own veiners using fresh radish leaves and food-grade silicone plastique as at the time of writing this book there are no commercial radish leaf veiners available. It is very satisfying being able to take a direct copy of the real thing and it also means that your own set of veiners is fairly unique too! (See p 10 for more details about making your own petal and leaf veiners.)

1 To make the fleshy stems of the leaves it is best to make them in advance so that they can dry a little before inserting into the leaf shape.

Cut a half-length of 26-gauge white wire and blend a small ball of pale green flowerpaste onto the dry wire, trying to leave the stem broader at the base and finer at the tip of the wire. The length of this fleshy stem varies, as does the size of the leaves. Work the paste quickly and firmly between your finger and thumb to coat the wire and then place in the fleshy part of your palms to roll and smooth the stem. Repeat to make the required number of stems. I usually use between three and five leaves per radish.

2 Next, roll out some pale green flowerpaste, leaving a thick ridge at the centre to hold the wire. Cut out the leaf shape using one of the rose petal cutters. Insert the tip of the fleshy-coated wire into the pointed end of the rose petal shape. Pinch the paste down onto the stem to secure a good, strong join. Some radish leaves have side sections too – these can sometimes be simply pinched from the base of the leaf between your finger and thumb. For larger side sections simply add extra pinched pieces of flowerpaste at the base of the upper leaf. A touch of fresh egg white might be needed to secure the two together.

3 Place the leaf down against the non-stick board and work the edge of the leaf with the broad end of the Dresden tool to create more of the untidy edge character that the leaves have. Pull the edges of the leaf at intervals down against the board. Don't forget the side sections too.

4 Place the leaf into an appropriate sized double-sided radish leaf veiner and press firmly to texture the surface. Remove from the veiner and pinch from the base of the leaf to the tip to accentuate the central veiner. Allow to firm up over a gentle curve. Repeat to make the required number of leaves.

5 Dust each leaf in layers with foliage and vine petal dusts. Keep the back of the leaves and the base of the stalk slightly paler.

6 Tape a group of leaves together using half-width nile green floristry tape. Trim the wires slightly before inserting into the main body of the radish.

RADISH

7 Roll a ball of well-kneaded white flowerpaste. Work the ball into a rounded teardrop shape. Insert the taped group of leaves into the rounded end of the teardrop and carefully squeeze and blend the main body of the radish against the foliage. Next, insert a short length of 28-gauge white wire into the fine end of the radish. Carefully and firmly work the paste onto the finer wire to create a fine strand at the tip of the radish. Trim off the excess wire and flowerpaste to the required length.

ROOTS

8 The next stage is optional – use fine fibre from the inside of a sweetcorn husk or fine lace maker's thread or even a little sisal to represent the roots. Cut a few short lengths of whichever medium you decide to use and carefully glue onto the fine end of the radish. Trim away any excess threads as you work.

COLOURING

9 The colouring of a radish can vary quite a bit. Use bright pinks and reds to create the vibrant colouring. I have used kiko and racy red on the radishes illustrated – these colours are from America. You could also use plum and ruby to create an intense colour. Tinges of aubergine help to give a little depth too. Add a tinge of foliage green too, if desired, to the radish and its roots. Allow to dry before lightly spraying with edible spray varnish.

Potato vine

Potato vine (*Solanum*) produces pretty flowers in white, pink and pale lilac through to dark blue, and a few mix-and-matches in between too. The plant also produces attractive berries that ripen from green through to yellow and red, and in some cases through to black. The trailing nature of the plant makes it an ideal addition to floral displays.

MATERIALS

Melon, white and pale green flowerpaste
33-, 30-, 28-, 26- and 22-gauge white wires
Small seed-head stamens
Daffodil, sunflower, foliage, African violet, white, plum, vine, aubergine and black petal dusts
Fresh egg white
Nile green floristry tape
Edible spray varnish

EQUIPMENT

Scissors
Plain-edge cutting wheel or scalpel
Dusting brushes
Celstick or smooth ceramic tool (HP)
Small calyx cutter (TT)
Ball tool
Tiny blossom cutter (Kemper)
Non-stick rolling pin
Simple leaf cutters (TT)
Bittersweet leaf veiner (SKGI)
Fine scissors

STAMENS

1 Attach a small cigar-shaped piece of melon-coloured flowerpaste onto the end of a 28-gauge white wire. Insert a short cut piece of a small seed-head stamen into the end to represent the pistil. Divide the flowerpaste into five sections using the plain-edge cutting wheel or a scalpel to represent the stamens. Dust with a mixture of daffodil and sunflower petal dusts.

PETALS

2 Pinch a ball of well-kneaded white flowerpaste to leave a raised 'pimple' at the centre. Thin out around the 'pimple' using a rolling action with a celstick or smooth ceramic tool. Cut out the flower shape using the small calyx cutter.

3 Elongate each petal very slightly and then roll each edge of the petals to broaden them with the smooth ceramic tool. Hollow out the back of each petal a little using the small end of the ball tool.

4 Pinch a central vein down each petal to accentuate a central vein. Moisten the base of the stamens with fresh egg white and thread through the centre of the flower. Pinch the pimple behind the flower to secure it in place.

5 Add a small calyx if time allows using the tiny blossom cutter and pale green flowerpaste. Thread and attach behind the petals. Otherwise, simply dust behind the flower with some foliage petal dust (not if entering competitions though!).

6 Leave to dry and then apply the petal dust as desired. Here I have used a very light mixture of African violet, white and plum petal dusts. Tape over each flower stem and then tape them into clusters using quarter-width nile green floristry tape.

LEAVES

7 Roll out some pale green flowerpaste, leaving a thick ridge for the wire. Cut out the leaf using one of the sizes of simple leaf cutters. Moisten a 30-, 28- or 26-gauge white wire with fresh egg white and insert it into the length (the gauge will depend on the size of leaf you are making). Soften the edge of the leaf with the ball tool and then texture using the bittersweet leaf veiner.

8 Pinch the leaf from the base to the tip to accentuate the central vein. Repeat to make numerous leaves in graduating sizes. Dust the leaves with foliage and vine petal dusts. Add a tinge of African violet mixed with aubergine on the edge. Spray lightly with edible spray varnish. Tape over each leaf stem with quarter-width nile green floristry tape.

BERRIES

9 Roll several balls of pale green flowerpaste and then form each into an egg shape. Insert a 33- or 30-gauge white wire into each fruit so that the wire almost pierces through the pointed end. Add a calyx as for the flower or add a quick-snipped five sepal calyx using fine scissors. Repeat to maker numerous berries in varying sizes.

10 Tape over each stem with quarter-width nile green floristry tape and then form small clusters of berries. Dust the berries in varying degrees of vine, aubergine and finally black petal dusts. Allow to dry and then spray with edible spray varnish.

11 Tape a few smaller leaves onto a 22-gauge white wire using half-width nile green floristry tape, alternating and graduating them down the stem. Introduce clusters of flowers or berries at a leaf axle. Dust the stems with aubergine and foliage petal dusts. Curve and bend the stems into shape.

Pink brunia

There are about seven species of Brunia from South Africa. At first glance, the flowers look rather like seed-heads. This variety is bright pink, making it an ideal subject for floral sugarcrafters to make. There are also grey, green and purple forms.

MATERIALS

28- and 24-gauge white wires
Pale green flowerpaste
Fresh egg white
Plum, coral, foliage, white and
myrtle bridal satin petal dusts
Edible spray varnish
Nile green floristry tape

EQUIPMENT

Fine-nose pliers
Fine curved scissors
Dusting brushes

FLOWER HEAD

1 Bend a hook in the end of a 24-gauge white wire using fine-nose pliers. Roll a ball of well-kneaded pale green flowerpaste. Moisten the hooked wire with fresh egg white and insert into the ball. Pinch the base of the ball onto the wire to secure it in place.

2 Use fine curved scissors to snip into the entire surface of the ball to create a rough texture.

3 When the surface is completely textured, go back and soften the cuts slightly by pressing gently into place. Repeat to make numerous flower heads in varying sizes.

4 Dust with a mixture of plum and coral petal dusts. Use foliage green at the base and over-dust with white or myrtle bridal satin dust. Spray very lightly with edible spray varnish.

5 Tape the flower heads into groups of three and five using nile green floristry tape.

LEAVES

6 Cut short lengths of 28-gauge white wire. Roll a small ball of pale green flowerpaste and work it onto the wire to create a thickened leaf stem. Smooth it between your palms.

7 Snip over the surface of the leaf to make a 'hairy' leaf. Curve into shape. Repeat to make lots of leaves and group into sets of three and five. Dust as for the flower heads.

8 Tape the leaves in groups of three to five at the base of the flowers using half-width nile green floristry tape. Dust over the stems with foliage and myrtle bridal satin dust and tinges of the plum/coral mixture used on the flowerheads.

Peony

Peonies have been used as medicinal plants for at least two thousand years. It is thought that the plant is named after Paeon, the Greek mythological figure who was a pupil of Asclepius, the Greek god of medicine and healing. The god was jealous that Paeon had used the plant to cure a wound that Pluto had received during a fight with Hercules so he had him killed. However, Pluto was so grateful that he changed him into a Paeonia plant!

INNER PETALS

1 Roll out some pink flowerpaste, leaving a thick ridge for the wire. Cut out the petal shape using the smallest rose petal cutter.

2 Insert a 26-gauge white wire moistened with fresh egg white into the thick ridge so that it supports about half the length of the petal. Cut into the petal using fine scissors to create long, slender 'V'-shaped cuts. The number of cuts will vary as this style of peony is quite random.

3 Use the broad end of the Dresden tool to work the very edges of the petal a little and then use the ceramic silk veining tool to texture and thin out each section of the shape. Repeat to make several wired petals.

4 It is best to make a few petals at a time and dust them while the paste is still pliable so that a strong colour can be achieved easily. Here I have used plum, aubergine and kiko petal dusts.

MATERIALS

Pink and holly/ivy flowerpaste
28-, 26- and 22-gauge white wire
Fresh egg white
Plum, aubergine, kiko, foliage, vine and forest petal dusts
Nile green floristry tape
Edible spray varnish

EQUIPMENT

Non-stick rolling pin
Large rose petal cutters (set of three) (TT549-551)
Fine scissors
Dresden tool
Ceramic silk veining tool (HP)
Dusting brushes
Peony petal veiner (SKGI) (optional)
Kitchen paper ring former (p 11)
Standard rose petal cutters (TT278-280)
Ball tool
Non-stick board
Single peony leaf veiner (SKGI)
Peony leaf cutters (optional)
Scalpel

5 Again, while the petals are still pliable, start to tape them together using half-width nile green floristry tape. Pinch and fold each petal as you tape them together to create the start of the almost fluffy centre of the flower. Continue to make the petals, gradually increasing the petals in size a little as you go. The number can vary – I generally work between 20 and 50 petals for this part of the flower.

OUTER PETALS

6 Roll out some pink flowerpaste, leaving a thick ridge. Cut out a petal shape using the largest rose petal cutter. Insert a 26-gauge white wire into the ridge to support about half the length of the petal.

7 Place the petal into a double-sided peony petal veiner or texture the surface by rolling over it with the ceramic silk veining tool, turning the petal over to vein the back too. Frills are optional – some varieties have very frilly outer petals while others are quite flat. Use the ceramic silk veining tool to apply short burst of pressure at the edges of the petal, rolling to create the desired frills.

8 Cup the centre of the petal and then dry in a kitchen paper ring former. Repeat to make between six and 10 outer petals – again the number varies between varieties. Dust as for the inner petals, adding more aubergine at the base to add depth to the flower.

9 Tape these outer petals around the inner fluffy petals using half-width nile green floristry tape. It is best if these petals are still slightly pliable which will allow you to cup and shape them a little more to create a relaxed finish.

CALYX

10 There are three rounded sepal shapes to the calyx that are made using pale holy/ivy flowerpaste (add a little white flowerpaste to lighten the colour) rolled out to leave a thick ridge. Cut out the shape using one of the standard rose petal cutters – there are three sizes used here and you will need to make one sepal of each size. Insert a 28-gauge wire moistened with fresh egg white into the thick ridge at the pointed end of the shape to support about half the length. Soften the edge of the sepal and then hollow out the centre using the ball tool. Pinch a slight point at the top curved edge. Repeat to make the other two sizes.

11 As well as the rounder inner sepals, there are two or three larger leaf-like sepals too. Roll a ball of holy/ivy flowerpaste onto a 28-gauge white wire, working it into a long leaf-like shape that is pointed at both ends. Place the shape against the non-stick board and flatten it using the flat side of the peony leaf veiner. Pick up the leaf and pinch from the base to the tip to create a central vein and curve into shape. Repeat to make the second sepal so that there is a variation in length.

12 Dust the sepals with foliage and vine petal dusts mixed together. Catch the edges with a mixture of plum and aubergine.

13 Tape the three sizes of rounded sepals onto the back of the flower so that they are evenly spaced. Add the two leaf-like sepals opposite each other using half-width nile green floristry tape.

LEAVES

14 There are several sets of peony leaf cutters. I generally make one large shape with two smaller shapes to sit on either side. The leaves can be made with cutters or using a scalpel and the leaf templates on p 246. Roll out the holly/ivy flowerpaste not too thinly, leaving a thicker tapered ridge for the wire. Cut out the leaf shape and insert a wire moistened with fresh egg white – a 22-gauge for the largest leaves through to a 28-gauge for the very smallest. The wire needs to support the leaf shape as it tends to be quite fragile.

15 Soften the edge of the leaf using a large ball tool. Vein each section of the leaf with the single double-sided peony leaf veiner.

16 Pinch the leaf from the base to the tip on each section to accentuate the central veins and also to give movement to the shape. Leave to dry fairly flat with a bit of curving at the tips. Repeat to make the required number of leaves.

COLOURING

17 Dust the edges of the leaves with a mixture of aubergine and plum petal dusts. Add a tinge at the base too. Use layers of forest, foliage and vine to colour the upper surface of each leaf. Use a lighter dusting on the back of the leaves.

18 Tape into sets of three using half-width nile green floristry tape. Spray lightly with edible spray varnish.

Ornamental cabbage

These decorative cabbages are actually edible but are not as tasty as other members of the brassica family and are grown for their highly decorative quality in landscape gardening and for flower arranging.

MATERIALS

28-, 26-, 20-gauge white wire
Pale green flowerpaste
Fresh egg white
Plum, African violet, moss, forest, foliage, vine and aubergine petal dusts
Isopropyl alcohol
White floristry tape
Edible spray varnish

EQUIPMENT

Fine-nose pliers
Non-stick rolling pin
Ornamental cabbage leaf veiner set (Aldaval)
Scissors, plain-edge cutting wheel or scalpel
Dresden tool
Large ball tool
Dusting brushes
Fine paintbrush

CENTRE

1 Bend a hook in the end of a 20-gauge white wire using fine-nose pliers. Attach a ball of pale green flowerpaste onto it and leave to dry.

2 Roll out some pale green flowerpaste not too thinly and place into one of the smaller ornamental cabbage leaf veiners. Press firmly and then release it from the veiner and cut around the outline using scissors, the plain-edge cutting wheel or a scalpel. Work the edges with the Dresden tool to create a slightly untidy finish. Repeat to make several of these smaller leaves and attach around the dried wired ball using fresh egg white.

OUTER LEAVES

3 Continue making outer leaves in various sizes, leaving a thick ridge for a wire strong enough to support the size of the leaf you are working on – 28-gauge for the small leaves and 26-gauge for the larger ones. Vein as before and trim around the shape. Work the edges with the Dresden tool and soften the edges with a large ball tool. Pinch the leaf to accentuate the central vein.

COLOURING AND ASSEMBLY

4 Dust the central area of each leaf on the back and front with a mixture of plum and African violet petal dusts. Use moss, forest and foliage on the edges of the leaves with tinges of vine green here and there too. Add a little depth in places with aubergine petal dust.

5 Mix some isopropyl alcohol with plum, African violet and aubergine petal dusts and then paint a strong central vein on each leaf along with finer side veins.

6 Tape the leaves around the tight centre using half-width white floristry tape. Gradually increase the size of the leaves as you work. Dust the stem with the plum/African violet mix and also a tinge of the greens used on the foliage too.

7 Spray lightly with edible spray varnish or steam gently to set the colour.

Begonia

There are over 900 species of begonia widely distributed throughout the tropics and subtropics but particularly in South America. It is the ornate leaves of Begonia rex that I like the most. They are great for filling spaces in a bouquet or arrangement, while providing interesting colour and texture.

MATERIALS

Pale green flowerpaste
20-, 22- and 24-gauge white wires
Aubergine, foliage, plum and African violet petal dusts
Isopropyl alcohol
Nile green floristry tape
Myrtle bridal satin dust (optional)
Edible spray varnish (Fabilo)

EQUIPMENT

Rolling pin
Non-stick board
Begonia leaf cutters (AD) or see templates on page 253
Sharp scalpel (optional)
Begonia leaf veiners (SKGI and Aldaval)
Dresden tool (J)
Dimpled foam (or similar)
No. 2 paintbrush
Dusting brushes

LEAVES

1 The paste needs to be rolled quite thickly for these leaves as the veiners have short, deep veining to them. You will find that at times they get hungry and bite into the paste – you can sort this out by overlapping the tear and persuading the leaf to mend itself. Roll out the paste leaving a thicker ridge for the wire. Cut out the leaf using a begonia leaf cutter or the templates on page 253 and a sharp scalpel.

2 Insert a moistened wire heavy enough to support the size of leaf you are working on. Place the leaf into the veiner so that the wire runs in line with the central vein on the back of the leaf. Squeeze the two sides of the veiner together to sandwich the leaf. Remove from the veiner and pinch the central and side veins to accentuate them and give them more movement. Turn the leaf over and use the broad end of the dresden tool to create a rough, slightly ragged, frilled edge. Allow the leaf to dry over dimpled foam or similar.

COLOURING

3 It is best to have a picture or a real leaf to copy when painting designs on the surface. Dilute some aubergine or foliage green petal dust (I used aubergine) with isopropyl alcohol. Paint in the main lines radiating from the base of the leaf with a no. 2 paintbrush. Add a border of colouring around the edge of the leaf too. Allow the lines to dry.

4 Dust the back of the leaf heavily with a mixture of plum and African violet petal dusts. Add a little of this colour to the upper surface of the leaf. Next, use some foliage green or aubergine, or both, from the edge of the leaf to the centre. If the painted lines look a little scary simply dust some foliage or aubergine over the lines to soften them. Thicken the stem with a few layers of nile green floristry tape and dust to match the leaf.

5 Add a light dusting of myrtle bridal satin dust or similar if you are making a shiny variety of begonia. Spray lightly with edible spray varnish.

Brassolaeliacattleya orchid

A few years ago I was invited to demonstrate at a sugarcraft exhibition in São Paulo along with my friends from the UK: Tombi Peck, Margaret Ford and David Ford. It was an intensive exhibition and one morning I was offered a quick trip to the flower market – this was just the diversion from cakes that I needed! There were hundreds of orchids as well as other flowers and plants on offer, and I was like a kid in a sweet shop! I managed to fill my hotel room with orchids and other plant material – even the mini-bar was used for storing some of the more tender flowers I had collected over the week! I managed to keep room service out of the room until all the flowers had been photographed by David Ford and then dissected by myself, Tombi and Margaret. It was a great sharing experience and kept us all entertained for days. Sadly, the following year David died, so I am very grateful for that wonderful week we all spent together in Brazil.

MATERIALS
White and green flowerpaste
26-, 24- and 22- gauge white wires
Fresh egg white
Kitchen paper ring former (p 11) or cotton wool
Nile green floristry tape
Daffodil, sunflower, white, vine, plum, African violet, foliage, forest and aubergine petal dusts
Isopropyl alcohol
Edible spray varnish

EQUIPMENT
Ceramic silk veining tool (HP)
Scalpel
Non-stick rolling pin
Amaryllis petal veiner (SKGI)
Dresden tool
Cocktail stick
Large ball tool
Non-stick board
Stargazer B petal veiner (SKGI)
Dusting brushes
Fine paintbrush
Plain-edge cutting wheel
Foam pad
Large tulip leaf veiner (SKGI)

COLUMN

This is the part of the flower that holds the throat petal (labellum). It is best if this can be made in advance and allowed to dry.

1 Roll a ball of well-kneaded white flowerpaste. Form the ball into a teardrop shape and insert a 22-gauge white wire moistened with fresh egg white into the pointed end to support about two-thirds the length of the shape.

2 Hollow out the underside of the column using the rounded smooth end of the ceramic silk veining tool. Firmly press the shape against the tool, pinching a gentle ridge down the back with your finger and thumb as you work. Curve the length of the shape. Allow to dry.

3 Add a tiny ball of white flowerpaste to represent the anther cap at the tip of the column. Divide the cap into two sections using a scalpel.

THROAT/LIP (LABELLUM)

4 Roll out some white flowerpaste, leaving a thick ridge for added support. The flowerpaste needs to be quite fleshy for this part of the flower to help create a heavily frilled throat. Cut out the throat template on p 246 using a scalpel.

5 Place the throat petal into the double-sided amaryllis petal veiner and press firmly to create a heavily veined effect.

6 Next, use the broad end of the Dresden tool to pull out the edge of the flowerpaste at intervals to create a heavy double-frilled effect. Soften the frill using the ceramic silk veining tool, again working at intervals over the frill and this time using a rolling action. The edge may also be thinned further using a cocktail stick.

7 Moisten the base of the throat petal with fresh egg white and wrap the petal around the column, making sure the column is positioned with the hollowed side down against the petal. Overlap the petal at the base and then curl back the edges slightly. There should be some space between the underside of the column and the petal – this can be corrected by opening up the area using the broad end of the Dresden tool. Leave to dry before colouring. The throat might need supporting with a kitchen paper ring former or cotton wool to hold it in place while it dries, or alternatively dry hanging upside down – checking and re-shaping as it firms to create a more relaxed finish.

WINGS/ARMS (LATERAL PETALS)

8 Roll out some white flowerpaste, leaving a thick ridge down the centre. Cut out the petal using the wing template on p 246 and a scalpel.

9 Insert a 24-gauge white wire moistened with fresh egg white into the thick ridge so that it holds about a third to half the length of the petal. Soften the edge with the ball tool. Place into the double-sided amaryllis petal veiner and press firmly to texture it.

10 Next, place the petal against the non-stick board or rest it against your index finger to frill the edges using the ceramic silk veining tool. Pinch a subtle ridge down the centre of the petal. Repeat to make the second wing petal. Allow to dry over a gentle curve of kitchen paper.

HEAD (DORSAL SEPAL)

11 Roll out some white flowerpaste, leaving a thick ridge as before. Cut out the sepal shape using the head template on p 246 and a scalpel.

12 Insert a 26-gauge white wire moistened with fresh egg white into the thick ridge. Soften the edges using the large ball tool. Vein using the double-sided stargazer B petal veiner. Curve the sepal forwards to create a curved shape.

LEGS (LATERAL SEPALS)

13 Repeat as for the dorsal sepal to create the two lateral petals. Curve backwards to dry.

COLOURING AND ASSEMBLY

14 Tape the two wing petals onto either side of the throat petal using half-width nile green floristry tape. Next, add the dorsal sepal to curve behind the wing petals and finally the lateral sepals at the base of the flower. A concentrated mix of daffodil and sunflower petal dusts is added at the centre of the orchid throat.

15 Dust the flower as desired. Here I have used a mixture of white, daffodil and vine green petal dusts to colour the outer petals and sepals. The throat has been coloured heavily with plum, African violet and white petal dusts mixed together. A further layer of just plum has been added to intensify the petal and then a final tinge of African violet has been used on the edge. Tinge the edges of the wing petals and sepals lightly with the plum mixture. Add a light dusting of vine green and foliage to the base of the petals.

16 Dilute some plum and African violet petal dusts with isopropyl alcohol and paint a series of markings onto the throat of the orchid using a fine paintbrush. Steam the flower to set the colour and to remove the dusty finish left by using the layers of petal dust.

LEAVES

17 The leaves are fairly fleshy so try not to roll the paste too fine. Roll out some green flowerpaste, leaving a thicker ridge running down the centre for a strong gauge wire. Cut out a long leaf shape using the large end of the plain-edge cutting wheel.

18 Carefully insert a length of 22-gauge white wire into the thick ridge, supporting the paste on either side as you feed the wire into about half the length of the leaf.

19 Place the leaf onto a foam pad and then soften the edges with a large ball tool, working the tool half on the edge of the leaf and half on the pad. Do not frill the edge.

20 Next, texture the leaf using the double-sided large tulip leaf veiner. Remove from the veiner and pinch the leaf from the base to the tip to accentuate the central vein. Allow the leaf to firm up a little prior to dusting.

21 Dust the leaf in layers with forest, foliage and vine green petal dusts. Catch the edges gently with aubergine petal dust. Leave the leaf to dry before spraying with edible spray varnish.

Epigeneium orchid

There are about 35 species of epigeneium orchid that are native to India, Nepal and across Asia to the Philippines. The colour variation is vast, making it an ideal addition to the flower-maker's repertoire. The method for making them is the same as that used for a dendrobium orchid. This type of orchid, along with the dendrobium orchid, tends to be very fragile as the outer sepals are unwired so care needs to be taken when arranging them into a bouquet.

MATERIALS

White and green flowerpaste
28-, 24- and 22-gauge white wires
Nile green floristry tape
Fresh egg white
Small piece of sponge
White, African violet, plum, vine, foliage and aubergine petal dusts
Edible spray varnish

EQUIPMENT

Ceramic silk veining tool (HP)
Fine-nose pliers
Non-stick rolling pin
Curly dendrobium orchid cutter set (TT)
Stargazer B petal veiner (SKGI)
Non-stick board
Dresden tool
Ball tool
Fine angled tweezers
Large scissors
Dusting brushes
Plain-edge cutting wheel
Large tulip leaf veiner (SKGI)

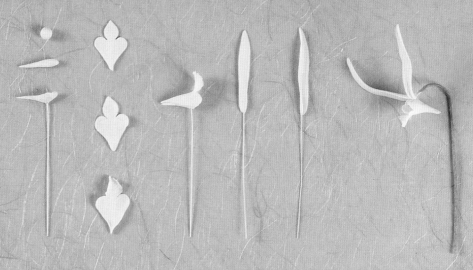

COLUMN

1 Form a small ball of white flowerpaste into a carrot shape. This should measure about a third of the length of the dendrobium orchid lip cutter from the set. Hollow out the underside of the column by pressing it against the rounded end of the ceramic silk veining tool – pinching the back slightly as you do to create a slight ridge.

2 Tape over the length of a 24-gauge white wire with nile green floristry tape. Bend a loop in the end of the wire using fine-nose pliers. Bend the loop against the main length of wire and then hold the loop with the pliers and bend it to form a ski stick shape. Moisten the hook with fresh egg white and pull it through the centre of the column to embed it into the paste. Curve slightly and leave to dry overnight. This section must be firm enough to support and hold the rest of the flower so it is important that it is given plenty of time to dry.

LIP (LABELLUM)

3 Roll out some well-kneaded white flowerpaste quite thinly and cut out the lip shape using one of the cutters from the dendrobium orchid set.

4 Soften the edges of the petal and then vein using the stargazer B petal veiner. Next, place the petal against the non-stick board and use the broad end of the Dresden tool to double frill the edge. Soften the frill using a rolling action with the ceramic silk veining tool.

5 Hollow out the two side sections of the petal using the ball tool. Pinch two ridges at the centre of the shape using fine angled tweezers to create a raised platform.

6 Moisten the sides of the shape with fresh egg white and attach onto the dried column, hollowed-side down, against the petal. Open up the throat slightly and curl back the two side edges. Leave to set a little.

LATERAL (WING) PETALS

7 Roll out some white flowerpaste thinly, leaving a thick ridge for a fine wire. Cut out the long, narrow wing petal shape using one of the cutters from the orchid set. Carefully remove the shape from cutter. Insert a 28-gauge white wire moistened with fresh egg white into the thick ridge of the petal to support about half the length of the petal.

8 Soften the edge and then vein using the stargazer B petal veiner. Pinch the petal from the base to the tip and curve back slightly. Repeat to make a second wing petal. Tape the two wing petals onto either side of the lip and column using half-width nile green floristry tape. Place to one side.

OUTER SEPALS

9 Roll out some white flowerpaste, leaving a ridge down the centre for added support. Cut out the tri-lobed sepal shape using one of the cutters from the orchid set – line up the thick ridge so that it runs into the middle of the central petal. Remove from the cutter and then soften the edge of each section using the ball tool. Vein each sepal in turn using the stargazer B petal veiner.

10 Pinch a central vein down the centre of each sepal. Next, moisten the back and base of the wired column and lip shape with fresh egg white and then thread the wire through the centre of the shape. Ease the shape to fit onto the back of the wired sections. Position each sepal into place and firmly squeeze them onto the dried centre to keep them in place. Curl the dorsal and lateral petals forwards and then backwards towards the tips.

11 Cut a square piece of sponge and then make a slit in it using a large pair of scissors. Slide the sponge behind the flower so that it supports the outer three sepals of the orchid until they firm up enough to support their own weight. When dry remove the sponge very carefully.

COLOURING

12 Mix together white, African violet and plum petal dusts. Use this mixture to colour the inside of the lip area fading towards the edges. Dust the base of the petals and sepals using the same mixture so that the colour fades about half way down the length of each petal/sepal.

13 Use a light mixture of vine and white to colour the sepals and petals from the tip towards the centre of the orchid. Add tinges of foliage green to the tips and the very back of the orchid. Tape over the stem of each orchid with half-width nile green floristry tape to thicken each of the stems. Use fine-nose pliers to bend the stems into a graceful curve.

LEAVES

14 Roll out some green flowerpaste, leaving a thick ridge for the wire. Use the plain-edge cutting wheel to cut out a freehand not-too-slender leaf shape.

15 Insert a 24- or 22-gauge white wire moistened with fresh egg white into about half the length of the leaf. The exact gauge will depend on the size of leaf you are making.

16 Place the leaf into the double-sided large tulip leaf veiner and press the two sides together firmly to texture the surface of the leaf. Remove the leaf from the veiner and carefully pinch it from the base to the tip to accentuate the central vein. Allow to dry in a slightly curved position.

17 Dust in layers with foliage and vine green petal dusts. Catch the edges with aubergine. Allow to dry further and then lightly glaze with edible spray varnish.

Hydrangea

There are many species of hydrangea. Here are the instructions for a crimped-edged variety. The decorative bracts of the hydrangea are formed into three, four or more sections looking rather like flower petals. The real flowers are actually tiny and are at the heart of the flower head.

MATERIALS

20-, 22-, 24-, 26-, 28-, 30-, 33- and
    35-gauge white wires
White and green flowerpaste
White and nile green floristry tape
African violet, aubergine, vine green,
    foliage, bluegrass, ultramarine, forest,
    plum and edelweiss white petal dusts
Clear alcohol
Half glaze or edible spray varnish (Fabilo)

EQUIPMENT

Wire cutters
Fine-nose pliers
Sharp scalpel or plain-edge cutting wheel
Dusting brushes
Crimped hydrangea petal cutters (AD) or
    hydrangea petal cutters (TT764, 765)
Medium metal ball tool
Hydrangea petal veiner (SKGI)
New fine toothbrush
Virginia creeper leaf cutters (AD)
Foam pad
Small, medium and large hydrangea leaf
    veiners (SKGI)
Edible spray varnish

BUDS

1 There are a mass of buds and flowers at the heart of the hydrangea and at the centre of each set of decorative bracts. I choose to make only the buds as they are much quicker to make than the tiny flowers. You will need to allow plenty of time to sit and make lots of buds. Cut several short lengths of 35- or 33-gauge white wires. Make a tiny hook in the end of each using fine-nose pliers. Roll several small balls of white paste and insert a dry, hooked wire into each. Work the base of the bud onto the wire to secure it in place.

2 Divide the bud into four or five sections using a sharp scalpel or plain-edge cutting wheel – the number varies on one flower head. Tape these buds into small groups using quarter-width white floristry tape. Dust as required. I have used a mixture of African violet and plum, with tinges of vine green and foliage. For the plain-edged blue hydrangea use a mixture of ultramarine and white.

MODIFIED BRACTS

3 At first glance these look like petals but they are actually modified decorative bracts. They occur in sets of three, four, five or even double forms. I usually use sets of three and four. Roll out some well-kneaded white flowerpaste leaving
a thick ridge for a fine wire. Cut out a bract shape using one of the hydrangea petal cutters. Insert a moistened 30- or 28-gauge wire into the thick ridge so that it supports about a third to half the length.

4 Soften the edge of the bract using a medium-sized metal ball tool. Texture the bract in the double-sided hydrangea bract/petal veiner. Pinch the base of the bract to the tip to accentuate a central vein. Repeat
to make the required number of bracts. The bracts can be all the same size or you can combine two small and two large.

COLOURING AND ASSEMBLY

5 Tape three or four bracts around a single bud using quarter-width white floristry tape. If you have varied the size then add the two small bracts first opposite each other followed by the two larger ones behind to fill
the gaps.

6 Dust the bracts as required. Here I have used patches of various colours – vine green mixed with a little edelweiss and then touches of bluegrass followed by a mixture of plum and African violet. Use ultramarine blue for the blue hydrangea pictured.

7 Tape a small group of buds onto the back of each of the bract flowers. Then start to build up the flower head, taping the flowers onto the end of a 20-gauge wire with nile green floristry tape. Add a group of buds and carry on adding further groups around this central one. Gradually encircle with the bract flowers to complete the flower head.

8 Dilute some African violet petal dust with clear alcohol. Load a new toothbrush with the dark purple colour and flick it over the whole flower head to add dark purple spots.

LEAVES

9 Roll out some green flowerpaste, leaving a thick ridge for the wire. Cut out the leaf using one of the Virginia creeper leaf cutters. Insert a moistened 28-, 26-, 24- or 22-gauge wire – depending upon the size of leaf you are making – into the thick ridge. Soften the edge using a medium ball tool working half on
the paste and half on a pad or your hand. Try not to frill the leaf.

10 Vein the leaf using one of the hydrangea leaf veiners. Pinch the leaf from the base to the tip to accentuate the central vein. Repeat to make graduating sizes of foliage.

COLOURING

11 Dust the edges of the leaves with aubergine petal dust. Add a little aubergine towards the base of the leaf also. Dust the upper surface of the leaf in light layers of forest green, from the base fading to the edges, and then heavier with foliage green and finally a little vine green. The backs of the leaves are much paler so use only a little of the colour left on the brush to catch the veins. Allow to dry and then glaze using a half glaze or spray lightly with edible spray varnish.

12 Add the leaves in pairs down the stem, starting with the small leaves and increasing in size as you work down the stem. Dust the main stem with foliage green and a touch of aubergine. Spray the stem with edible spray varnish or steam to seal the colour

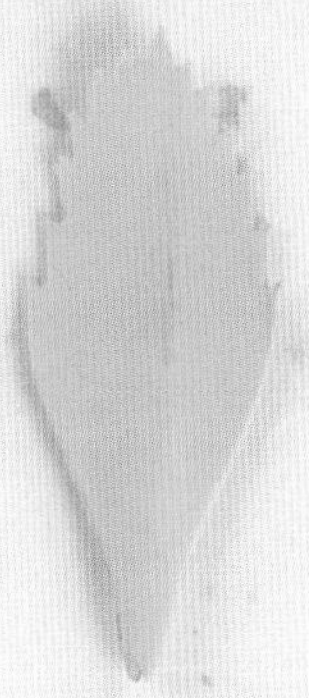

59

Moth orchid

There are many species of moth orchid (*Phalaenopsis*) and many more hybridised forms. The flower illustrated here is based on one that I have growing at home and that flowers very regularly. This is a difficult flower to make look realistic as it is quite flat looking. Most people crave the need to make the very flat, pure white moth orchids but I much prefer the hybridised, unusually coloured and spotted forms.

MATERIALS

White and yellow flowerpaste
26-gauge white wire
Fresh egg white
Sunflower, plum, African violet, daffodil, vine, white and foliage petal dusts
Isopropyl alcohol
White floristry tape

EQUIPMENT

Non-stick rolling pin
Scalpel
Morth orchid lip cutters (TT28, 25)
Non-stick board
Celstick or smooth ceramic tool
Scissors
Fine-nose pliers
Tweezers
Dusting brushes
Fine paintbrush
Ball tool

THROAT/LIP (LABELLUM)

1 Roll out some white flowerpaste, leaving a thick ridge for the wire. Cut out the labellum shape using the throat template on p 247 and a scalpel. Otherwise use one of the two sizes of moth orchid lip cutters to cut out the shape – the shape can vary a little between a just-opened and a fully opened orchid. Insert a 26-gauge white wire into the length of the thick ridge – this is quite a fragile shape so it is important that the wire passes through the narrow section of the shape.

2 Place the shape onto the non-stick board, elongate and broaden the two rounded side sections using a rolling action with the celstick or smooth ceramic tool to make them more oval in shape. Next, soften the edge of the whole shape and hollow out the two oval side sections. Pinch the length of the petal down the centre slightly back on itself to create a gentle ridge. The tip of the labellum may be left very pointed or trimmed into less of a point using scissors. In some moth orchids it can be fairly blunt.

3 Use fine-nose pliers to bend the wire and create a small hook at the base of the shape. Twist the hook slightly to tighten it. Next, attach a small cone-shaped piece of white flowerpaste over the hook to represent the column. Hollow out the underside by positioning the rounded end of the smooth ceramic tool under the shape and pressing the top of the column against it, creating a hollowed-out shape to the underside and a slight ridge to the upper surface. Curve the whole length of the labellum into the required curved shape.

4 To create the yellow ridged platform at the centre of the throat, simply form a small ball of yellow flowerpaste into a teardrop shape. Divide the broad end using the back of a scalpel blade or with tweezers to create a heart shape profile. Pinch the edges of the shape to thin them slightly. Trim the point off the base of the heart and attach at the heart of the throat/labellum petal with a small amount of fresh egg white. Leave to dry.

5 This step is optional, depending on the type of moth orchid you are making. There are often two fine strands at the very tip of the labellum that form a moustache shape. Roll these from white flowerpaste and attach to the tip of the labellum using fresh egg white or a tacky mixture of egg white and flowerpaste. In some varieties, the moustache curls and curves forwards at the tip, and in others it bends and curls backwards.

6 Carefully dust the raised platform and around its base onto the petal using sunflower petal dust. Dust the edges and base of the lip as required – here I have used a mixture of plum and African violet petal dusts and added fine detail spots using this colour mix diluted with isopropyl alcohol.

WINGS/ARMS (LATERAL PETALS)

7 Roll out some white flowerpaste, leaving a thick ridge for the wire. Cut out the petal shape using the wing template on p 247 and cut around it with a scalpel. Insert a moistened 26-gauge white wire into the thick ridge of the petal so that it supports a third to half the length of the petal. Pinch the base of the petal down onto the wire to neaten it and secure it in place. Soften the edge with a ball tool.

8 Place the petal into the wide petal veiner from the moth orchid veiner set. Press firmly to texture the surface. Remove from the veiner and pinch slightly at the base and the tip to create a little movement in the petal. Repeat to make a second petal – a mirror image of the first.

HEAD (DORSAL SEPAL)

9 Roll out some white flowerpaste leaving a thick ridge and cut out the sepal shape using a sharp scalpel and the head template on p 247. Insert a 26-gauge white wire into the central ridge to support about half the length. Soften the edge of the sepal using the ball tool. Next, place the sepal into the narrow veiner from the moth orchid set. Pinch the sepal at the base and at the tip, and then allow to dry, curved gently backwards – sometimes the tip curves forwards too.

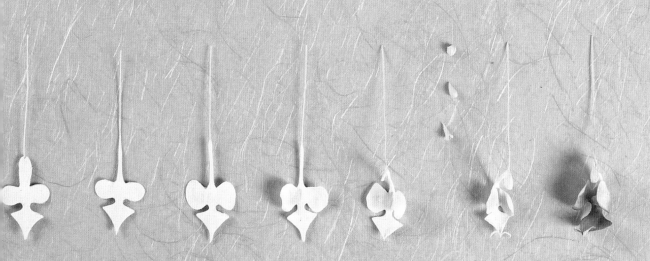

LEGS (LATERAL SEPALS)

10 Repeat the method described for the dorsal sepal in step 9, using the more curved lateral sepal template on p 247. To create the second lateral sepal, flip the template over prior to cutting with the scalpel so that you create a left and a right sepal shape.

ASSEMBLY AND COLOURING

11 It is best to assemble the petals and sepals while they are still on the pliable side as this will allow you to curve and form them into a more relaxed shape, thereby creating a more realistic end result. Use half-width white floristry tape to tape the two wing petals onto either side of the labellum petal. Next, add the dorsal sepal tightly behind the wings to fill the gap that they have created. Finally, add and tape the lateral sepals (legs) behind the wings to fill in and complete the flower shape. Reshape the petals if needed.

12 Dust the petals and sepals with a light mixture of daffodil, vine green and white petal dusts, working from the base of each shape fading towards the edges and then dusting from the edge towards the centre. Don't forget to dust the backs too.

13 Add spotted detail using a mixture of African violet, plum and white petal dusts diluted with isopropyl alcohol. Use a dry mixture of these colours to catch the edges of the petals and sepals. Use a mixture of vine green and foliage to add a tinge of colour at the back of the flower where the petals and sepals join the main stem.

14 Allow the flower to dry and then hold over the steam from a just-boiled kettle, or if you are worried about the heat, try using a clothes steamer instead.

Anemone

Native to Mediterranean countries and also parts of Asia, the anemone has been cultivated since ancient times. They are wonderful to make in sugar because of their intense colouring and beautiful stamen-packed centres.

MATERIALS

22-, 26- and 28-gauge white wires
Pale green cold porcelain (optional)
Semolina coloured with black and deep purple petal dusts
White seed-head stamens
Hi-tack non-toxic craft glue (Impex)
African violet, plum, aubergine, ruby, black, foliage, forest and vine green petal dusts
Clear alcohol (Cointreau or kirsch)
White and pale green flowerpaste
Pale green or white floristry tape
Edible spray varnish (Fabilo)
Fresh egg white

EQUIPMENT

Fine-nose pliers
Sharp fine curved scissors
Sharp scissors
Tweezers
Rolling pin
Non-stick board
Grooved board
Anemone petal and leaf cutter set (AD) or see templates on page 253
Sharp scalpel
Foam pad
Large ball tool
Anemone petal veiner (Aldaval)
Kitchen paper
Wild geranium leaf veiner (SKGI) dresden tool

CENTRE AND STAMENS

1 The centre of the flower can be made with flowerpaste however, I prefer to use craft glue to bond the stamens around the centre to create a neater finish so it is advisable to make an inedible centre using cold porcelain instead. Bend a hook in the end of a 22-gauge wire using fine-nose pliers. Roll a ball of pale green cold porcelain and insert the hooked wire into it. Pinch the ball onto the wire to secure in place. Texture the surface of the ball using the curved scissors. Moisten the surface of the ball and dip into the coloured semolina. Shake off the excess and leave to dry.

2 Make several small groups of seed-head stamens. Line up their tips at both ends. Use a little non-toxic craft glue at the centre of each bunch to bond the stamens together. Work the glue from the centre towards the tips leaving a little of the stamen length unglued at each end to create movement in the finished flower. Flatten the glue into the stamens and leave to set – it will only take about 4–5 minutes for the glue to firm up sufficiently. Cut the stamens in half using sharp scissors and trim off the excess length – the stamens should be a little longer than the black centre.

3 Apply a little glue to each cropped stamen group and attach around the base of the black centre to create a neat ring. Leave to dry, and then pinch with tweezers to create a little movement and realism. Dust the stamens to match the flower – a purple flower has purple stamens, a red flower has red stamens etc. Dilute a little black petal dust with clear alcohol and add a touch of deep purple petal dust to create a thick paint to colour the tips of the stamens. Leave to dry.

PETALS

4 Roll out some white paste leaving a ridge thick enough to insert a fine wire. (A grooved board may also be used for this job.) Cut out a petal shape using one of the anemone petal cutters or use a sharp scalpel and one of the templates on page 253. The number of petals can vary on each flower. I usually use between 5 and 15 petals per flower and vary the size a little.

COLOURING

7 It is best to dust the petals while the paste is still pliable to create strong colouring. In this example I used African violet and plum petal dust to create a very intense purple flower. It is important to leave a white area at the base and use less on the back of the petal. (If you make a mistake and colour the whole petal it is possible to remove a bit of colour with an anti-bacterial wipe.)

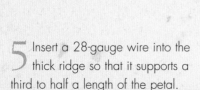

5 Insert a 28-gauge wire into the thick ridge so that it supports a third to half a length of the petal.

6 Place the petal onto a foam pad and soften the edges with a large ball tool. Texture the petal using a double-sided anemone petal veiner or something with a similar fine fan formation texture. Hollow the centre of the petal very gently and allow to firm up a little in a kitchen-paper ring former. Repeat to make the required number of petals.

ASSEMBLY

8 Start by taping the smaller petals onto the stamens using half-width white or pale green floristry tape. Continue to add the larger petals a few at a time to build up the complete flower head. You will find that some flowers look better with fewer petals and some with more. Tape over the stem a few times to create a fleshy stem.

10 Using a sharp scalpel or fine scissors make a series of V-shaped cuts in the edge of the leaf to make a finer effect. The edge may also be worked on using the broad end of the dresden tool to create a 'frillier' effect. Repeat to make three leaves for each flower and bud.

11 Dust the edges of each leaf with a little of the flower colour plus a tinge of aubergine.
Next, dust in layers from the base with foliage green, adding a touch of forest green, fading the colour a little towards the edges. Overdust with vine green. Glaze lightly with an edible spray varnish or dip into a quarter glaze. Leave to dry.

12 Tape three or four leaves behind the flower so that they are all at the same level on the stem. The more mature the flower, the further down the stem the leaves will be. Dust the stem lightly with foliage, vine, aubergine and perhaps a little of the flower colour too.

BUD

13 Bend a hook in the end of a 20-gauge wire. Form a ball of white paste into an almost egg shape. Moisten, and insert the hook into the broad base of the bud. Leave to dry. Roll out some white paste and cut out five petals using the smaller anemone petal cutter. Soften the edges of each petal and vein using the anemone petal veiner.

14 Moisten the bud with fresh egg white and position the petals around the centre in a fairly informal way, adding them opposite each other. Flatten the bud shape if a tighter bud is required. Dust to match the flower, remembering that the back of the petals is usually paler than the inside. Add leaves as for the flower.

LEAVES

9 Roll out some pale green paste leaving a thick ridge for the wire. Cut out the leaf shape using an anemone leaf cutter. Insert a moistened 26-gauge wire into the thick ridge so that it supports quite a bit of the length in the central section. Soften the edge of the leaf using a large ball tool. Vein the leaf using a wild geranium leaf veiner.

Ornamental grass

I was lucky enough to watch a demonstration by Gregor Lersch – a wonderful florist and flower arranger. He used grasses amongst the flowers and when asked which variety he was using he joked that one was called Grassius Roadside-ius and the other Grassius Carpark-ius! Just after this introduction into the fun side of grasses, three friends of mine created a beautiful wedding cake with roses and grasses.

MATERIALS
25-, 26-, 28-, 30- and 33-gauge white wires
White or pale green flowerpaste
Ruby, aubergine and foliage green
    petal dusts
Edible spray varnish (Fabilo)
Quarter glaze (optional)

EQUIPMENT
Fine curved scissors
Flat dusting brushes

GRASS

1 Choose a wire strong enough to hold the size of grass you intend to make. The one illustrated here was made on 33-gauge wires.

2 Blend a small amount of white or pale green flowerpaste onto the end of a wire to create the required length. Hold the wire upside down and quickly snip fine cuts into the paste using a pair of fine curved scissors. Flick some of the cuts back on themselves to open up the shape slightly. Repeat to create a whole bunch of grass.

I generally find the more grass used in a bouquet or arrangement the more realistic it looks.

COLOURING

3 Dust as required. Here I have used a touch of foliage green at the base of the grass and then lots of ruby and an overdusting of aubergine. Allow to dry and then spray very lightly with edible spray varnish or dip into a quarter glaze, shake and dry. Use *en masse* for delicate impact.

Geraldton waxplant

This pretty plant from Western Australia produces tiny lilac, rose, red and also white flowers. They are readily available from florists during spring and are useful for bouquets and arrangements.

MATERIALS

28-, 30-, 33- and 35-gauge white wires
Non-toxic hi-tack craft glue (Impex)
White seed-head stamens
Aubergine, plum, vine, moss and foliage petal dusts
Tiny white stamens
White and green flowerpaste
Nile green floristry tape

EQUIPMENT

Wire cutters
Dusting brushes
Rolling pin
Non-stick board
Small five-petal blossom cutter
Smooth ceramic tool
Leaf/petal veiner
Fine sharp curved scissors

STAMENS

1 Cut several short lengths of 30- or 28-gauge white wires. Glue a short length of a seed-head stamen onto the end with a touch of hi-tack glue – this represents the pistil. Leave to set and then paint with some diluted aubergine petal dust.

2 Attach five fine stamens around the pistil using a little glue. These should have their tips lower than the tip of the pistil. Dust the tips with plum petal dust and a little touch of vine green at the base.

FLOWER

3 Form a ball of white paste into a cone and then pinch the base to form a small hat shape. Roll out the base to thin the brim and then cut out the flower using a five-petal blossom cutter.

4 Hollow out the centre of the flower and soften the petals using the ceramic tool. Moisten the base of the stamens and pull through the centre. Neaten the back. Dust the edges with plum petal dust and the base with vine green and foliage.

5 Make tiny round buds on 35- or 33-gauge wires. Dust to match the flowers.

LEAVES

6 Cut short lengths of 35- or 33-gauge wire. Attach a ball of green paste to the wire and work the paste to form a thin strand. Flatten the leaf using the flat side of any leaf/petal veiner. If needed, use fine sharp curved scissors to tidy up the shape. Next, pinch a central vein. Repeat to make lots of leaves. Dust with moss and foliage petal dusts.

7 Tape the leaves onto a 28-gauge wire using quarter-width nile green floristry tape. Gradually introduce the buds and flowers to snuggle in amongst the foliage.

67

Golden spider lily

This Chinese species – Lycoris aurea – is one of about 20 species of spider lily that produce beautifully fragile flowers that help to add impact to any floral arrangement. There are also other species that have white, orange, pink or red flowers.

MATERIALS
26-, 28- and 30-gauge white wires
Pale yellow and green flowerpaste
Daffodil, sunflower, African violet, aubergine, coral, vine green and foliage petal dusts
Nile green floristry tape
Clear alcohol

EQUIPMENT
Wire cutters
Dusting brushes
Non-stick board
Stargazer B petal veiner (SKGI)
Dresden tool (Jem)
Plain-edge cutting wheel
Fine-nose pliers

PISTIL

1 Take a half length of 30-gauge wire and blend a small ball of yellow paste onto the wire about 5 cm (2 in) from the tip. Work the paste to the tip to create a fine, smooth pistil. Flatten the tip slightly by pinching with your finger and thumb and flattening with another finger. Curve gracefully. Dust the pistil with a touch of vine green at the tip and a mixture of daffodil and sunflower from the base fading towards the tip.

STAMENS

2 Repeat the above process to create the stamens – they should be very slightly shorter than the pistil and do not flatten their tips. Next, add a tiny sausage shape pointed at both ends, to the tip. (As with other fine stamens of this nature I prefer to use cold porcelain, making the final result much stronger.) Make six more.

3 Curve the length of the stamens to follow the line of the pistil. Dust the length of the stamens as for the pistil. Colour the tips yellow with African violet and aubergine. Tape the six stamens around the pistil using quarter-width nile green floristry tape.

PETALS

4 Use 28-gauge white wires for the petals. Roll a ball of yellow paste onto the wire to create a slightly shorter length but with more bulk than the stamens. Flatten the shape against the non-stick board using the flat side of the stargazer B petal veiner. Texture the surface using the stargazer B veiner, pressing firmly to leave fine veining.

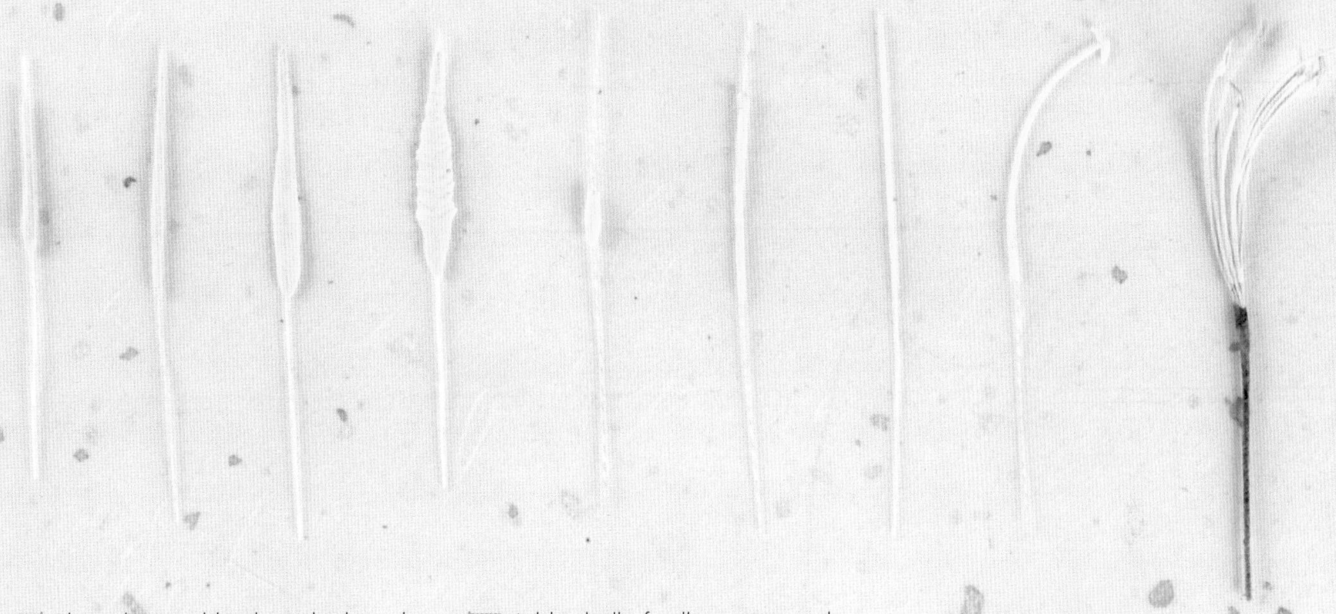

5 Place the petal back on the board and double frill the edge using the broad end of the dresden tool. Work at intervals along both edges of the petal pulling out with the broad end of the tool to create a very tight frilled effect. Curl the petal back on itself. Repeat to make six petals.

COLOURING AND ASSEMBLY

6 It is up to you if you dust now or when the flower is taped together. I prefer to wire the petals around the stamens first using half-width nile green tape and then colour. This allows me to create a more balanced finish between the petals. Tape three petals on first and then position the other three slightly behind and in between the joins.

It helps at this stage if the petals are still pliable as you will be able to create more interesting curls.

7 Add a ball of yellow paste at the back of the flower and work it to create an elongated neck shape. Use the broad end of the dresden tool with a touch of clear alcohol to try and blend the paste into the base of the petals.

8 Dust the flower using a mixture of daffodil and sunflower. Add tinges of coral to the edges.

OVARY

9 Add a ball of green paste at the base of the flower to represent the ovary. Divide into three sections using the plain-edge cutting wheel. Pinch each section between your finger and thumb. Dust with foliage and vine green.

BUDS

10 Bend a hook in the end of a third of a length of 26-gauge wire. Form a cone-shaped bud using pale yellow paste. Insert the hooked wire into about half the length of the bud and then work the base of the bud down onto the wire to elongate its shape. Divide the length into three using the plain-edge cutting wheel. Dust as for the flower and add an ovary.

Winterberry

Winterberry (Ilex verticillata) is a type of holly native to America and Canada. The plant loses its foliage during the autumn allowing these stunning berries to show themselves off to their full potential! The berries are mostly red but there are yellow and orange forms too.

MATERIALS

18-, 20-, 22-, 33- and 35-gauge wires
Red, yellow or orange flowerpaste (depending on colour of berries you want to make)
Ruby, red, tangerine, aubergine, sunflower, nutkin brown and foliage petal dusts
Edible spray varnish or full glaze
Brown floristry tape

EQUIPMENT

Wire cutters
Fine-nose pliers
Tealight
Cigarette lighter or matches
Flat dusting brushes

BERRIES

1 Cut several lengths of 35- or 33-gauge wire into very short lengths. Take several wires at a time, line up the ends and then bend them all in one go with a pair of fine-nose pliers.

2 Light the tealight and burn the hooked end of the wires. This will leave them looking black.

3 Roll balls of your chosen colour of flowerpaste. Moisten the hook and push a single wire into each berry. Leave to firm up a little before the next stage.

COLOURING AND ASSEMBLY

4 Dust the berries to create the desired effect. I use red, ruby and a tinge of aubergine for the very red forms; tangerine and red for the orange varieties; and sunflower and tangerine for the yellow. Allow to dry, then spray with edible spray varnish or dip into a full glaze. You might need a few layers of glaze to create very shiny berries. Allow to dry. Dust the short stems with foliage and aubergine petal dusts.

5 Tape over a short length of 22-gauge wire with half-width brown tape to create a twig effect. Tape the berries quite tightly onto the twig. To create a larger piece, tape several smaller twigs onto a 20- or 18-gauge wire. I mostly use short twigs in a spray of flowers. Dust over the twigs with nutkin brown petal dust.

Wire vine

This delicate trailing foliage has a very complicated Latin name for such a small leaf – Muehlenbeckia axillaris! Its common names are just as much fun – maindenhair vine, creeping wire vine and my favourite, the mattress vine! Although the plant has a very small leaf it both builds structure within a bouquet and softens a design at the same time.

LEAVES

1 Cut several lengths of 33- or 35-gauge wire into very short lengths. Blend a tiny ball of pale green paste onto the end of a dry wire. Work the ball between your finger and thumb to create a slight point at both ends.

2 Place the shape against the non-stick board and using the flat side of a leaf veiner simply flatten, or as I prefer to call it, 'splat', the shape to thin it out and form the leaf shape. Remove the veiner and take a look at the form – it might need a trim here and there with fine scissors to keep a more uniform shape. However, with practice you will find that the 'splatted' shapes start to form a uniform shape of their own.

3 Soften the edges with a small ball tool and then vein using a tiny rose leaf veiner or use the tighter, smaller veined section of a larger briar rose leaf veiner. Remove the leaf from the veiner and pinch from the base to the tip. Repeat to create what will seem like a few million leaves. I suggest listening to some music while you work!

4 Tape the leaves onto a fine-gauge wire, gradually adding slightly stronger wires for support if needed. Use quarter-width nile green tape and alternate the leaves down the stem, starting with the smallest and gradually increasing in size.

COLOURING

5 Dust the upper surface of each leaf using a touch of forest green and overdust with foliage green. Add a tinge of aubergine around the edges and to the main trailing stem and short stems that might be visible too. Spray lightly with edible spray varnish.

MATERIALS
26-, 28-, 33- and 35-gauge white
    wires
Pale green flowerpaste
Nile green floristry tape
Foliage, forest and aubergine petal
    dusts
Edible spray varnish (Fabilo)

EQUIPMENT
Wire cutters
Non-stick board
Small rose leaf veiner or large briar
    rose leaf veiner (SKGI)
Fine curved scissors
Small ball tool
Flat dusting brushes

Lilac

It was John Tradescant, the naturalist who became gardener to Charles I, who introduced lilac (*Syringa*) to Great Britain in 1621. Lilac is native to eastern Europe and Asia Minor. My friend, Alex Julian, kindly donated this sprig of lilac for the book – she has a lot more patience than me with tiny flowers!

BUDS

1 Cut short lengths of 33-gauge white wires. Form a ball of white flowerpaste into a cone shape. Insert a dry wire into the fine end. Thin down the neck slightly and pinch off any excess using your finger and thumb. Divide the top of the bud into four using fine scissors. Make lots of buds in varying sizes of small!

FLOWERS

2 These are made using a pulled flower method. Form a teardrop of well-kneaded white flowerpaste. Open up the broad end using the pointed end of the smooth ceramic tool.

3 Cut four sections using fine scissors. Pinch each section between your finger and thumb to form pointed petals. Next, 'pull' the petals between your finger and thumb to flatten and thin them a little.

4 Use the broad end of the Dresden tool to hollow out and mark a central vein on each petal.

5 Insert a hooked 30-gauge white wire moistened with fresh egg white through the centre of the flower. Thin the back of the flower if needed. Trim off the excess. Repeat to make numerous flowers – some should be slightly open and others fully open in shape.

COLOURING AND ASSEMBLY

6 Dust the buds and flowers as required. Here, the flowers were dusted with a mixture of empress purple, plum and African violet.

7 Tape the buds into small tight groups using quarter-width nile green floristry tape. Use these at the tip of the sprig. Continue to add other groups of flowers and buds mixed together as you work down the sprig.

MATERIALS
33- and 30-gauge white wires
White flowerpaste
Fresh egg white
Empress purple, plum and African violet petal dusts
Nile green floristry tape

EQUIPMENT
Wire cutters
Fine scissors
Smooth ceramic tool
Dresden tool
Dusting brushes

French lavender

I adore lavender. The scent is amazing and is without doubt my favourite scented plant of all time. There are many forms of lavender, with the petal-like bracts occurring in white, pink and pale blue through to strong purples and an almost black variety too. The plant is a wonderful herb that can be used to cook with and has anti-bacterial and healing qualities too.

MATERIALS

33-gauge white wire
White and pale holly/ivy flowerpaste
African violet, plum, deep purple, white, foliage and aubergine petal dusts
Nile green floristry tape

EQUIPMENT

Wire cutters
Non-stick board
Briar rose leaf veiner (SKGI)
Dresden tool
Dusting brushes
Cocktail stick
Fine curved scissors
Fine angled tweezers

MODIFIED BRACTS

1 At first glance you could be mistaken for thinking that French lavender has large colourful petals. These are in fact modified bracts/leaves. To make the bracts, cut short lengths of 33-gauge white wire. Blend a small ball of white flowerpaste onto the wire to create a slender shape that is slightly pointed at both the base and the tip. Place the shape against the non-stick board and flatten it using the flat side of the briar rose leaf veiner. Repeat to make four bracts of varying sizes.

2 Work the edges of each bract with the broad end of the Dresden tool to create a thinned out, slightly untidy, frill effect. Next, vein each bract using the double-sided briar rose leaf veiner.

3 Pinch each bract from the base to the tip to accentuate the central vein. Curve each bract slightly.

4 Dust the bracts to the desired intensity – it is best to apply the colour before the paste dries to create a strong effect. Here I have used a mixture of African violet, plum and deep purple petal dusts. Fade the colour towards the edge a little.

5 Tape the four bracts together with quarter-width nile green floristry tape, making sure that the ridged veins of the back of each bract are facing the outer edges. If the paste is still pliable you will find that now is a good time to reshape the bracts to create a more relaxed/realistic effect.

FLOWERS AND BUDS

6 These are tiny and not always in flower, so you might prefer not to make them. I have only used buds in the lavender illustrated here and if I am making flowers, then I tend to create very simple, almost abstract, forms, as to create an accurate replica takes too much time. For the buds, form tiny sausage shapes of African violet-coloured flowerpaste. Taper both ends. Make lots and leave to set hard. For the flowers, hollow out the broad end of a tiny cone of African violet-coloured flowerpaste using a cocktail stick. Thin the edges at intervals with the Dresden tool to create a five-petal effect. Leave to dry.

GREEN BRACTS/CALYX

7 Attach a ball of pale holly/ivy flowerpaste at the base of the wired bracts. Blend the paste into a tight waistline where it meets the base of the bracts. Elongate and thin the base of the green paste too and remove any excess. The size and shape of this green section can vary quite a bit. I have kept it fairly slender in my sugar version to create a daintier effect for cake decorating purposes.

8 Use fine curved scissors to snip a scale effect into the surface of the green flowerpaste – this is to represent the numerous green bracts that occur in this section. Add a few pinched lines with fine angled tweezers onto each bract.

9 Before the flowerpaste dries, quickly insert the required amount of dried buds and flowers into the paste so that they appear out of the bract shapes. Leave to dry before colouring.

10 Dust the whole of the green bract shape with a mixture of white and foliage petal dusts. Add tinges of African violet mixed with aubergine. Dust the buds and flowers as desired – these can be a clean purple through to an almost dark purple-black colour.

LEAVES

11 Cut several short lengths of 33-gauge white wire. Attach a tiny ball of pale holly/ivy flowerpaste onto the end of a dry wire and work the paste onto the wire to create a fine strand shape. Flatten the shape against the non-stick board using the flat side of the briar rose leaf veiner. Soften the edge if needed and then pinch from the base to the tip to create a central vein. Repeat to make the leaves in pairs.

12 Tape the leaves in pairs down the stem of the lavender using quarter-width nile green floristry tape. Dust the stem to match the green bract/calyx. Steam to set the colour.

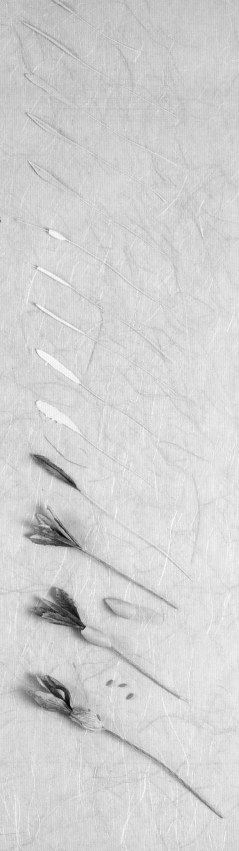

White bombax

There are eight species of bombax tree native to India and the drier parts of Burma. The flowers are very large and the petals vary in width and length between varieties. There are also red and orange forms. Usually, the white bombax has narrower petals than its coloured counterparts but I have used a little artistic licence here, preferring the broader petals of the red and orange varieties. The tree also produces a fruit, which when ripe, splits to reveal a silky material similar to that from the kapok tree which is often used for stuffing cushions. These flowers are very useful for filling spaces in floral displays and create maximum impact too.

EQUIPMENT

Fine scissors
Fine angled tweezers
Dusting brushes
Fine paintbrushes
Non-stick rolling pin
Amaryllis cutter (TT748)
Large metal ball tool
Stargazer B petal veiner (SKGI)
Rose petal cutter set (TT276-280)
Fine-nose pliers
Plain-edge cutting wheel
Large gardenia leaf veiner (SKGI or Aldaval)
Large scissors

MATERIALS

White and green cold porcelain
26-, 24-, 22-, 20- and 18-gauge white wires
White seed-head stamens
Hi-tack non-toxic craft glue
Vine, sunflower, white, plum, foliage, aubergine, forest, nutkin, tangerine and coral petal dusts
Isopropyl alcohol
White and holly/ivy flowerpaste
Fresh egg white
Nile green and brown floristry tape
Edible spray varnish
Kitchen paper
Tangerine paste food colour

PISTIL AND STAMENS

To create a neat centre it is best to use a non-toxic craft glue to hold the stamens and pistil together – because of this I prefer to make the pistil with cold porcelain as the glue bonds far easier than it would with flowerpaste.

1 Form a ball of white cold porcelain and insert a 24-gauge white wire. Leaving a slightly rounded tip to the pistil, work the paste down onto the wire to cover about 5 cm (2 in). Smooth the length of the pistil, working it between the fleshy part of your palms. Gently curve the pistil. Next, divide the bulbous tip into five sections using fine scissors. Open up the five sections and carefully pinch each section between your finger and thumb to neaten them and then curl them back slightly. Attach a ball of green cold porcelain at the base of the pistil and work into an oval shape.

2 Next, you will need at least one to two full bunches of seed-head stamens. Divide the bunches into groups of about 15 stamens and line up their tips. Use a small amount of non-toxic craft glue to bond one end of each bunch together. Allow to dry for several minutes. Try not to use too much glue as this will take much longer to dry. Clean the excess glue from your fingers before trimming off the excess stamens from the glued end. You might need to shorten the groups, bearing in mind that the pistil should stand slightly higher than the stamens. Once the stamens are dry enough, simply apply a touch more glue to the glued ends and then attach to the green ovary at the base of the pistil. Continue to add more groups of stamen until the desired effect is achieved – some flowers have larger, bushier stamens than others. Leave to dry, then curl back the stamens slightly using fine angled tweezers.

3 Dust the stamens from the base fading towards the tips with a light dusting of vine green petal dust. Next, dilute some sunflower petal dust with isopropyl alcohol and carefully paint the tips of each of the stamens using the fine paintbrush. As the flower fades, the stamens have brown tinges to them – but with a white flower I prefer to keep the stamens a fresh yellow colour.

PETALS

4 Now back to using flowerpaste! Roll out some well-kneaded white flowerpaste, leaving a thick ridge for the wire. The petals of this flower are quite fleshy so be careful not to roll too heavily. Use the amaryllis cutter to cut out the petal shape. Insert a 26-gauge white wire moistened with fresh egg white into about half the length of the petal. Soften the edge of the petal using the large ball tool – try not to frill the petals.

5 Place the petal into the double-sided stargazer B petal veiner and squeeze firmly to create strong veining. Remove from the veiner and then pinch the petal from the base to the tip to accentuate the central vein and also to curve the shape slightly. Repeat the process to create five petals.

COLOURING AND ASSEMBLY

6 Dust the base of each petal with a mixture of vine green and white petal dusts. Tinge the back of each petal down the centre and at the tips with this light mixture too. Add delicate tinges to the side edges using a light mixture of plum and white petal dusts if desired.

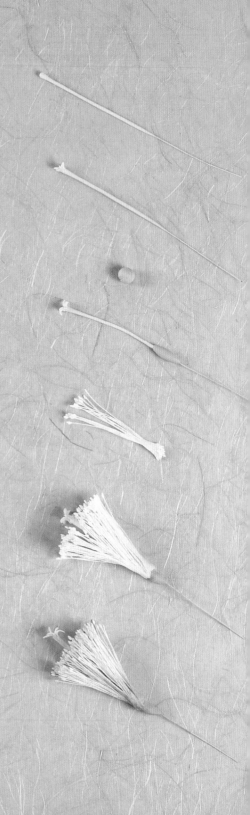

7 It is best to tape the petals around the stamens with half-width nile green floristry tape while they are still slightly pliable so that you may reshape them slightly and create a more realistic balanced result. The back of the flower is quite bulbous so at this stage you will need to attach a ball of holly/ivy flowerpaste over the base of the petals to create a padded finish which will then be covered by the sepals of the calyx.

CALYX

8 Roll out some holly/ivy flowerpaste not too thinly and cut out three large rose petal shapes using the largest rose petal cutter. Soften the edges and cup the centre of each sepal using the large metal ball tool. Attach over the padded base of the flower using fresh egg white. Pinch the tip of each sepal into a sharp point. Dust with vine and foliage petal dusts.

BUDS

9 Bend an open hook in the end of a 20-gauge white wire using fine-nose pliers. Form a cone shape of well-kneaded white flowerpaste and insert the hooked wire moistened with fresh egg white into the rounded base. Pinch five petals from the sides of the cone using your finger and thumb – you might need a pair of fine angled tweezers too to get tight into the base of each petal. Keep pinching each of the petals to make them finer. Next, twist to spiral the petals around the bud. Add a calyx as described for the flower, using a slightly smaller rose petal cutter.

LEAVES

10 Roll out some holly/ivy flowerpaste, leaving a thick ridge for the wire. Cut out a long, pointed freestyle leaf shape using the plain-edge cutting wheel. Insert a moistened 26- or 24-gauge white wire into about half the length of the leaf – the gauge will depend on the size of the leaf you are making. Next, work the thick base of the leaf between your finger and thumb to elongate it and create a thickened stem. Repeat to make leaves in varying sizes.

11 Soften the edge of the leaf and then place it into the double-sided large gardenia leaf veiner and press firmly to texture the leaf. Remove from the veiner and then pinch from the base to the tip to accentuate the central vein. Repeat to make five leaves for each set of foliage.

12 Tape the five leaves together to form a hand-like formation using half-width nile green floristry tape.

COLOURING

13 Dust the edges of each leaf with aubergine petal dust. Use layers of forest, foliage and vine to colour the main body of the leaves. Dust the back of the leaves much lighter than the front. Tape the group onto an extra 22-gauge white wire to give support using half-width nile green floristry tape. Spray lightly with edible spray varnish.

ASSEMBLY

14 If you wish to create a branch of bombax, simply tape the flowers, buds and foliage onto 18-gauge white wire. Thicken the branch using strips of kitchen paper wrapped around the wire and tape over with brown floristry tape. Smooth the stem using the side of a large pair of scissors to polish it. Every time you add a flower or a bud, add a set of leaves too. To create added texture, twist some brown floristry tape back onto itself to form a long strand. Wrap this around the branch at intervals, focusing mostly at the base of the buds, flowers and leaves.

15 Dust the branch with nutkin petal dust and spray lightly with edible spray varnish.

ORANGE FLOWERS

16 If you decide to make the orange form featured here, then you will need to colour the paste with some tangerine paste food colour to form the base colouring and then over-dust with tangerine and coral petal dusts. The stamens' tips are coloured with nutkin rather than sunflower yellow petal dust and the calyx is often a stronger brown/aubergine colour. There are also red forms of bombax; for these, use red-coloured flowerpaste for the petals and dust them with red and ruby petal dusts. The stamens are brown-tipped, as described for the orange flower above.

Oxalis

There are about 800 oxalis species that are native in various forms throughout most of the world with a particular diverse group in Argentina, Brazil, Mexico and South Africa. The plant illustrated here is based on a plant that was posted to me by a very kind sugarcrafter. The plant is mostly grown for its very decorative foliage, which has the fascinating ability to open in daylight and close as the light diminishes.

MATERIALS

Pale pink, pale green and white flowerpaste

Fresh egg white

Plum, African violet, foliage, aubergine, vine, sunflower and white petal dusts

Edible spray varnish

White floristry tape

Fine white stamens

33-gauge white wire

Hi-tack non-toxic craft glue

EQUIPMENT

Non-stick rolling pin

Heart-shaped leaf cutter set (optional)

Plain-edge cutting wheel

Fine scissors

Large ball tool

Dusting brushes

Non-stick board

Stargazer B petal veiner (SKGI)

Cocktail stick

Scalpel

LEAVES

1 The leaves vary in the depth of colour so you will need to make some leaves with pale pink flowerpaste and others with pale green flowerpaste. Roll out some pale pink or pale green flowerpaste very thinly, leaving a fine ridge for the wire. Cut out the leaf shape using one of the sizes of heart-shaped leaf cutters or with the plain-edge cutting wheel and the template on p 247.

2 Insert a wire moistened with fresh egg white into the fine pointed end of the heart – the gauge will depend on the size of the leaf you are making. Next, use fine scissors to trim off the two curves of the heart shape to create a more angular leaf shape.

3

Soften the edge of the leaf using the large ball tool, which will help to thin the edge too. Use the small wheel of the plain-edge cutting wheel to add a faint central vein and several side veins to the leaf. Pinch the leaf from behind to accentuate the central vein. Repeat to make another two leaves of the same size.

COLOURING AND ASSEMBLY

4

Dust the base of each leaf, fading to the centre with plum petal dust. Add a light dusting of African violet over the top. Next, add a border of foliage green followed by a dense colouring to the edge with aubergine and a touch of plum. The smaller leaves tend to be more green in colour and less aubergine. Allow to dry, then gently steam or spray lightly with edible spray varnish.

5

Tape the leaves into their sets of three using quarter-width white floristry tape. Dust the stem with plum petal dust and a touch of foliage.

FLOWERS

6

Glue ten short fine white stamens to the end of a 33-gauge white wire using a small amount of non-toxic craft glue. Leave to dry and then dust the base with vine petal dust and the tips with sunflower petal dust.

7

Insert a 33-gauge white wire into the pointed base of a teardrop-shaped piece of white flowerpaste. Smooth the shape and remove any excess. Flatten it against the non-stick board using the flat side of the stargazer B petal veiner. Next, soften the edges with the ball tool and then texture using the double-sided stargazer B petal veiner.

8

Pinch the petal to create a central vein and then curl the edges slightly using a cocktail stick. Repeat to make five petals.

9

Tape the petals around the stamens using quarter-width white floristry tape. It is good if they are still pliable as this allows you to reshape and curl the petals as desired.

10

Dust the edges of the petals with a light mixture of plum, African violet and white petal dusts. Add a light tinge of vine mixed with foliage at the base of the flower to represent the calyx. Or if you have the time and patience, cut five fine sepals of pale green flowerpaste using the scalpel and attach them to the base of the flower. Dust the stem very lightly with a tinge of the flower colour and a little of the pale green colours used on the calyx.

Caper

It is the unopened flower buds that most people are familiar with – gathered and pickled in wine vinegar for cooking purposes. The fruit too is used in the same way, and even the foliage of the plant can be used pickled in salads. The plant originates from the Mediterranean area and has been introduced and grown widely in other warm territories. The beautiful flowers are very short-lived, lasting not even a day.

MATERIALS

Pale green cold porcelain (p 14–5)
33-, 28-, 26- and 22-gauge white wires
Vine, plum, African violet, white, foliage, aubergine and forest petal dusts
Seed-head stamens
Hi-tack non-toxic craft glue
White and pale green flowerpaste
Fresh egg white
Nile green floristry tape
Edible spray varnish

EQUIPMENT

Plain-edge cutting wheel
Dusting brushes
Scissors
Tweezers
Non-stick rolling pin
Rose petal or gardenia petal cutters
Large ball tool
Cupped Christmas rose petal veiner (SKGI)
Stargazer B petal veiner
Ceramic silk veining tool
Non-stick board
Fine-nose pliers
Briar rose leaf veiner (SKGI)

PISTIL

1 It is best to make the pistil with cold porcelain as this enables the stamens to be glued onto it with non-toxic craft glue. Roll a small ball of pale green cold porcelain and insert a 28-gauge white wire into it. Form the ball into a cone shape and then quickly work the base of the cone down the wire to form a long, fine pistil. Smooth the length between your palms. Divide the tip into four sections using the plain-edge cutting wheel. Curve the pistil slightly. Dust lightly with vine green and then add a tinge of aubergine onto the pointed tip.

STAMENS

2 The number of stamens can vary. It is best to assemble and glue small groups together and gradually add them to the pistil until the desired effect is achieved. Take groups of five to 10 stamens, line up the tips and glue one end with a small amount of non-toxic craft glue – try not to add too much as this will slow down the drying time and cut down the bulk.

3 Trim off the glued ends of the stamens, apply a little more glue and attach at the base of the pistil so that it protrudes higher than the stamen tips. Hold each bunch to the count of ten to hold them in place. Allow to dry and then open up the stamens using a pair of tweezers to pull and give the odd curl here and there.

4 Dust the base of the stamens with a mixture of plum and African violet. There are some varieties that have pure white stamens and others with green-tinged stamens.

PETALS

5 Roll out some well-kneaded white flowerpaste thinly, leaving a thick ridge for the wire. Cut out the petal shape using a rose petal cutter or a gardenia petal cutter – the shape can vary between varieties. Insert a 28-gauge white wire moistened with fresh egg white into the base of the thick ridge to support about a third of the length.

6 Soften the edge of the petal using the large ball tool and then texture using the double-sided cupped Christmas rose or stargazer B petal veiner. Remove from the veiner and cup the petal slightly. Sometimes the edges of the petals are slightly frilled – this can be achieved by rolling the edges with the ceramic silk veining tool. Repeat to make four petals.

COLOURING AND ASSEMBLY

7 Mix together African violet, plum and white petal dusts. Brush the colour from the base of each petal, fading a little at the edges. There are varieties with pure white petals, white petals tinged with green and pale pink too.

8 Tape the four petals evenly around the base of the stamens using quarter-width nile green floristry tape. Some varieties look as if they have only three petals but this is because they are almost fused together at the base.

CALYX

9 Cut short lengths of 33-gauge white wire. Insert a wire into a small teardrop-shaped piece of pale green flowerpaste. Place the shape against the non-stick board and flatten it using the flat side of one of the double-sided veiners. Next, hollow it out using the ball tool. Repeat to make four sepals – these may be of the same size or sometimes two large and two smaller sepals. Dust with foliage and vine petal dusts. Tinge with aubergine.

10 Tape the sepals onto the back of the flower using half-width nile green floristry tape. Dust the sepals with a mixture of white, vine and foliage petal dusts. Catch the edges with aubergine petal dust.

BUDS

11 These are the wonderful creatures we mostly buy pickled in wine vinegar – for years I was led to believe that they were the fruit of the nasturtium – however, these too can be pickled and used in the same way. These need to vary in size down the stem. Use 33- through to 28-gauge white wire, depending on the size you are working on. Bend a hook in the end of the wire. Form a small rounded cone shape and insert the hook moistened with fresh egg white into the base. Pinch a sharp point at the tip. Divide the surface into four to represent the outer sepals. Pinch a subtle ridge on each sepal.

12 Tape over the stem with quarter-width nile green floristry tape. Dust with various green petal dusts. The smaller buds tend to be a brighter green and benefit from a dusting of vine and foliage. The larger buds need more foliage and a touch of forest green too. All need a tinge of aubergine on the tips and a light dusting of white. Spray lightly with edible spray varnish.

FRUIT

13 These are much larger than the buds. Use 26-gauge white wire hooked in one end. Roll a ball of pale green flowerpaste and insert the wire into it. Work the ball into a slight point and then work the base of the shape down onto the wire to create a slender neck. Use the plain-edge cutting wheel to make a series of fine lines down the length of the shape. Dust with a mixture of foliage, white and forest green petal dusts. Tinge with aubergine. Spray lightly with edible spray varnish.

LEAVES

14 Use the rose petal cutters in various sizes for the foliage. Roll out some pale green flowerpaste, leaving a thick ridge for the wire. Cut out the leaf shape using one of the sizes of rose petal cutters. Position the cutter so that the point of the rose petal shape becomes the pointed tip of the leaf.

15 Insert a 28- or 26-gauge wire into the thick ridge to support about half the length of the leaf. Pinch the base of the leaf down onto the wire to create a more tapered appearance.

16 Soften the edge of the leaf and then texture using the double-sided briar rose leaf veiner. Pinch the leaf to accentuate the central vein. Repeat to make numerous leaves of various sizes.

17 Dust in layers with foliage, forest and white petal dusts. Tinge the base and the edges with aubergine. Tape over each leaf stem with quarter-width nile green floristry tape. Spray lightly with edible spray varnish.

18 Start taping the smallest leaves onto a 22-gauge white wire with half-width nile green floristry tape, alternating their position down the stem. Gradually increase the leaf size as you work down the stem. Introduce the buds at the same point that the leaves appear, increasing these in size too. Next, add the flowers again partnered with a single leaf.

19 Tape together other trailing stems using only the caper fruit and foliage. The buds and flowers are not usually on the same stems as the more mature fruiting parts of the plant.

Old-fashioned rose

The centre of this rose is a little tricky to make but with a bit of patience and practice the results can be most effective. I love the depth of colour that some of these old-fashioned roses have, but of course you might prefer to use more delicate colouring.

MATERIALS

Pale pink and pale green flowerpaste

30-, 28- and 26-gauge white wires

Fresh egg white

Aubergine, plum, African violet, white, vine, daffodil, foliage, forest and ruby petal dusts

Nile green floristry tape

Kitchen paper ring former (p 11)

Edible spray varnish

EQUIPMENT

Non-stick rolling pin

Rose petal cutter set (TT276-280)

Ceramic silk veining tool (HP)

Ball tool

Dusting brushes

Rose petal veiner (SKGI)

Wire cutters

Non-stick board

Scissors

Rose calyx cutter (optional)

Celstick (optional)

Foam pad

Curved scissors

Rose leaf cutters (Jem)

Large briar rose leaf veiner (SKGI)

INNER PETALS

1 Roll out some pale pink flowerpaste, leaving a thick ridge for the wire. Cut out a small rose petal shape using the smallest cutter from the rose petal cutter set and then insert a 26-gauge white wire moistened with fresh egg white into the thick ridge. Vein and thin out the petal using the ceramic silk veining tool to roll over the surface. Soften the edge with the ball tool.

2 Next, curl the petal into a spiral shape using a tiny amount of fresh egg white to hold it in place. Leave to dry. Repeat to make four more of these spiralled petals.

3 Roll out some more pale pink flowerpaste and cut out more petals using the same size cutter, plus the next size up in the set. Vein and soften as before.

4 Attach three or four petals around each of the wired spiralled petals using fresh egg white. Curl the edges a little as you add each petal.

5 Dust the petals heavily with a mixture of aubergine, plum and African violet. Dust the back of the petals with white petal dust.

6 Tape the five sections together using half-width nile green floristry tape. Leave to dry.

OUTER PETALS

7 Roll out some more pale pink flowerpaste, leaving a thick ridge for the wire. Insert a 26-gauge white wire moistened with fresh egg white into the thick ridge to support about half the length of the petal. Soften the edge of the petal and then vein using the rose petal veiner.

8 Hollow out the centre of the petal using the ball tool. Curl back the edges of the petal and leave to firm up slightly in a kitchen paper ring former. Repeat to make the required number of petals – usually about eight to 10. The size can vary a little too.

COLOURING

9 Dust the upper surface heavily with the same aubergine/plum/African violet mixture used earlier. Dust the back of each petal with white petal dust and introduce a little of the dark mixture to the edges too. A light glow of white mixed with vine green and daffodil can help to lighten the rose a little.

ASSEMBLY

10 Tape the outer petals around the inner curled petals using half-width nile green floristry tape. Curl the edges of the petals if they are still pliable. Allow to dry and then steam the flower lightly. Re-dust if a velvety effect is desired.

CALYX

11 Cut five lengths of 30-gauge white wire. Work a ball of pale green flowerpaste onto the wire, creating a long tapered carrot shape. Place the shape against the non-stick board and flatten using the flat side of one of the double-sided veiners. If the shape looks distorted, simply trim it into shape with scissors.

12 Place the flattened shape onto a foam pad or the palm of your hand, and soften and hollow out the length using the ball tool. Pinch the sepal from the base to the tip. Cut fine 'hairs' into the edge of the sepal using curved scissors. Repeat to make five sepals.

I tend to leave one sepal without hairs – although remember there are some varieties of rose that have no hairs to their calyces at all.

13 Dust each sepal on the outer surface with a mixture of foliage and forest petal dusts. Add tinges of aubergine mixed with plum or ruby petal dusts. Use the same brush used for the green mixture and dust lightly on the inner surface of each sepal with white petal dust. Lightly glaze the back of each sepal with edible spray varnish.

14 Tape the five sepals to the base of the rose, positioning a sepal over a join. Add a ball of pale green flowerpaste for the ovary and pinch and squeeze it into a neat shape. Dust the ovary to match the colouring of the sepal.

15 Alternatively, the calyx can be cut out in one piece using the rose calyx cutter. To do this, roll a ball of pale green flowerpaste and form it into a cone shape. Pinch the cone into a hat shape using your fingers and thumbs, leaving a rose hip shape at the centre to represent the ovary. Place the shape against the non-stick board and use a celstick or ceramic silk veining tool to roll out the brim of the 'hat'. Place the cutter over the paste with the rose hip/ovary shape at the centre and cut out the calyx shape. Remove the shape from the cutter and elongate each sepal using the ceramic silk veining tool or celstick. Hollow out the centre of each sepal using the ball tool and then add snipped hairy bits, as in step 12. Moisten the centre of the calyx and thread onto the back of the rose so that a sepal hides a join in the outer petals.

LEAVES

16 Roll out some pale green flowerpaste, leaving a thick ridge for the wire (a grooved board can speed up this process greatly). Cut out the leaves using the rose leaf cutters. You will find that the black rose leaf set does not allow for very thick leaves – these tend to stick in the cutter. Insert a moistened 26-, 28- or 30-gauge white wire into the leaf, depending on its size.

17 Soften the edge of the leaf and vein using the large briar rose leaf veiner. Pinch from behind the leaf to accentuate the central vein and give more movement to the leaf. Repeat to make leaves of various sizes. Tape over a little of each wire stem with quarter-width nile green floristry tape. Tape the leaves into sets of three or five, starting with the largest leaf and two medium-size leaves, one on either side. Finally, add the two smaller leaves at the base.

18 Dust the edges with aubergine and plum or ruby mixed together. Use this colour on the upper stems too. Dust the upper surface of the leaf in layers lightly with forest and heavier with foliage and vine petal dusts. Dust the backs with white petal dust using the brush used for the greens. Spray with edible spray varnish.

ROSE BUDS

19 These can be made following the instructions on page 84 (steps 1 to 5). You will need to keep the rose cone centre fairly small and use one of the smaller rose petal cutters from the rose petal set.

Degarmoara orchid

The Degarmoara orchid has actually been created by cross-hybridising three orchid genus from South America: the Brassia, Miltonia and Odontoglossum orchids. In fact, the cutter set I use for this orchid is used to create another cross-hybrid, the Miltassia orchid. It is always good to know that one set of cutters can be used for other projects too! This is another of the orchids that I bought at the early morning flower market in Brazil a few years ago. I love using this style of spidery orchid and the range of colours that these three species of orchid provide. They are fairly easy to make and add an unusual delicate yet exotic touch to floral sprays.

MATERIALS

33-, 26-, 24-, 22- and 20-gauge white wire
White and mid-green flowerpaste
Cornflour bag (p 11)
Nile green floristry tape
Vine, white, daffodil, plum, sunflower, aubergine, ruby, foliage and forest petal dusts
Isopropyl alcohol
Fresh egg white
Edible spray varnish

EQUIPMENT

Scissors or wire cutters
Ceramic silk veining tool (HP)
Miltassia orchid cutters (TT878-880)
Metal ball tool
Stargazer B petal veiner (SKGI)
Dresden tool
Non-stick board
Fine-nose tweezers
Non-stick rolling pin
Foam pad
Dusting brushes
Fine paintbrush
Plain-edge cutting wheel
Large tulip leaf veiner (SKGI)

COLUMN

1 Cut a short length of 33-gauge white wire. Roll a tiny ball of white flowerpaste and then form it into a cone shape. Insert the wire into the pointed end of the teardrop. Work the paste down the wire slightly to create a more slender shape. Place the wired cone against the rounded end of the ceramic silk veining tool and press against it to hollow out the underside of the column. Use your finger and thumb to pinch and press against the tool, which will in turn create a slight ridge down the back of the column. Leave to dry.

LIP/THROAT (LABELLUM)

2 Squash the lip/labellum cutter from the miltassia orchid set into a more slender shape. Roll out some well-kneaded white flowerpaste, leaving a thick ridge for the wire. Cut out the labellum petal using the cutter.

3 Insert a moistened 26-gauge white wire into the thick ridge of the petal. Soften the edges using the metal ball tool to take away the cut edge effect.

4 Dust the surface of the petal lightly with cornflour and then place into the double-sided stargazer B petal veiner and press firmly to texture the surface of the petal.

5 Use the broad end of the Dresden tool to work the edges of the petal against the non-stick board and then go back over the edge to frill with the ceramic silk veining tool.

6 Use fine-nose tweezers to pinch two fine ridges at the base (wire end) of the petal to create a platform. Pinch the petal down the centre and then push and pinch back a waistline shape on the petal. Allow to firm up a little before taping onto the column with half-width nile green floristry tape. Make sure the column is facing with the hollowed side down towards the surface of the petal.

WINGS/ARMS (LATERAL PETALS)

7 Roll out some white flowerpaste, leaving a fine ridge for the wire. Cut out the wing petal shape using the wing template on p 247. Insert a moistened 26-gauge white wire into the thick ridge so that it supports about a third to half the length of the petal. Soften the edge using the metal ball tool, working half on the paste and half on your hand or foam pad.

8 Texture the petal using the stargazer B petal veiner. Pinch from the base to the tip and curve the petal backwards slightly. Repeat to make a second wing petal, which should create a mirror image of the first.

HEAD (DORSAL SEPAL)

9 Roll out some white flowerpaste and cut out the dorsal shape using the longer cutter in the set or the head template on p 247.

10 Insert a moistened 26-gauge white wire into the thick ridge to support about half the length of the petal. Soften the edge and vein as for the wing petals. Curve the dorsal backwards and allow to firm up slightly.

LEGS (LATERAL SEPALS)

11 Repeat as for the dorsal sepal to create a mirror image of the lateral sepals. Curve the legs and allow to dry a little.

ASSEMBLY AND COLOURING

12 Tape the two lateral petals onto either side of the labellum and column using half-width nile green floristry tape. Next, add the dorsal sepal followed by the lateral sepals. If the flowerpaste is still pliable at this stage, it will give you a chance to create more interesting curves and a realistic finish.

13 Dust the petals with a light mixture of vine green, white and a touch of daffodil petal dusts mixed together. Start dusting at the base of each petal and fade out towards the tip. Tinge the edges of the petals with plum petal dust. Use sunflower petal dust to colour the two ridges at the base of the labellum.

14 Dilute a mixture of aubergine, ruby and plum petal dusts with isopropyl alcohol and paint detail spots onto the labellum and outer petals. There are some varieties with no spots if you are feeling nervous about painting. Dust the back of the flower at the base of each petal/sepal with foliage petal dust.

BUDS

15 Roll a ball of well-kneaded white flowerpaste and form it into an elongated teardrop shape. Insert a hooked 26-gauge white moistened with fresh egg white into the broader end of the teardrop to support about half the length of the bud.

16 Use the plain-edge cutting wheel to divide the bud into three sections. Curve the bud slightly. Repeat to make buds of varying sizes. Dust as for the flower.

17 Tape the buds, starting with the smallest, onto a 20-gauge white wire with half-width nile green floristry tape.

LEAVES

18 Roll out a long length of mid-green flowerpaste, leaving a thick ridge for the wire. Cut out the long strap-like leaf shape using the plain-edge cutting wheel. Insert a 24-or 22-gauge white wire into the ridge, depending on the size of the leaf.

19 Soften the edge and vein using the double-sided large tulip leaf veiner. Pinch from the base to the tip. Dry to create a graceful curve. Repeat to make another leaf slightly shorter in length.

20 Dust in layers with forest and foliage green. Tinge the edges with aubergine. Spray lightly with edible spray varnish.

Brassada orchid

This spider-like orchid is from South America and is actually a cultivated cross-hybrid between a Brassia orchid and an Ada orchid. I love the long curly petals that these flowers have. These orchids tend to be mostly orange or yellow in colour but I see no reason why the colour scheme could not be given a touch of artistic licence!

MATERIALS
White/cream and green flowerpaste
33-, 28-, 26-, 24-, 22- and 20-gauge white wires
Cyclamen liquid food colour
Fresh egg white
Nile green floristry tape
Sunflower, daffodil, aubergine, tangerine, coral, foliage and vine petal dusts
Edible spray varnish

EQUIPMENT
Ceramic silk veining tool (HP)
Scalpel
Fine paintbrush
Non-stick rolling pin
Small alstromeria petal cutter (TT438)
Dresden tool
Stargazer B veiner (SKGI)
Fine angled tweezers
Non-stick board
Scissors
Dusting brushes
Plain-edge cutting wheel
Large tulip leaf veiner (SKGI)

COLUMN

1 Attach a small ball of white/cream flowerpaste onto the end of a 33-gauge white wire. Work the paste down the wire to form a teardrop shape. Place the shape against the rounded end of the ceramic silk veining tool to hollow out the underside. Curve the shape. Add another cap if desired by adding a tiny ball of flowerpaste onto the tip of the column. Split the ball in half using a scalpel. Paint spots on the underside with cyclamen liquid food colour.

LIP (LABELLUM)

2 Roll out some well-kneaded white/cream flowerpaste, leaving a thicker ridge at the centre for the wire. Cut out the lip shape using the alstromeria petal cutter. Insert a 28-gauge white wire moistened with fresh egg white into the ridge. Broaden the base of the petal to create a flap on either side using the broad end of the Dresden tool. Soften the edges of the petal and vein using the double-sided Stargazer B veiner.

3 Frill the edges of the lip using the ceramic silk veining tool. Pinch back the base of the lip and pinch the tip into a sharp point.

4 Pinch two ridges at the base of the petal using fine angled tweezers to create the characteristic raised platform. Allow to dry a little before colouring.

WING/LATERAL PETALS

5 There are two wing petals. Work a small ball of white/cream flowerpaste onto a length of 28-gauge white wire. Form the shape into a long pointed petal shape. Place against the non-stick board and flatten the shape using the flat side of the stargazer B veiner. Trim the edges if required using scissors. Vein using the Stargazer B veiner. Pinch the petal from the base to the tip to accentuate the central vein. Curve each petal back slightly so that they are a mirror image of each other.

DORSAL (HEAD) AND LATERAL (LEGS) SEPALS

6 These are made in the same way as the wing petals but you need to make the legs much longer. Curve the dorsal petal back slightly and curl the tips of the leg petals before the flowerpaste has a chance to dry.

COLOURING/ASSEMBLY

7 Tape the column onto the labellum petal using half-width nile green floristry tape. Next add the two shorter outer petals (arms) and finally the outer three petals. If the flowerpaste is still pliable at this stage you can reshape it to create a more natural finish.

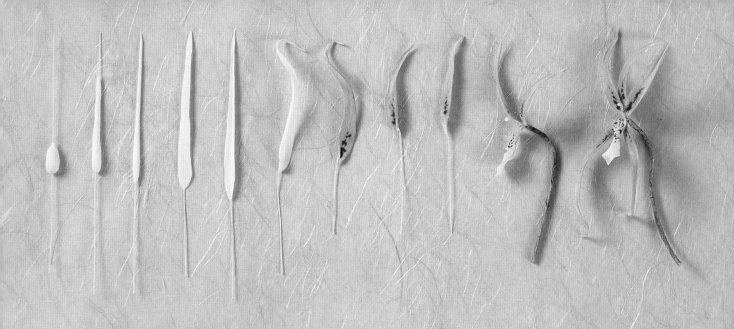

8 Dust the lip lightly with a mixture of sunflower and daffodil petal dusts. Paint spots onto the lip using cyclamen liquid food colour mixed with aubergine petal dust. Some Brassada orchids have raised spots on the throat while others have simple spotted markings.

9 Dust the outer petals and sepals with tangerine petal dust to create an intense colouring. Add a tinge of coral to the petal edges too. Paint spots at the base of each petal.

BUDS

10 These are long and slender. Add teardrop-shaped piece of white/cream flowerpaste onto a 26-gauge white wire. Work into a slender point. Divide into three using the plain-edge cutting wheel or scalpel. Curve into shape. Dust as for the flower.

ASSEMBLY

11 Tape the buds onto a 20-gauge white wire using half-width nile green floristry tape. Alternate the buds starting with the smallest and graduating the size as you work. Finally add the flowers. Dust the stem with foliage green. Add tinges of aubergine to the tips and the base of the buds.

LEAVES

12 Roll out some green flowerpaste, leaving a thick ridge for the wire. Use the plain-edge cutting wheel to cut out a freehand, not-too-slender leaf shape.

13 Insert a moistened 24- or 22-gauge white wire into about half the length of the leaf. The exact gauge will depend on the size of leaf you are making.

14 Place the leaf into the double-sided large tulip leaf veiner and press the two sides together firmly to texture the surface of the leaf. Remove the leaf from the veiner and carefully pinch it from the base to the tip to accentuate the central vein. Allow to dry in a slightly curved position.

15 Dust in layers with foliage green and vine green petal dusts. Catch the edges with aubergine. Allow to dry further and then glaze using edible spray varnish.

93

Scorpion orchid

There are more than 20 species and many hybrid forms of *Arachnis* orchid, also commonly known as the scorpion orchid. These flowers make an unusual addition to the flower-maker's repertoire and can be almost any colour except blue. Petals are often spotted or striped.

COLUMN

1 Cut a short length of 26-gauge white wire. Insert it into a small ball of well-kneaded white flowerpaste. Work the ball of flowerpaste down the wire very slightly to create a short neck. Hollow out the underside of the column by pressing it gently but firmly against the rounded end of the smooth ceramic tool. This will also create a subtle ridge on the upper surface of the column.

2 Roll a tiny ball of white flowerpaste to represent the anther cap. Attach the tip of the column so that it sits in between the hollowed area and the upper surface. Use the plain-edge cutting wheel to divide the anther cap down the centre. Leave to dry.

LIP (LABELLUM)

3 Take a ball of well-kneaded pale vine green flowerpaste and form it into a teardrop shape. Next, pinch and form a short fine node at the pointed end of the teardrop and pinch out the flowerpaste around it. Place the shape against the non-stick board and roll out the flowerpaste around the node. Place the lip cutter over the flowerpaste so the node is at the base of the shape. If you are using the template on page 251, cut a hole in the template so it fits over the node.

4 Soften the edges and hollow out the inside of the tool side sections. Use fine angled tweezers to pinch a few ridges down the length of the middle section. Use the pointed end of the smooth ceramic tool to indent the area above the node to hollow it out, creating a nectary. Moisten the edges of the column with fresh egg white and attach the lip/labellum to it with the hollowed side facing the petal. Curl the edges of the two side sections back slightly and curve the very tip of the lip. Allow to set before colouring.

COLOURING

5 Dust the tip of the lip intensely with plum petal dust. Catch the curled side edges gently with colour. Add a little daffodil and sunflower petal dusts at the very centre of the lip. Use a light mixture of edelweiss and vine on the underside of the nectary area.

MATERIALS

26-gauge white wires
White and pale vine green flowerpaste
Fresh egg white
Plum, daffodil, sunflower, edelweiss, vine, aubergine, moss and foliage petal dusts
Nile green floristry tape
Isopropyl alcohol
Edible spray varnish

EQUIPMENT

Wire cutters
Smooth ceramic tool
Plain-edge cutting wheel
Non-stick board
Lip cutter
Fine angled tweezers
Non-stick rolling pin
Scorpion orchid cutter set or templates on p 251
Foam pad
Metal ball tool
Stargazer B petal veiner
Dusting brushes, including a flat dusting brush
Fine paintbrush
Fine-nose pliers

OUTER PETALS AND SEPALS

6 I think of an orchid as a figure with a head and four limbs. The dorsal is the head sepal. Roll out some pale vine green flowerpaste, leaving a thick ridge for the wire. Cut out the dorsal sepal using the straightest cutter from the set or the template on page 251 and a sharp scalpel. Insert a 26-gauge white wire moistened with fresh egg white into the petal to support a third to half its length. Pinch the flowerpaste at the base of the petal down onto the wire to secure it.

7 Place the petal onto the foam pad and soften the edges using the metal ball tool. Texture the petal using the double-sided stargazer B petal veiner. Remove petal from the veiner and pinch it back from the base through to tip to create a hollowed-out look at the back of the petal. Curve the petal forwards slightly. Allow to firm up before colouring/assembly. Repeat the process using the other cutters to create two curved wing petal shapes, turning the cutter over to create a left and right petal shape. Do the same with the leg sepal cutter. Create more of a curved bow legged shape to these two.

ASSEMBLY AND COLOURING

8 The colouring can be done before assembly or once the flower has been taped up. Start by taping the two larger curved lateral petals onto either side of the column and lip/labellum using half-width nile green floristry tape. Next, add the head/dorsal sepal followed by the legs/lateral sepals. If the flowerpaste is still pliable, this will allow you to reshape to create a more realistic flower shape.

9 Dust the petals/sepals with a mixture of vine, a touch of daffodil and edelweiss petal dusts. To create the markings, dilute a mixture of aubergine and plum petal dusts with isopropyl alcohol and use a fine paintbrush to paint on the detail. Try not to paint the stripes too neatly. Allow to dry.

10 Mix together some more plum and aubergine petal dusts and use a flat dusting brush to over-dust the edges of the petals/sepals, bringing the colour over some of the painted stripes to calm the colour down.

11 Mix a little moss and foliage petal dusts to tinge the back of the petals. Allow to dry, then spray with edible spray varnish.

OVARY

12 Attach a ball of pale vine green flowerpaste behind the flower and work it down the stem to create a fleshy stem-like ovary. Use the plain-edge cutting wheel to mark a series of fine lines down the length. Dust to match the petals/sepals.

BUDS

13 Using fine-nose pliers, bend a hook in the end of a 26-gauge white wire. Form a ball of pale vine green flowerpaste and insert the hooked wire moistened with fresh egg white into the base. Pinch it onto the wire to secure the two together to create a strong join. Pinch a small node/nectary at the base of the bud. Use the plain-edge cutting wheel to mark lines to give the impression of the outer sepals tightly formed around the bud. Repeat to make buds in graduating sizes.

Christmas orchid

This is a terrestrial orchid that was prized by the Victorians and nicknamed the 'Christmas orchid' as it flowers profusely during that period. It actually flowers from the autumn through to February. Its Latin name, Calanthe, translated means 'with lovely flowers'. There are pure white, pink, red and burgundy forms.

MATERIALS
White and pale green flowerpaste
22-, 26-, 28-, 30-, 33- and 35-gauge white wires
Plum, vine, foliage and aubergine petal dusts
Nile green floristry tape

EQUIPMENT
Rolling pin
Non-stick board
Simple leaf cutters (TT229, 230)
Wire cutters
Sharp fine scissors
Silk veining tool (HP)
Sharp scalpel
Cupped Christmas rose petal veiner (SKGI)

LIP/LABELLUM

1 Roll out some well-kneaded white flowerpaste leaving a thick ridge for the wire. Cut out the lip shape using one of the two sizes of simple leaf cutter. Cut a length of 26-gauge wire into thirds. Moisten the end of one of the wires and insert into the pointed end of the petal. Work the base of the petal down onto the wire to elongate the shape slightly.

2 Use sharp fine scissors to alter the shape of the petal, cutting out one V-shaped cut at the top of the lip and one either side of the lip.

3 Broaden, vein and slightly frill each section of the lip using the silk veining tool. Rest the petal against your finger or on the board while the tool is being rolled against the petal.

4 Open up the base of the petal to create an opening that will form the column of the flower. Pinch the petal from the base to the tip to create a central vein and curve it slightly. Leave to set a little before the next stage.

5 Attach a small ball of paste just above the hollowed-out area of the lip. This represents the anther cap. Divide the cap into two sections using a sharp scalpel.

COLOURING

6 Dust the petal with plum petal dust. In this example I have faded the colour towards the edges of the petal but some of the Christmas orchids have a very intense pink, red or burgundy lip. Add a tinge of aubergine into the throat of the orchid.

LATERAL (WING) PETALS

7 I find these petals easier to make using a freehand technique. Cut short lengths of 30-gauge white wires. Roll a ball of white well-kneaded flowerpaste and then form into a cone shape. Insert a wire into the broad end of the cone. Work the base of the cone down onto the wire to create an elongated petal shape.

8 Place the wired shape against a non-stick board and 'flatten the petal using the flat side of the Christmas rose petal veiner. You might need to trim the thinned petal into shape but with practice you will create a more consistent petal shape.

9 Soften the edge of the petal and then vein using the cupped Christmas rose veiner. Pinch the petal to create a central vein. Repeat to make two lateral petals.

DORSAL AND LATERAL SEPALS

10 Repeat the above process to create a dorsal and two lateral sepals – you should aim to make these a little narrower in shape.

NECTARY/SPUR

11 There is a very fine nectary that follows through from the column and the lip. It is easiest to make this as a separate wired piece. Use a short length of 33- or 35-gauge white wire and roll a tiny ball onto the end. Work the paste down the wire to create a fine coating. The length of the nectary varies between different varieties of Christmas orchids – just make sure that you are fairly consistent with the length you create if making a lot of these orchids for a cake. Curve the nectary and then tape onto the base of the lip so that it curves below it.

97

ASSEMBLY

12 Use half-width nile green floristry tape to attach the two lateral petals onto either side of the lip. Position the dorsal sepal behind the petals to fill the gap and the two lateral sepals at the base of the flower. Encourage them all to fall away from the lip.

BUDS

13 Cut a length of 28-gauge wire into thirds. Roll a ball of white flowerpaste and form it into a cone shape. Work the base of the cone to create the long fine nectary/spur shape. Bend a hook in the end of a length of 28-gauge wire and insert into the centre of the bud. Pinch into place and then create a three-sided angular effect to the broader end by simply pressing it between two fingers and a thumb.

14 Divide the top section into three to represent the three outer sepals. Curve the nectary to the underside of the bud.

BRACTS

15 These are made in the same way as the outer petals of the orchid but use finer wire for the smaller bracts and pale green paste. Make one bract for each flower and bud, plus a few extras for the top of the stem. Dust lightly with vine green and foliage petal dust.

FINAL ASSEMBLY

16 Start by snuggling a few of the tiny green bracts at the end of a 22-gauge wire. Tape them into place using half-width nile green tape. Gradually introduce a small bud accompanied by a leaf and continue down the stem, increasing the size of the buds and bracts until you are ready to introduce a flower and a bract. Bend the stem into a graceful curve. Dust the stem with foliage and vine green. Add tinges of aubergine to the tips of the bracts if desired.

Gum nuts

This funny name has been given to the woody seed pods of the eucalyptus tree or gum tree. There are more than 700 species of eucalyptus, mostly native to Australia. Eucalyptus are cultivated throughout the tropics and subtropics.

GUM NUTS

1 Form a ball of well-kneaded pale green flowerpaste into a teardrop shape. Use the pointed end of the smooth ceramic tool to open up the pointed end of the shape, then use the rounded end of the tool to open up the shape a little more. Use the small ball tool to hollow out the inner rim of the shape. To create a slight waist, insert the fine celstick into the centre and squeeze the shape against it. You may need to re-hollow the rim and re-form the waist until the desired shape is achieved.

2 Bend an open hook in the end of a 24- or 22-gauge white wire, depending on the size of gum nut. Moisten the hook with fresh egg white and pull the wire through the centre of the pod, embedding the hook into the fleshier area. Pinch the flowerpaste at the base of the pod and work it down onto the wire. Work the flowerpaste with your finger and thumb to create a fine neck. Curve the stem. Allow to firm up a little before dusting.

LEAVES

3 Roll out some well-kneaded pale green flowerpaste, leaving a thick ridge for the wire. Use one of the gum leaf cutters or refer to the template on page 252 and use the plain-edge cutting wheel to cut out the leaf shape. Insert a 26- or 24-gauge white wire moistened with fresh egg white into the thick ridge to support about half the length of the leaf. Pinch the base of the leaf down onto the wire then work the flowerpaste between finger and thumb to create a fine stem coating.

4 Place the leaf on the foam pad and soften the edge using the ball tool. Use the plain-edge cutting wheel to draw a central vein down the leaf and then use the small wheel to mark some finer side veins tapering out from the central vein. Pinch the leaf from base to tip to shape it and define the central vein. Allow to firm before colouring. Repeat to make leaves in various sizes.

COLOURING

5 Dust the leaves with a mixture of woodland, foliage and edelweiss petal dusts. Catch the edges with a touch of aubergine. Allow to dry and then spray very lightly with edible spray varnish.

6 Dust the gum nut pods with the same mixture, adding aubergine and nutkin brown into the very heart and very edges of the pod and slightly at the base. Allow to dry and spray lightly with edible spray varnish. Tape over each leaf stem with quarter-width nile green floristry tape. Tape the leaves alternating down the length of a 22-gauge white wire with half-width nile green tape. Add the gum nuts in clusters from the leaf axils.

MATERIALS

Pale green flowerpaste
26-, 24- and 22-gauge white wires
Fresh egg white
Woodland, foliage, edelweiss, aubergine and nutkin brown petal dusts
Edible spray varnish
Nile green floristry tape

EQUIPMENT

Smooth ceramic tool
Small ball tool
Fine celstick
Fine-nose pliers
Non-stick rolling pin
Gum leaf cutters
Plain-edge cutting wheel
Foam pad
Dusting brushes

99

Umbrella tree stalks

I first saw these wonderful things being used in an Australian floristry book. I had no idea what they were! It turns out they are the stalks of the Australian umbrella tree, the leaves removed by the florist, to leave these exciting firework-style stalks. They can be very pale green or, as I prefer, tinged with a dark red. They are very simple to make and add an instant touch of drama.

STALKS

1 The number of stems per stalk varies, with as few as five stems creating a complete stalk. Cut several 33-gauge white wires into four sections using wire cutters.

2 Roll a very small ball of well-kneaded pale green flowerpaste. Wrap the flowerpaste around a short length of wire and work it to the tip of the wire to create the required stalk length. Keep working the flowerpaste firmly between your finger and thumb, removing the excess flowerpaste at the tip of the wire. Place the stalk between your palms and roll it firmly to create a smoother finish. Repeat to make several stalks. Don't worry about making them all the same length as they vary in length a little on one stalk.

ASSEMBLY AND COLOURING

3 Use fine-nose pliers to bend each wire at the base of the stalk as you tape them together using half-width nile green floristry tape. Tape together several stems to create a stalk. Use the side of a pair of scissors to rub against the tape to smooth it and leave a slight shine. Trim any of the sections that need shortening.

4 Roll a very tiny ball of pale green flowerpaste and stick it into the very centre where each of the stems join together. Use the broad end of the dresden tool to indent the centre of the ball and bond it to the stalk.

5 Dust the undersides and the upper side at the very centre with a mixture of vine, a touch of daffodil and a touch of edelweiss petal dusts. Use a mixture of plum, ruby and aubergine to dust the upper surface of each section, leaving the very heart of the stalk a bright green. Allow to dry and then spray with edible spray varnish.

MATERIALS

33-gauge white wires
Pale green flowerpaste
Nile green floristry tape
Vine, daffodil, edelweiss, plum, ruby and aubergine petal dusts
Edible spray varnish

EQUIPMENT

Wire cutters
Fine-nose pliers
Non-stick rolling pin
Scissors
Dresden tool
Dusting brushes

Tillandsia

Another member of the bromeliad Tillandsia, are air plants native to southeast of the USA although most are native to South America. The flowers can be yellow, pink, orange or purple with brightly coloured bracts that look very much like flower petals.

FLOWERS

1 Form three balls of white flowerpaste into cone shapes. Flatten them against the board and roll out each petal in a fan formation using the silk veining tool. Pinch each petal to create a central vein and attach them onto the end of a 28-gauge wire. Twist and blend the base of each petal onto the wire. Curl the tips back slightly.

2 Allow the paste to firm up a little before colouring. Here I used African violet however, you can colour them pink, yellow, orange or purple.

BRACTS

3 Twist a length of half-width white floristry tape and stretch it slightly to create a subtle point. Trim off the extreme twisted section to leave a neat point. Repeat to make numerous bracts. Tape a few onto the back of the flower, gradually working down the stem as you add them.

4 Dust the bracts with plum petal dust. Dust the stem with a little of the bract colour and add tinges of foliage green mixed with white.

LEAVES

5 Use a 35- or 33-gauge white wire for the leaves. Work a tiny ball of pale green flowerpaste onto the wire and work it towards the end of the wire so that most or all of the length is supported. Smooth the paste between your palms and then flatten against the board using the flat side of the stargazer B veiner. Place in the veiner to texture and pinch the leaf from the base to the tip to create a central vein, twisting and curling it into shape.

6 Dust with foliage, edelweiss and forest green. Tape the leaves around the base of the flower. Dust the base and tips of the leaves and the base of the stem with aubergine. Spray with edible spray varnish.

MATERIALS

White and pale green flowerpaste
28-, 33- and 35-gauge white wires
Forest, foliage, edelweiss, plum, aubergine and African violet petal dusts
White floristry tape
Edible spray varnish (Fabilo)

EQUIPMENT

Non-stick board
Silk veining ceramic tool (HP)
Dusting brushes
Scissors
Stargazer B petal veiner

Clematis

There are around 200 species of clematis distributed across the world and many more hybrid forms. The flowers can have four to eight outer petal-like segments and many of the hybrid varieties are double in form. The size, colour and form of this family are vast, providing the cake decorator with a good variety to work with.

MATERIALS

Seed-head and hammerhead stamens
Hi-tack non-toxic craft glue
28-, 26-, 24- and 22-gauge white wires
Vine, white, aubergine, plum, foliage and
African violet petal dusts
Isopropyl alcohol
Edible spray varnish
White and mid-green flowerpaste
Fresh egg white
Nile green floristry tape

EQUIPMENT

Scissors
Fine angled tweezers
Dusting brushes
Non-stick rolling pin
Clematis petal cutter (optional)
Plain-edge cutting wheel
Large ball tool
Asiatic lily or clematis petal veiner (Aldaval)
Ceramic silk veining tool (HP)
Fine-nose pliers
Simple leaf cutters (TT225-232)
Clematis Montana leaf veiners (SKGI)

STAMENS

1 Take a few small groups of seed-head stamens and apply non-toxic craft glue at the centre of each group to bond and hold them together. Flatten the glue as you apply it and try not to add too much as it will take much longer to dry. Cut each group in half using scissors and trim off the tips and some excess from the un-glued ends. Next, apply a little more glue to one of the groups and wrap around the end of a 22-gauge white wire, pinching it firmly onto the wire to create a good, strong bond. Leave to dry and then continue to add the other small groups in the same way to create a tight, compact centre. Allow to dry and trim shorter again if necessary.

2 The threads of the hammerhead stamens are a little thicker, making them ideal for the longer outer stamens. Glue a few stamens at a time and repeat the above trimming process prior to attaching these longer stamens around the tighter group on the wire. Once the glue has dried, trim the stamens and curve these outer stamens using fine angled tweezers.

COLOURING AND ASSEMBLY

3 Dust the stamens lightly with a mixture of vine green and white petal dusts. The colouring does vary between varieties of clematis. I have painted the tips of the stamens with aubergine and plum mixed with isopropyl alcohol. Leave to dry and then set the colour onto the stamens using a light spray of edible spray varnish.

PETALS

4 Roll out some well-kneaded white flowerpaste, leaving a thick ridge for the wire. Cut out the petal shape using the clematis petal cutter or refer to the clematis petal template on p 247 and use a plain-edge cutting wheel to cut around the shape.

5 Insert a 26-gauge white wire moistened with fresh egg white into about a third of the length of the thick ridge of the petal. Work the base of the petal down onto the wire to give a strong join. Soften the edge of the petal gently with the large ball tool.

6 Place the petal in the double-sided Asiatic lily or clematis petal veiner and press firmly to texture the petal. Remove from the veiner and rest the petal against your index finger which will act as a platform while you frill at intervals around the edges of the petal with the ceramic silk veining tool.

7 Pinch the petal from the base to the tip to accentuate the central veins and curve the tip slightly. Allow to firm up a little before colouring. Repeat to make eight petals.

8 Dust the base and tip of each petal lightly with a mixture of vine green and white petal dusts. Add a strip of this colour down the back of the petals. Over-dust the back at the base slightly with foliage green. Mix together African violet and plum petal dusts with a touch of white and dust a stripe down the centre of the upper surface of each petal. Add a stronger stripe of colour over the top if you wish.

9 Tape the petals around the stamens using half-width nile green floristry tape. If the petals are still pliable at this stage it will help you reshape and give a more relaxed feel to the finished flower.

BUDS

10 Bend a hook in a 24- or 22-gauge white wire using fine-nose pliers – the gauge will depend on how big the bud is to be. Form a cone of well-kneaded white flowerpaste and insert the hooked wire moistened with fresh egg white into the broad end. Divide the surface of the bud into eight sections using the plain-edge cutting wheel or a knife. Pinch a central ridge down the length of each using fine angled tweezers (preferably without teeth!). Twist the bud slightly. Dust the base of the bud to match the flower with a tinge of vine green at the tip. The smaller buds should have more green to their make-up. The odd tinge of aubergine helps too.

LEAVES

11 These come in sets of three – generally one large and two slightly smaller leaves, one on either side. I prefer the toothed edge of the clematis Montana leaves and so I create my own hybrid forms combining them with the larger showy clematis types. Roll out some mid-green flowerpaste, leaving a thick ridge for the wire.

12 Cut out the leaf shape using one of the simple leaf cutters. Insert a 28-, 26- or 24-gauge white wire into the thick ridge of the leaf to support about half its length. Soften the edge of the leaf and vein using one of the clematis Montana leaf veiners. Pinch from the base gently to the tip to accentuate the central vein. Repeat to make leaves in sets of three.

13 Dust in layers with foliage and vine green petal dusts. Tinge the edges with aubergine. Glaze lightly with edible spray varnish. Tape the leaves into their sets of three using half-width nile green floristry tape. Dust the taped stems on the upper surface with aubergine petal dust.

Hazelnuts

Hazels (*Corylus*) are a genus of deciduous trees and large shrubs that are native to the temperate northern hemisphere. The nuts of all hazels are edible, with the common hazel being the most extensively grown, followed by the Filbert.

MATERIALS

Pale green and cream flowerpaste
26- and 24-gauge white wires
Fresh egg white
Foliage, vine, terracotta, tangerine, nutkin, champagne and cream petal dusts
Edible spray varnish
Nile green floristry tape

EQUIPMENT

Non-stick rolling pin
Hazel leaf veiner set (SKGI)
Plain-edge cutting wheel
Metal ball tool
Rose petal cutters (optional)
Non-stick board
Dresden tool
Dusting brushes
Scriber or needle
Fine-nose pliers
Scalpel
Six-petal pointed blossom cutters (OP)

LEAVES

1 Roll out some well-kneaded pale green flowerpaste, leaving a thick ridge for the wire – do not roll the flowerpaste too fine as the hazel leaf veiners are quite heavily veined and will cut through the paste if it is too fine. Insert a 26-gauge white wire moistened with fresh egg white into about half the length of the thick ridge (use 24-gauge for larger leaves).

2 Place the wired flowerpaste into one of the double-sided hazel leaf veiners, lining up the central vein with the wire. Press the two sides together firmly to texture the leaf. Remove from the veiner and trim the excess paste away using the plain-edge cutting wheel. Soften the edge with the metal ball tool. To speed up the process a little, you might prefer to use rose petal cutters to cut out the basic leaf shape. This does tend to make the leaves a little too regular but will save you a little time.

3 Place the front side of the leaf down against the non-stick board and work the edges with the broad end of the Dresden tool to create a more serrated, ragged finish. Next, pinch the leaf down the centre to accentuate the central vein. Allow to firm up a little before dusting with petal dusts.

COLOURING

4 Dust the leaves as required. The smaller new growth is a fresher green so use layers of foliage and vine green. For the larger autumnal foliage, use terracotta, tangerine and nutkin on the edges. Dust foliage and vine green from the base towards the edges. Leave to dry and then spray lightly with edible spray varnish. Add insect nibbles and weather damage to the edges by attacking the leaves with a scriber, needle or wire that has been heated until red hot (using a cigarette lighter or tea-light). Tape over the wire with half-width nile green floristry tape.

NUTS

5 Roll a ball of well-kneaded cream-coloured flowerpaste. Form it into more of an oval shape and then insert a hooked 24-gauge white wire moistened with fresh egg white into the base.

6 Pinch the upper edge on either side of the nut to create a slight ridge on either side, keeping the base still rounded. Pinch the tip into a sharper point.

7 Use a scalpel, scriber or plain-edge cutting wheel to make a series of lines down the sides of the nuts. Dust with champagne and cream petal dusts. Add a slight tinge of vine green and foliage mixed with champagne petal dusts. Spray lightly with edible spray varnish.

HUSK

8 Roll out some pale green flowerpaste not too thinly. Cut out a shape using the six-petal pointed blossom cutter. Elongate the central petal on either side of the shape so that they are longer than the other petals which also need increasing only very slightly in length.

9 Use the broad end of the Dresden tool to work the edges of each section to thin it and create a more ragged husk-like finish. Attach onto the back of the nut with the shortest sections at the side of the nut. Curl back the edges using your fingers.

10 Dust the husk with foliage and vine green. Add tinges of cream and nutkin.

11 Repeat to make the nuts in pairs or sets of three. Snuggle them tightly together before they have a chance to dry.

Chinese lantern

These ornamental forms of physalis are native to China, Korea and Japan, and are related to the popular Cape gooseberry, which is actually South American in origin but cultivated in South Africa and other parts of the world too for its edible fruits. The ornamental forms also produce an inedible fruit that is concealed inside the inflated and very decorative calyx, which turns orange as the stems mature. Florists often strip the leaves from the plant to make more of a feature of the lanterns – I personally prefer them with the foliage. There are instructions for the flowers too, although these are optional. When I started to demonstrate years ago it was these and the nasturtium that became my signature flowers!

MATERIALS

28-, 26-, 24-, 22- and 20-gauge white wires
White, pale green, orange and pale melon flowerpaste
Small white seed-head stamens
Hi-tack non-toxic craft glue
Daffodil, sunflower, white, vine, tangerine, coral, foliage and aubergine petal dusts
Fresh egg white
Clear alcohol (Cointreau or kirsch)
Piece of polystyrene
Edible spray varnish
Nile green floristry tape

EQUIPMENT

Fine-nose pliers
Scalpel or plain-edge cutting wheel
Dusting brushes
Celstick
Small rose calyx cutters (OP or TT)
Non-stick rolling pin
Physalis leaf veiners (SKGI)
Clematis leaf veiner (SKGI)
Fine paintbrush
Large rose calyx cutters (OP or TT244)
Non-stick board
Fine scissors
Angled tweezers

BUD

1 Insert a hooked 26-gauge white wire into the base of a teardrop-shaped piece of white flowerpaste. Thin down the neck slightly. Divide the tip into five using a scalpel or plain-edge cutting wheel.

FLOWER

2 Glue five short seed-head stamens to the end of a 26-gauge white wire using non-toxic craft glue. Add a sixth stamen with the tip cut off to represent the pistil. Leave to dry and then curl them slightly. Dust the tips with a mixture of daffodil, sunflower and white petal dusts. Dust the base with vine petal dust.

107

3 Form a teardrop-shaped piece of white flowerpaste and pinch the base to form a hat shape. Roll out the 'brim' of the hat using the celstick. Cut out the flower shape using one of the small rose calyx cutters.

4 Broaden each petal with the celstick, rolling either edge of each petal and leaving a thicker area at the centre of each. Open up the centre of the flower using the pointed end of the celstick. Pinch a central vein down each petal and then thread the stamens through the centre of the flower. Thin the back of the flower a little and remove any excess flowerpaste.

CALYX

5 Add a ball of pale green flowerpaste at the base of the flower and the bud. Roll out some pale green flowerpaste and cut out a small calyx shape using the same size cutter as used to make the flower. Roll each sepal and broaden them with a celstick. Vein each sepal using the small physalis leaf veiner or clematis leaf veiner. Thread onto the back of the ball of flowerpaste, so that the raised veins produced by the back of the leaf veiner are on show. Moisten the edges of each sepal with fresh egg white and carefully join them together around the back of the flower/leaf so that it looks like a small lantern shape. Leave to dry. Dust with vine green and catch the edges with a little tangerine petal dust. Paint fine spots using sunflower, daffodil and white petal dusts diluted with clear alcohol. Add tinges of vine to the tips of the bud and the petals.

'LANTERNS'

6 These can be made with orange-coloured flowerpaste or with a pale melon base dusted to the varying degrees of green through to bright orange. Form a large teardrop-shaped piece of flowerpaste and then pinch out the broad end to form a large hat shape. Roll out the paste around the centre – not too thinly at this stage.

7 Use a large rose calyx cutter to cut out the basic shape of the lantern. You will need a few sizes of cutter to create a variation in lantern size down the stem.

8 Next, place the shape flat against the non-stick board and broaden each sepal with the celstick, leaving a thick ridge running down the centre of each. This will create wider sepals and thin the paste too. Elongate the sepals slightly too.

9 Vein each sepal using the physalis or clematis leaf veiner, making sure that the raised veins on the back of the leaf are used to create the texture on the upper surface of each sepal.

10 Bend a hook in the end of a 22-gauge white wire. Heat the wire using a tea-light until it goes red hot. Quickly thread the wire through the solid centre of the shape, embedding the hot hook into the flowerpaste. This caramelises the sugar to form a good instant bond. Be very careful not to burn your fingers on the hot sugar!

11 Next, moisten the edges of each sepal with fresh egg white. At this stage it is often best to insert the other end of the wire into a piece of polystyrene to hold the shape and give you both hands free to join and squeeze the edges of each sepal together. I often find it best to join two pairs together and then join these together leaving the fifth sepal to simply slot in. Trim off any excess paste from the edges of the sepals using fine scissors.

12 Use angled tweezers to continue the ridged vein made by the veiner to the centre of the shape where the wire comes out. Leave to set for a little while, but not dry completely, before dusting.

13 Dust the lantern in layers of tangerine, a touch of coral, tinges of foliage green, and on some you can introduce tinges of aubergine. The smaller lanterns at the top of the stem will be more green in colour, with gradual introduction of the orange and coral. Allow to dry before spraying lightly with edible spray varnish.

LEAVES

14 The leaves occur singular and in pairs, and sometimes even in sets of three. I generally use one leaf to each bud, flower and lantern. Roll out some pale green flowerpaste, leaving a thick ridge for the wire. Press the flat side of the chosen size of physalis leaf veiner against the paste to leave an outline. Use the plain-edge cutting wheel to cut out the shape.

15 Insert a 28-, 26- or 24-gauge white wire into the leaf so that it supports about half the length of the leaf.

16 Soften the edge of the leaf and then place into the double-sided physalis leaf veiner to texture it. Remove from the veiner and pinch from the base to the tip to accentuate the central vein. Tape over each leaf stem with half-width nile green floristry tape.

17 Dust with vine green, foliage and tinges of aubergine. Spray lightly with edible spray varnish or steam the leaves to set the colour.

ASSEMBLY

18 Tape a few smaller leaves at the end of a 20-gauge white wire using half-width nile green floristry tape. Gradually introduce the buds accompanied by one or two leaves. Next, add the flowers, again with leaves at the same point and then finally use the smaller lanterns with their heads hanging downwards with foliage at the same point gradually working through to the larger, more mature, lanterns. Dust the stem with vine, foliage and tinges of aubergine petal dusts. Spray the stem lightly with edible spray varnish to seal the colour onto the stems. Bend the stem slightly to create a bit of movement.

Ilex berries

Ilex verticillata is a native holly from America and Canada. The plant loses its foliage during the autumn, allowing these glossy berries to shine brightly on naked stems. The berries can be yellow, orange or red, making them a very useful addition to autumn and winter displays.

MATERIALS

35-, 33-, 22-, 20- and 18-gauge white wires
Sunflower yellow flowerpaste
Fresh egg white
Sunflower, tangerine, foliage, aubergine and nutkin petal dusts
Edible spray varnish
Full glaze (p 12) (optional)
Brown floristry tape

EQUIPMENT

Wire cutters
Fine-nose pliers
Tea light
Flat dusting brushes

BERRIES

1 Cut 35- or 33-gauge white wire into five or six short lengths. Take five or six short wires at a time and line up the ends to then bend them all in one fell swoop using fine-nose pliers.

2 Using the tea light, burn the hooked end of the wires to leave them looking black.

3 Roll balls of sunflower yellow flowerpaste to make the berries. Moisten the hook with fresh egg white and pull through a single wire into each ball. Leave to firm up a little before the next stage.

4 Dust the berries to create the desired effect. Here, I have dusted in layers with sunflower and over-dusted with tangerine petal dusts. Allow to dry and then spray with edible spray varnish or dip into a full glaze. You might need a few layers of glaze to create very shiny berries. Allow to dry. Dust the short stems with foliage and aubergine petal dusts.

5 Tape over a short length of 22-gauge white wire with half-width brown floristry tape to create a twig effect. Tape the berries tightly onto the twig. To create a larger piece, tape several smaller twigs onto a 20- or 18-gauge white wire.

6 Dust the twigs carefully with nutkin petal dust. Be very careful not to catch the berries too much with this colour. Spray lightly again with edible spray varnish.

Acer

There are around 120 species of Acer throughout the northern hemisphere. The variety I have chosen to use in this book has leaves made up of three to seven finer individual leaves. The beautiful autumnal colouring of the foliage makes the Acer an ideal addition to the flower-maker's repertoire.

LEAVES

1 Cut short lengths of 33-, 30- or 28-gauge white wires. The gauge of wire will depend on the size of foliage you are planning to make.

2 Roll a ball of well-kneaded pale green flowerpaste. Wrap it around the wire at the length required and then work the paste to the tip to form it into a fine point. You will need to work firmly and quickly to create a smooth finish.

Next, place the coated wire between the fleshy part of your palms and smooth the whole shape.

3 Place the wired shape against the non-stick board and flatten it using the flat side of the large briar rose leaf veiner — a method that I commonly refer to as SPLAT! Remove the veiner and check to see that the shape is good — if it isn't, you will need to trim the edge using the plain-edge cutting wheel or small scissors.

4 Soften the edge of the leaf with the small ball tool and then texture using the double-sided large briar rose leaf veiner. Remove from the veiner and pinch from the base to the tip to accentuate the central vein. Curve accordingly. Repeat to make varying sizes of leaf.

5 Tape the leaves into 'hand' shapes using quarter-width nile green floristry tape — these groupings can be made up of three to nine sections. If the leaves are still pliable, then reshape them to create a more natural overall design.

MATERIALS
33-, 30-, 28-gauge white wires
Pale green flowerpaste
Nile green floristry tape
Sunflower, tangerine, coral, ruby, aubergine and foliage petal dusts
Edible spray varnish

EQUIPMENT
Wire cutters
Non-stick board
Large briar rose leaf veiner (SKGI)
Plain-edge cutting wheel or small scissors
Small ball tool
Dusting brushes

6 Dust the leaves in varying layers while the paste is still wet. Use sunflower, tangerine, coral, ruby and aubergine in turn until the desired depth of colour is achieved. Add tinges of foliage too if required. Allow to dry and then spray lightly with edible spray varnish.

111

Cucumis fruit

These decorative fruit belong to the *Cucurbitaceae* family that includes the more familiar pumpkin, marrow, melon, gherkin and gourd. They are great for autumnal and winter floral displays and because of their size fill a good space too. The foliage is mostly stripped away by florists to reveal the brightly coloured fruit.

MATERIALS

33-, 28-, 26- and 24-gauge white wires

Nile green floristry tape

Pale cream flowerpaste

Fresh egg white

Sunflower, tangerine, coral, red, ruby, foliage, vine and aubergine petal dusts

Isopropyl alcohol

Edible spray varnish

EQUIPMENT

Scissors

Plain-edge cutting wheel

Dusting brushes

Fine paintbrush

TENDRILS

1 Tape over lengths of 33-gauge white wire with quarter-width nile green floristry tape. Smooth over the tape by rubbing the sides of a pair of scissors against it. Curl and tangle the tendril to give plenty of movement. Repeat to make several tendrils.

FRUIT

2 Roll a ball of well-kneaded pale cream flowerpaste. Form it into an oval, almost egg shape. Insert a 28- or 26-gauge white wire moistened with fresh egg white into the fruit so that the wire protrudes through the end. Pinch the paste at the tip and at the base to secure it in place. Texture the surface slightly with lines created with the plain-edge cutting wheel. Repeat to make varying sizes of fruit.

COLOURING AND ASSEMBLY

3 Dust to varying degrees with sunflower, tangerine, coral, red and ruby petal dusts. Add tinges of foliage mixed with vine and also tinges of aubergine.

4 Dilute some of the foliage and vine petal dusts with isopropyl alcohol to paint very fine lines onto the surface.

5 Tape a tendril onto the end of a 24-gauge white wire with half-width nile green floristry tape. Start to add smaller fruit and graduate down the stem, adding tendrils at the same point as each fruit. Curl the stem as required. Dust it with foliage and aubergine petal dusts. Glaze the fruit with edible spray varnish.

Chincherinchee

I love the name of this South African flowering bulb. I have chosen to use orange chincherinchees in this book but there are also white and yellow forms.

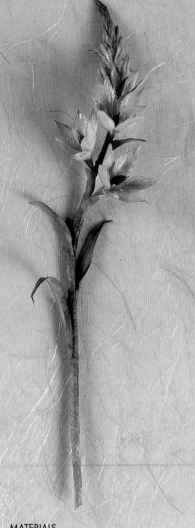

OVARY AND STAMENS

1 Attach a small cone-shaped piece of green cold porcelain onto the end of a 33-gauge white wire so that the tip of the wire very slightly protrudes. Work the base of the cone into a more slender shape. Squeeze the sides of the ovary between two fingers and a thumb to create three sides. Mark a line on each side using the scalpel. Dust with a mixture of foliage and navy petal dusts. Using non-toxic craft glue, glue six short seed-head stamens around the ovary and leave to dry. Dust the tips of the stamens with sunflower petal dust.

PETALS

2 Work a ball of cream flowerpaste onto the end of a short length of 33-gauge white wire. Form it into a cigar shape slightly pointed at both ends. Place the shape on the non-stick board and flatten it using the back of the cupped Christmas rose petal veiner. Soften the edges and then texture using the veined side of the same veiner.

3 Cup and pinch the petal into shape. Repeat to make six petals. Tape the petals around the stamen centre using quarter-width nile green floristry tape. Dust the petals with tangerine and tinges of coral petal dusts.

BUDS

4 Insert a 22-gauge white wire into a slender teardrop piece of pale green flowerpaste. Smooth the sides between your palms. Use fine scissors to snip into the surface of the flowerpaste to create the bracts that form a scaled effect at the top of the stem.

5 Add small, wired cigar-shaped buds to the stem, adding a bract to each bud made by cutting a pointed shape from some pale green flowerpaste. Attach to the stem with fresh egg white. Dust the buds to match the flowers. Dust the green bracts with vine and foliage petal dusts. Add tinges of aubergine.

6 Tape the flowers onto the stem using half-width nile green floristry tape. Add a flowerpaste bract at the base of each of these flowers where the short flower stems meet the main stem. Dust the bracts as for the smaller bracts at the top of the stem. Dust the main stem with vine green and a touch of foliage green.

MATERIALS

Green cold porcelain (p 14–5)
33- and 22-gauge white wires
Foliage, navy, sunflower, tangerine, coral, vine and aubergine petal dusts
Hi-tack non-toxic craft glue
Seed-head stamens
Cream and pale green flowerpaste
Nile green floristry tape
Fresh egg white

EQUIPMENT

Scalpel
Dusting brushes
Non-stick board
Cupped Christmas rose petal veiner (SKGI)
Fine scissors

Hawaiian perfume flower tree

There are about 50 species of *Fagraea* – often known as the perfume flower tree. The tree takes an epiphytic form, not as a parasite, but uses other trees as a support. The trees are native to South East Asia through to northern Australia and the Pacific Islands. The flowers are thick and fleshy in form, opening in the morning and lasting for two days. They fade from a green-tinged white flower through to a cream yellow. The flowers are pollinated by insects and birds, which return later to feed on the red pulp in which the seeds are embedded.

MATERIALS

26-, 24-, 22- and 20-gauge white wires

Wire cutters

Mid-green, pale lemon and white flowerpaste

Edelweiss, vine, sunflower, daffodil, plum, foliage, aubergine and woodland petal dusts

Edible spray varnish

Fresh egg white

Nile green floristry tape

EQUIPMENT

Large rose petal cutters (TT776-778) or see templates on p 250

Non-stick board

Fine tweezers

Fine-nose pliers

Dusting brushes, including a flat dusting brush

Plain-edge cutting wheel

Non-stick rolling pin

Standard set of rose petal cutters (TT276-280)

Foam pad

Large metal ball tool

Wide amaryllis petal veiner (SKGI)

Curved former or kitchen paper

Large datura leaf veiner (Aldaval)

PISTIL

1 Cut a length of 26-gauge white wire in half using wire cutters. Take a small ball of well-kneaded mid-green flowerpaste and insert the wire into it. Work the flowerpaste quickly and firmly down the wire to create a length that measures about two-thirds the length of the petal cutter/template. Leave a small ball/bead of flowerpaste at the tip of the wire and keep the length of the pistil fairly fine. Smooth the length between your palms or against the non-stick board. Use fine tweezers to pinch three very subtle sections to the tip. Curve the length slightly using fine-nose pliers.

2 Dust the tip and length of the pistil with a mixture of edelweiss petal dust mixed with vine. Allow to dry and then spray gently with edible spray varnish.

STAMEN – FILAMENTS

3 Cut three 26-gauge white wires in half and set one piece of wire to one side as you only need to make five stamens for this flower. Attach a ball of well-kneaded white flowerpaste to the wire and work the paste up to the tip of the wire to create a thickened filament. Remove any excess flowerpaste and smooth the length between your palms or against the non-stick board. Repeat to make five stamens. Allow them to rest a little before curving them into a lazy 'S' shape.

ANTHERS

4 Form a ball of pale lemon flowerpaste into a cigar shape. Moisten the tip of the wired filament with fresh egg white and attach the cigar to the end of it. Pinch it firmly in place to secure the two together. Use the plain-edge cutting wheel to mark a single line down the length of the upper surface. Repeat with all five stamens and then leave to dry.

114

5 Dust the tips of the stamens with a light mixture of sunflower, daffodil and edelweiss petal dusts. Use plum petal dust to colour the filaments. Spray lightly with edible spray varnish to prevent the plum colour marking the pure white petals.

6 Tape the five stamens to the underside of the pistil using half-width nile green floristry tape.

PETALS

7 The petals are fairly fleshy so don't roll the flowerpaste too fine, however, be careful not to make it too heavy either, otherwise the wires will not support the weight of the petals. Roll out some well-kneaded white flowerpaste, leaving a thicker ridge to hold the wire. Cut out the petal shape using one of the three sizes of squashed rose petal cutters or using a plain-edge cutting wheel and the petal template on page 250.

8 Insert a moistened half-length of 24-gauge white wire into the ridge to support about half the length of the petal. As you insert the wire, support the thick ridge on either side of the petal between your finger and thumb and hold the wire very close to the end that is being inserted

so that the wire does not pierce through the flowerpaste or bend and change direction while you are carrying out this step.

9 Place the petal onto the foam pad or the palm of your hand and soften the edges using a rolling action with the large end of a metal ball tool. Next, place the petal in between the double-sided wide amaryllis petal veiner and press firmly to texture the surface. Repeat to make five petals. Cover the petals with a plastic bag as you make them to stop them from drying out too much.

10 Take each petal in turn and pinch them from the base very gently through to the tip to create a more natural shape, curving gracefully at the tip. Repeat with each petal and allow them to firm up a little over a curved former or use a few sheets of kitchen paper rolled up. Keep checking on the petals as they are quite large and often lose their shape over the former so you will need to reshape them a little from time to time.

11 Using a flat dusting brush, colour the base of each petal with a mixture of vine and edelweiss petal dusts, fading the colour out as it hits the mid section of the petals.

12 Tape the five petals around the curved stamens and pistil using half-width nile green floristry tape. If the petals are still pliable, then this is good as it will enable you to reshape one last time to create a more realistic effect.

13 The back of the flower fuses the petals together into a tube. To create this, add a ball of white flowerpaste at the

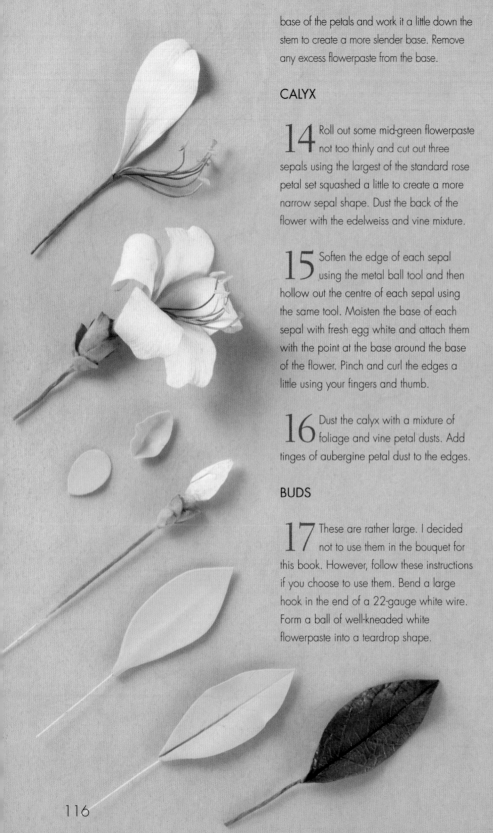

base of the petals and work it a little down the stem to create a more slender base. Remove any excess flowerpaste from the base.

CALYX

14 Roll out some mid-green flowerpaste not too thinly and cut out three sepals using the largest of the standard rose petal set squashed a little to create a more narrow sepal shape. Dust the back of the flower with the edelweiss and vine mixture.

15 Soften the edge of each sepal using the metal ball tool and then hollow out the centre of each sepal using the same tool. Moisten the base of each sepal with fresh egg white and attach them with the point at the base around the base of the flower. Pinch and curl the edges a little using your fingers and thumb.

16 Dust the calyx with a mixture of foliage and vine petal dusts. Add tinges of aubergine petal dust to the edges.

BUDS

17 These are rather large. I decided not to use them in the bouquet for this book. However, follow these instructions if you choose to use them. Bend a large hook in the end of a 22-gauge white wire. Form a ball of well-kneaded white flowerpaste into a teardrop shape.

18 Moisten the hooked wire with fresh egg white and insert it into the broad base of the teardrop. Work the base down onto the wire to create a more slender neck shape.

19 Next, pinch five flanges to represent petals using your fingers and fine tweezers. Twist the petals around the bud. Dust as for the back of the flower. The smaller buds would be greener than the larger forms. Add a calyx as for the flower, gauging the size of cutter accordingly.

LEAVES

20 These, like the flowers, are rather large and fairly fleshy. Roll out some mid-green well-kneaded flowerpaste, leaving a thick ridge for the wire. Cut out the leaf either freehand using the plain-edge cutting wheel or use one of the templates on page 250.

21 Insert a 24- or 22-gauge white wire into the thick ridge to support about a third to two-thirds the length of the leaf. Pinch the base of the leaf down onto the wire. Place the leaf onto the foam pad and soften the edges using the large metal ball tool.

22 Texture the leaf using the large double-sided datura leaf veiner. Remove the leaf from the veiner and pinch it from the base through to the tip to accentuate the central vein. Allow to dry fairly flat.

23 Dust in layers with woodland petal dust, fading towards the edges and then over-dust with foliage and a touch of vine. The backs are much paler with more vine colouring. Add aubergine tinges very lightly to the edges. Allow to dry and then glaze lightly with edible spray varnish.

Chinese yam (*Dioscorea*)

This plant belongs to a genus that contains around 600 tropical and subtropical herbaceous climbing plants. There are many decorative forms, some with spotted leaves, others with silver and dark green margins. The backs of the leaves are often decorative too, with plum, magenta or aubergine colouring.

PREPARATION

1 The heart-shaped golden wings rose cutters and the black bryony leaf cutters are ideal for making these decorative yam leaves, however, they will need to be squashed to reshape the design a little to match the templates on page 250.

LEAVES

2 Roll out some mid-green flowerpaste, leaving a thick ridge for the wire. Cut out the leaf shape using one of the various sizes of golden wings rose or black bryony leaf cutters, or refer to the templates on page 250.

3 Insert a 28-, 26- or 24-gauge white wire moistened with fresh egg white into the central thick ridge to support about half the length of the leaf. The exact gauge will depend on the size of the leaf, but remember: the higher the wire gauge number, the finer the wire is.

4 Place the leaf on the foam pad or the palm of your hand and soften the cut edge of the leaf using the medium or large metal ball tool. Use a rolling action with the tool, working half on the flowerpaste and half on your pad/hand.

5 Place the leaf into the double-sided galex or black bryony leaf veiner and press firmly to create a realistic leaf texture. Remove the leaf from the veiner and carefully pinch it from the base through to the tip to accentuate the central vein and add movement to the leaf. Dry over some dimpled foam or crumpled kitchen paper to help support the leaf in a natural shape. Repeat to make the required number of leaves in varying sizes.

6 Dust the leaves in layers on the front surface using a mixture of moss, foliage and vine petal dusts. Dust the back of the leaves with a mixture of plum and aubergine, fading towards the edges. Next, dilute a little plum and aubergine petal dusts with isopropyl alcohol and, using a fine paintbrush, add detail veining from the base of the leaf fading into a fine point on each of the radiating textured veins. Allow to dry. Add a tinge of dry plum/aubergine to the painted area. Spray lightly with edible spray varnish.

7 Tape the leaves onto a length of 22-gauge white wire using half-width nile green floristry tape. Leave a little of each leaf stem showing and stagger them down the stem graduating in size. Add tendrils using curled lengths of pale green 33-gauge wire if desired. I decided to omit the tendrils for the perfume perfection project.

MATERIALS

Mid-green flowerpaste

28-, 26-, 24- and 22-gauge white wires

Fresh egg white

33-gauge pale green wires (optional)

Moss, foliage, vine, plum and aubergine petal dusts

Isopropyl alcohol

Edible spray varnish

Nile green floristry tape

EQUIPMENT

Golden wings rose cutters (TT770-775) or Black bryony leaf cutters (TT652-654) or see templates on p 250

Non-stick rolling pin

Foam pad

Medium or large metal ball tool

Galex leaf veiner (SC) or Black bryony leaf veiner (SKGI)

Dimpled foam or kitchen paper

Dusting brushes

Fine paintbrush

Ylang-ylang

The genus *Cananga* contains two species ranging through tropical Asia into Australia. *Cananga odorata*, a native of Malaysia, is now cultivated in many other tropical areas of the world and is often grown as a commercial crop to create the perfume known as ylang-ylang. The flowers can be yellow or more green in form, and the green-black berries also form a very useful decorative addition to the sugarcrafter's repertoire.

MATERIALS

28-, 26-, 24- and 22-gauge white wires

Pale vine green and mid-green flowerpaste

Vine, moss, sunflower, daffodil, foliage, black, aubergine and edelweiss petal dusts

Fresh egg white

Nile green floristry tape

Edible spray varnish

EQUIPMENT

Piping bag fitted with a no.3 piping tube

Fine paintbrush, dusting brushes

Non-stick rolling pin

Single petal daisy cutter

Scalpel

Foam pad

Medium metal ball tool

Stargazer B petal veiner

Plain-edge cutting wheel

Large gardenia leaf veiner (SKGI)

Fine-nose pliers

Ceramic tool

STAMEN CENTRE

1 Bend a hook in the end of a third length of 28-gauge white wire. Attach a small ball of pale vine green flowerpaste onto the hook. Squeeze the flowerpaste around the wire to secure the two together. Next, use two fingers and thumb to pinch and form the flowerpaste into a triangular shape. Keep the top of the shape flat. Use the no.3 piping tube to emboss a spot at the centre of the shape.

2 Use a mixture of vine and moss petal dusts to dust the embossed spot an intense green. Dust the outer area with sunflower petal dust. Allow to dry.

PETALS

3 Roll out some well-kneaded pale green flowerpaste, leaving a thick ridge for the wire. Angle the rolling pin as you roll the flowerpaste to create a tapered ridge. Cut out the petal shape with the ridge running down the centre using the single petal daisy cutter or a scalpel and the template on page 250.

4 Insert a 28-gauge white wire moistened with fresh egg white into the rounded broader base of the petal to support about a third of the length of the petal. Hold the ridge firmly as you insert the wire to prevent the wire piercing through the flowerpaste. Next, place the petal onto the foam pad or on the palm of your hand and soften the edge using the medium metal ball tool, working half on your pad/hand and half on the edge of the flowerpaste. Take care not to ruffle or frill the edges – you are simply trying to thin and remove the harsh cut edge left by the cutter.

5 Texture the surface of the petal using the double-sided stargazer B petal veiner. Remove the petal from the veiner and carefully pinch the base of the petal through to the tip. Use the metal ball tool to hollow out the base of the petal. Repeat to make six petals. The petals can curve inwards or outwards on one flower – they are quite random in form.

COLOURING AND ASSEMBLY

6 It is best to dust the petals while they are freshly made and still pliable so that the colour sticks well and you can reshape the petals during assembly. Dust the petals as desired: they can be green in form, green-yellow or a golden yellow. Here I have used a mixture of daffodil, sunflower and edelweiss white petal dusts.

7 Tape three inner petals evenly spaced around the stamen centre using quarter-width nile green floristry tape. Pinch and curl the tips of each petal to create more movement. Next, tape the remaining three petals to fill the gaps in the first layer. Once again, pinch the tips and curl them inwards or outwards as desired. Dust the base and the tips of each petal with a mixture of moss and vine petal dusts. Allow to dry and hold them over a jet of steam from a just-boiled kettle or use a clothes steamer to set the colour and take away the dusty effect left by the dusting process.

CALYX

8 There are three tiny sepals at the base of the flower. Form three cone-shaped pieces of pale-green flowerpaste and flatten using the flat side of a veiner. Soften the edges and then pinch at the tip. Attach to the base of the flower using fresh egg white.

LEAVES

9 Roll out some well-kneaded mid-green flowerpaste, leaving a central thick ridge for the wire. Use the plain-edge cutting wheel to cut out a pointed oval-shaped leaf.

10 Insert a 28-, 26- or 24-gauge white wire, depending on the leaf size, moistened with fresh egg white. Soften the edge of the leaf and then texture using the large gardenia leaf veiner. Remove the leaf from the veiner and pinch it from the base to the tip quite firmly to accentuate the central vein. Curve the leaf slightly. Repeat to make numerous leaves in graduating sizes.

11 Dust the leaves in layers, starting with foliage and moss mixed together to add depth at the base and centre of each leaf and fading towards the edges. Over-dust with vine petal dust. Leave to dry and then glaze lightly with edible spray varnish or dip into a half glaze (see page 12).

BERRIES

12 Bend a hook in the end of a 28-gauge white wire using fine-nose pliers. Roll a ball of mid-green flowerpaste and insert the hooked end into it. Work the base of the ball down onto the wire to create a more tear-dropped shaped fruit.

13 Use the rounded end of the ceramic tool to create indents and bumps over the surface of the fruit. Repeat to make berries in varying sizes. Tape over each wire with quarter-width nile green floristry tape.

14 Dust the fruit to the desired stage of ripeness using layers of vine and foliage, gradually introducing black and aubergine petal dusts, and then just black. It is wise to dust these quickly so that the colour is intense and sticks easily to the flowerpaste.

Allow to dry, then spray the berries to create a glossy finish using edible spray glaze or dip into a full glaze (see page 12).

15 Using quarter-width nile green floristry tape, tape the berries into clusters of varying numbers, leaving a little of each stem showing.

119

Butterfly flower tree

The flowers of this beautiful tree from Central to Southern America are between 15–20 cm (6–8 in) across. Here, I have scaled the flower down for use on cakes. The flowers can be yellow, apricot, through to a deep orange in colour. The scent of the flower is almost like that of an apricot. They are fairly simple to make, only having five petals, and yet form a stunning focal flower for cake design.

PISTIL

1 The pistil is split into three very fine sections. Cut three short lengths of 33-gauge white wire. Take a tiny ball of pale tangerine flowerpaste and work it onto one length of wire, about 2.5 cm (1 in) from the tip. Hold the wire firmly between one finger and thumb and use the other finger and thumb to twiddle the paste towards the end. Keep thinning the paste and remove any excess as you work to create a very finely coated wire. Repeat with the other two wires and gently curve them.

2 Tape the three sections together using quarter-width nile green floristry tape. Next, attach a ball of pale green flowerpaste at the base of the pistil. Work the base into a slightly oval shape and divide into three sections using the plain-edge cutting wheel. Set to one side.

STAMENS

3 To make the filaments (lengths of the stamens), cut five short lengths of 33-gauge white wire. Attach a slightly larger ball of pale green flowerpaste than that used for the pistil onto a wire. Work the flowerpaste as for the pistil, creating a tapered shape slightly broader at the base and fine at the tip. Smooth the length between your palms or against the non-stick board. Next, flatten the shape using the flat side of the stargazer B petal veiner. If the shape is too heavy or has very uneven edges, simply trim them into shape using a pair of fine scissors.

MATERIALS

33-, 28-, 26-, 24- and 22-gauge white wires

Pale tangerine, pale green, pale yellow and mid-green flowerpaste

Nile green floristry tape

Coral, tangerine, vine, daffodil, sunflower, white, foliage and aubergine petal dusts

Fresh egg white

Edible spray varnish

EQUIPMENT

Wire cutters

Plain-edge cutting wheel

Non-stick board

Stargazer B petal veiner

Fine scissors

Dusting brushes

Non-stick rolling pin

Amaryllis petal cutter (TT) or see template on p 250

Foam pad

Large metal ball tool

Ceramic silk veining tool

Fine scissors

Sage leaf or cattleya orchid wing petal cutter

Mandevilla leaf veiner (SKGI)

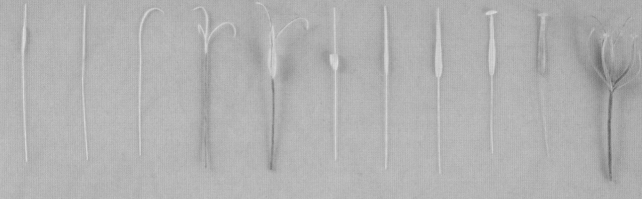

4 To create the anther, take a tiny piece of pale yellow flowerpaste and form it into a cigar shape. Moisten the tip of the filament with water and embed it into the centre of the anther to secure the two together. Mark a line down the length of the anther using the plain-edge cutting wheel. Repeat to complete the five stamens. Curve the length of each stamen before they have a chance to dry.

COLOURING AND ASSEMBLY

5 Dust each fine section of the pistil and the length of each stamen filament with a mixture of coral and tangerine petal dusts. Dust the green ovary with vine petal dust. Use a mixture of daffodil and sunflower petal dusts to colour the anthers.

6 Tape the five stamens around the ovary/pistil using quarter-width nile green floristry tape so that they curve in towards the pistil. Set to one side.

PETALS

7 Take a piece of well-kneaded pale tangerine flowerpaste and roll it out using the non-stick rolling pin to leave a thick ridge for the wire. As you roll the flowerpaste, try to angle it so that it creates a tapered ridge. Cut out the petal shape using the amaryllis petal cutter or use the template on page 250 and the plain-edge cutting wheel. Insert a 26-gauge white wire moistened with fresh egg white into the thick ridge to support about a third of the length of the petal – hold the wire very close to the end that is being inserted so that it can't wiggle and pierce through the flowerpaste.

8 Place the petal onto your palm or a firm foam pad and soften the edge using the large metal ball tool, working half on the edge of the petal and half on your palm/foam pad. Next, place the petal into the double-sided stargazer B petal veiner and press firmly to texture the surface.

9 Remove the petal from the veiner and place it back onto the foam pad. Use the plain-edge cutting wheel to draw three fine lines down the centre of the petal. Pick up the petal and pinch it gently from behind at the base working through to the tip to accentuate the central veins and give the petal more shape and movement. The tip should be pinched slightly harder.

10 The edges can be fairly flat or slightly frilled. I prefer the frilled effect as it gives the flower more movement. Rest the petal against your index finger and use the ceramic silk veining tool to frill the upper edges of the petal. Take care not to point the tip of the tool into the flowerpaste as this will create ugly indents. Finally, curve the petal and dry over a dimpled foam pad or curved former. Repeat to make five petals for each flower.

COLOURING AND ASSEMBLY

11 Dust each petal to the required colour/depth. Here I have used a mixture of coral and tangerine petal dusts. Add white petal dust for a paler colour. Start by adding a streak of colour from the base of each petal fading out towards the edges on the back and front. Bring some of the colour in from the edge of each petal, catching the side of the brush against the edges to make it more intense on the very edge.

12 Tape the petals evenly spaced around the base of the stamens using half-width nile green floristry tape. If the petals are still pliable reshape them as required.

CALYX

13 There are five sepals to the calyx. I find it best to wire each section giving the whole flower a lot more movement. Cut five short lengths of 28-gauge white wire. Work a small ball of well-kneaded pale yellow flowerpaste onto the wire to create a tapered shape measuring just under 3.5 cm (1.5 in) long. Work the paste onto the wire in the same way that the stamen filaments were made. Smooth the length of the shape between your palms and then place onto the non-stick board and flatten it with the flat side of the stargazer B petal veiner. Trim the shape with a pair of fine scissors if needed.

14 Place the sepal into the stargazer B veiner and press firmly to texture it. Remove the sepal from the veiner and pinch it from the base through to the tip to create a central vein and a sharper point. Repeat to make five sepals. Dust each sepal with a mixture of sunflower and a touch of daffodil petal dusts, starting at the base and fading out towards the tip. Add a tinge of vine to the very tips to break up the space.

15 Tape the five sepals onto the back of the flower using half-width nile green floristry tape. Position them in the spaces in between each petal.

LEAVES

16 Cut lengths of 26-, 24- or 22-gauge white wire into half lengths. Roll out well-kneaded mid-green flowerpaste, leaving a thick ridge for the wire. Use a sage leaf or cattleya orchid wing petal cutter to cut out the shape.

17 Insert a 24-gauge white wire into the thick ridge of the leaf to support half the length of the leaf. Place leaf on foam pad and soften edges using the large metal ball tool. Place the leaf in mandevilla leaf veiner, lining the tip of the leaf and the base with the central vein. Remove and pinch from base to tip to accentuate the central vein. Allow to dry slightly.

COLOURING AND GLAZING

18 Dust the leaf in layers, starting with foliage petal dust from the base of the leaf, aiming the colour down the central vein first of all and then fading towards the edges. Over-dust with vine petal dust. Add a tinge of aubergine here and there to break up the space. Allow to dry and then spray very lightly with edible spray varnish.

Zantedeschia berries

The red, green and gold berries of the African *zantedeschia* family can be a wonderful addition to exotic flower arrangements. The plant is often called calla lily, although strictly speaking it does not belong to the lily family.

BERRIES

1 Cut several lengths of 30-gauge white wire into fifths using wire cutters or sharp florist's scissors. Use fine-nose pliers to bend a hook in the end of each wire. Use a lighter or tea-light flame to singe the white paper off the wires to give a black finish.

2 Roll the pale green, pale yellow and orange-red flowerpaste into lots of small berries. Moisten the hooked end of a singed wire with fresh egg white and thread it through the centre of a berry, leaving a little of the wire showing through.

3 Create a series of indents radiating from the hook into the berry. Repeat to create numerous berries – the number varies quite a bit, which is good for flower arranging as more variation can be created.

4 Tape over a 22-gauge white wire with white floristry tape and then start to tape the berries to the wire in no particular colour order – although I usually fix the green berries at the top of the stem.

5 It is easier to dust the berries once they are all taped onto the stem. Dust vine, moss, sunflower, tangerine, red and ruby petal dusts over the berries, creating a natural ripening process from green through to a rich red. The odd tinge of aubergine to the rich red berries can help to add extra depth. Allow to dry and then dip into a full confectioner's glaze or spray a few times with edible spray varnish, allowing the glaze to set in between coats.

6 Next, thicken the stem with a strip of shredded kitchen paper. Tape over the top with half-width nile green floristry tape. Use the side of a pair of scissors to rub the blade against the tape to smooth out the joins in the tape and leave a slightly polished finish.

BRACT

7 This is the left-over dead flower often removed by florists so you might feel that you don't want to add it. I use a short length of white floristry tape dusted with cream and nutkin brown petal dusts. Use the fine end of the dresden tool to draw a series of fine lines onto the tape. Cut into the edge with a scalpel or sharp pair of scissors to give a ragged finish. Tape the bract onto the base of the berries using half-width nile green floristry tape. Polish the stem and then dust lightly with vine and foliage petal dusts. Spray the stem lightly with edible spray varnish.

MATERIALS

30- and 22-gauge white wires

Pale green, pale yellow and orange-red flowerpaste

Fresh egg white

White and nile green floristry tape

Vine, moss, sunflower, tangerine, red, ruby, aubergine, cream, nutkin brown and foliage petal dusts

Full confectioner's glaze (see p 12) or edible spray varnish

Kitchen paper

EQUIPMENT

Wire cutters or sharp florist's scissors

Fine-nose pliers

Lighter or tea light

Dusting brushes

Scissors

Dresden tool

Scalpel or sharp scissors

Joseph's coat foliage

There are about 16 species of *Codiaeum* that are found native from Malaysia to the Pacific, as well as many cultivated forms that are grown in other areas of the world too. In the UK, the plants are often cultivated as houseplants and known as *Croton*, or affectionately as Joseph's coat because of the interesting colour range of their leathery ornate foliage. They are very useful leaves, filling lots of space and providing extra colour to floral displays. The size and shape of each variety is different, as are the colour variations. Here I have illustrated some of my favourites.

MATERIALS

Pale green or cream flowerpaste
24-, 22- or 20-gauge white wires
Cornflour
Sunflower, daffodil, coral, plum, foliage, vine, woodland, ruby and forest petal dusts
Isopropyl alcohol
Edible spray varnish

EQUIPMENT

Non-stick rolling pin
Grooved board
Scalpel
Plain-edge cutting wheel
Foam pad
Large metal ball tool
Large, flat dusting brushes
Large gardenia or mandevilla leaf veiner (SKGI)
Dimpled foam
Cotton wool or kitchen paper
Fine paintbrush
Toothbrush or stencil brush
Rubber gloves (optional)

LEAVES

1 These leaves are quite fleshy so there is no need to roll the flowerpaste super fine. Take some well-kneaded pale green or cream flowerpaste and roll it out, leaving a thicker ridged area for the wire. A grooved board may be used for this if desired.

2 Cut out the Croton leaf shape using one of the templates on page 251 and a scalpel or plain-edge cutting wheel.

3 Insert a white wire, the size of which is dependent on the size of the leaf, moistened with fresh egg white into the thick ridge of the leaf to support at least half the length. For the finer tri-lobed shapes it is important to support as much of the leaf length as possible.

4 Place the leaf against the foam pad and soften the edges of the leaf with the large metal ball tool, working half on the very edge of the leaf and half on the foam pad using a rolling action with the tool rather than rubbing it, which would create a frilled edge.

5 Next, dust the leaf with cornflour to prevent sticking and place it into the large gardenia or mandevilla leaf veiner. Line up the tip of the leaf and the base with the central vein of the leaf veiner. Press firmly to texture the surface of the leaf.

6 Remove the leaf from the veiner and carefully pinch it from the base through to the tip to shape it and emphasize the central vein. If you are making a tri-lobed leaf, you will need to pinch the leaf down to the tip too.

7 The thick flowerpaste at the very base of the leaf now needs to be worked between your finger and thumb to create a fleshy stem. Alternatively, extra flowerpaste can be added to the stem when the leaf has dried and blended between your finger and thumb. Allow the leaf to dry slightly before colouring. Rest it on some dimpled foam. Use cotton wool or kitchen paper under the side sections of a tri-lobed leaf to give it support and more movement.

COLOURING

8 The leaves illustrated here have various colour combinations. The first leaf pictured is dusted gently with a mixture of sunflower and daffodil petal dusts and then over-dusted from the base with a mixture of coral and plum petal dusts. The edges of the leaf are dusted with foliage and vine petal dusts. Painted veins are added using isopropyl alcohol mixed with foliage petal dust and a touch of woodland. Use a fine paintbrush to paint in the stronger central vein and then add finer side veins. Allow to dry, then spray with edible spray varnish – this works better if built up in layers, otherwise the leaves become too shiny.

9 The smaller red leaf pictured was dusted with a mixture of ruby and plum petal dusts. Darker green shading was dusted onto the base and the tip using woodland petal dust. Spots and a central vein were painted on using woodland diluted with isopropyl alcohol. Other variations use ruby petal dust diluted with isopropyl alcohol.

10 The fine spotted effect on the larger three leaves can be created using a mixture of foliage with a touch of forest or woodland diluted with isopropyl alcohol and then flicked over the leaves using a toothbrush kept only for this purpose or a stencil brush – something with stiff bristles is required here. A pair of food-safety rubber gloves could be good here too to avoid green fingers. Stains can be removed, however, using diluted bicarbonate of soda.

Crane flower

There are five species of *strelitzia* and all are native to South Africa where they are often known as crane flowers or birds of paradise. In fact, they are pollinated by sun birds and bats too. Most folk think of the orange-petalled flowers although they can be yellow, white and creamy-green. The blue arrow-like petals are actually stamens. The white-petalled forms of *strelitzia* are much larger than the more common orange forms and the beak colouring varies too, often being quite strikingly black in colour. I was shocked when I first saw this plant on a brief trip to South Africa – it was about the height of two-storey house!

MATERIALS

White and mid-green flowerpaste
26-, 24-, 20- and 18-gauge white wires
Fresh egg white
Ultramarine and Prussian blue craft dusts
White, vine, daffodil, edelweiss, plum, aubergine, foliage, woodland and forest petal dusts
Edible spray varnish

White and nile green floristry tape
Isopropyl alcohol

EQUIPMENT

Non-stick rolling pin
Plain-edge cutting wheel
Scalpel
Strelitzia cutters (AD)

Dresden tool
Foam pad
Medium and large metal ball tools
Large dusting brushes
Very large tulip leaf veiner (SKGI) or a piece of dried sweetcorn husk
Sharp scissors
Fine angled tweezers

STAMENS

1 Although these dramatic blue structures look like petals they are actually the stamens! As with most blue and purple flowers it is best to use white flowerpaste and then dust to create a clean colour to the finished piece – using a blue flowerpaste tends to create a rather grey finish. Roll out some well-kneaded white flowerpaste, leaving a thick ridge that will run down the length of the stamen. Angle the non-stick rolling pin on either side of the ridge to create a tapered ridge. Use the stamen template on page 251 and the plain-edge cutting wheel or scalpel to cut out the shape or use the stamen cutter from the *strelitzia* cutter set.

2 Insert a 26-gauge white wire moistened with fresh egg white into the thick ridge of the stamen so that it supports most of the length. Next, thin down the narrow part of the

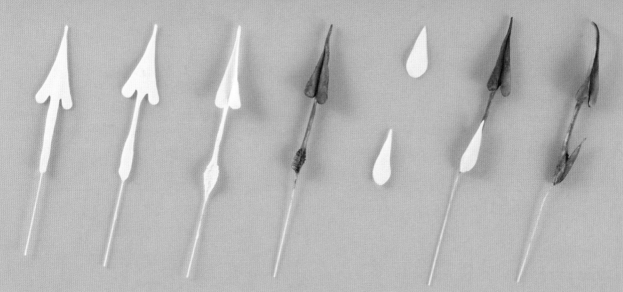

stamen by working the flowerpaste firmly between your finger and thumb. Leave some of the excess bulk that will be gathered at the base and trim off any excess so the length is about that of the original template or cutter shape. Use the broad end of the dresden tool to thin the edges of this section, leaving a slight texture at the same time and a slightly serrated finish to the edges.

3 Place the shape onto the foam pad or the palm of your hand with the ridged side uppermost and soften the edges using the medium metal ball tool. Use the tool to hollow out either side of the arrowhead shape. Pinch the length of the stamen from the base to the tip to create a strong central vein to the front surface of the stamen and to create a sharper point to the shape.

4 Roll out some more white flowerpaste and cut out the small stamen bract shape using the template on page 251 or the appropriate cutter from the *strelitzia* cutter set. Soften the edges using the metal ball tool and then pinch slightly at the tip and the base to create a gentle central vein. Moisten the base of the stamen with fresh egg white and attach the bract onto it. Repeat to make the required number of stamens – there is one stamen to

every three petals and the number does vary depending on the stage of the flower's life. I generally use two or three stamens per flower.

COLOURING

5 Dust the stamens with ultramarine and Prussian blue craft dusts, leaving the very tip and the very base a little paler. Dust the tip of the stamen heavily with white petal dust to represent the pollen. Spray lightly with edible spray varnish.

LARGE PETAL

6 You will need to make two large petals and one smaller petal to add to each stamen. Roll out some well-kneaded white flowerpaste, leaving a central ridge for the wire. Cut out a petal shape using the large petal template on page 251 and the plain-edge cutting wheel or the larger petal cutter from the *strelitzia* cutter set.

7 Insert a 24-gauge white wire moistened with fresh egg white into the thick ridge of the petal to support about half its length. Thin the base of the petal down onto the wire slightly and then trim off any excess flowerpaste. Place the petal onto the foam

pad and soften the edges using the large metal ball tool. Next, place the petal into the very large tulip leaf veiner or sweetcorn husk to texture both sides of the petal.

8 Pinch the petal from the base through to the tip to accentuate the central vein and create a sharper point to the petal too. Repeat to make another large petal.

SMALL PETAL

9 This is made in exactly the same way as the larger petals but you will only need to make one of them and the tip needs to be pinched into a finer, sharper point.

COLOURING AND ASSEMBLY

10 It is best to dust and assemble the petals while still pliable so they can be reshaped to create a more realistic form. Mix together some daffodil, edelweiss and vine petal dusts. Dust each of the petals from the base to the tip, fading the colour towards the tip on both sides of each petal. Use plum petal dust to add an intense colouring at the base of each petal, fading it out as it enters the main petal area. Tinge the very tips of the petals gently with aubergine petal dust.

127

11 Use half-width white floristry tape to tape the two larger petals together. Next, add a blue stamen followed by a smaller petal. This creates one flowerhead group. You will need two or three groups to make one flower. Tape the groups together onto the end of a few 18-gauge white wires using full-width nile green floristry tape.

12 To form the start of the 'beak' structure, tape over a few 18-gauge white wires with nile green floristry tape and add to the main stem at an angle, taping the two together with full-width nile green floristry tape. Use white flowerpaste to build up the remainder of the beak, blending the flowerpaste against the wire. Smooth the flowerpaste to form a fine point at the tip and work it at the base down onto the main stem to create a neck shape. Allow to dry. The remainder of the stem may be thickened with flowerpaste or with lengths of shredded kitchen paper taped onto the stem with full-width nile green floristry tape.

LARGE BRACT FOR THE 'BEAK'

13 Roll out a large piece of mid-green flowerpaste not too thinly. Cut out the large bract shape using the template on page 251 or cut freehand using plain-edge cutting wheel. Soften the edges of the shape using a foam pad and the large metal ball tool. Pinch a central vein down the length of the shape. Moisten the bract with water and then cover the beak, stretching the mid-green flowerpaste to cover the white flowerpaste beneath. Trim the flowerpaste if the shape is too large. Pinch the tip of the beak into a fine point. Stretch and smooth the bract shape at the base, down onto the main stem.

STEM BRACTS

14 Roll out more mid-green flowerpaste and cut out some pointed bract shapes, wide enough to wrap around the flower neck. Soften the edges as for the large bract. Moisten each of the bracts with fresh egg white and attach them to the main stem. Alternate the bracts at intervals down the stem, trimming off any excess length as you work. Pinch the points of the bracts and curve them slightly. Repeat this process to cover the length of stem required for your arrangement.

COLOURING

15 Use plum petal dust to tinge the edges and tips of each bract, especially where the two long edges of the larger bract join. Use foliage mixed with vine petal dusts to add colour from the tip of the large beak fading towards the main section. Add this colour to each of the smaller bracts, too. Layer Prussian blue and ultramarine craft dusts and aubergine and edelweiss petal dusts to colour the majority of the beak and the base of each of the smaller bracts. When dry, spray lightly with edible spray varnish.

LEAVES

16 These are huge! I tend to only make new growth foliage for use on cakes. Roll out a large piece of well-kneaded mid-green flowerpaste, leaving a thick ridge at the centre for the wire. Note that these leaves are quite leathery in texture. Cut out a long, pointed oval leaf shape using the large end of the plain-edge cutting wheel.

17 Insert a 20- or 18-gauge white wire moistened with fresh egg white into the ridge to support about half to three-quarters of the length of the leaf. The exact gauge will depend on the size of the leaf you are making.

18 Soften the edges of the shape using a foam pad and the large metal ball tool. Use fine angled tweezers to pinch a long, ridged central vein. Flip the leaf and use the dresden tool to draw alternating veins from the central vein down the length of the leaf to create raised veins on the upper surface.

19 Turn the leaf again and use the medium metal ball tool to hollow out the areas between the raised veins. Pinch the leaf to accentuate the central vein. Curve as required but note these leaves are flatish in form. Allow to firm up a little before colouring.

COLOURING

20 Use aubergine petal dust to catch the edges, tip and very base of the leaf. Use a large flat dusting brush to colour the main body of the leaf in layers with woodland, forest and foliage petal dusts. Allow to dry and then spray with edible spray varnish or dip into a half-glaze (see page 12). Allow to dry and then highlight the central vein with some white and vine petal dusts mixed together with isopropyl alcohol. If the highlight is too extreme, gently over-dust with a light mixture of vine and foliage petal dusts.

Gingko

Considered to be the most ancient of all living trees with fossil samples dating back to the Jurassic period, the leaves of this plant are highly decorative and useful for floral sprays for cakes. Even the fruit of the plant can add an interesting decorative edge to a floral display.

MATERIALS

Pale green flowerpaste

28-, 26-, 24- and 22-gauge white wires

Fresh egg white

Forest, foliage, vine, ruby and aubergine petal dusts

Edible spray varnish

EQUIPMENT

Non-stick rolling pin

Gingko leaf cutters (TT)

Plain-edge cutting wheel or scalpel

Metal ball tool

Non-stick board

Dresden tool

Gingko leaf veiners (SKGI or SC)

Dimpled foam

Dusting brushes

Fine-nose pliers

LEAVES

1 Roll out some pale green flowerpaste, leaving a thick ridge for the wire. Cut out the leaves using one of the four sizes of gingko leaf cutters or refer to the templates on page 250 and use the plain-edge cutting wheel or scalpel to cut out the shapes.

2 Insert a 28-, 26- or 24-gauge white wire moistened with fresh egg white into the central ridge to support most of the length of the leaf. The exact gauge will depend on the size of the leaf you are making. Pinch the base of the leaf firmly against the wire and work the flowerpaste down the wire to create an elongated, slightly fleshy, tapered stem. Trim off any excess as you thin the flowerpaste out. Alternatively, you could wait for the leaf to dry and then add some extra flowerpaste onto the wire, blending it into the base of the leaf and working it to create the same effect.

3 Soften the edges of the leaf with the metal ball tool and then place the leaf onto the non-stick board and work the bottom edge of the leaf with the broad end of the dresden tool, repeating the pulling/thinning process at close intervals along the edge to create a slightly frilled effect.

4 Next, place the leaf into one of the gingko leaf veiners and press firmly to texture the surface of the leaf. Remove the leaf from the veiner and pinch it down the centre to accentuate the central vein. Place it onto some dimpled foam to support the leaf as it dries slightly. Repeat to make numerous leaves in graduating sizes.

5 Dust the leaves in layers, starting with a light dusting of forest petal dust followed by foliage and an over-dusting of vine petal dusts. Add tinges to the bottom edge using a mixture of ruby and aubergine petal dusts. Allow to dry and then spray lightly with edible spray varnish.

FRUIT

6 Bend a hook in the end of a 26- or 24-gauge white wire using fine-nose pliers. Form a ball of well-kneaded pale green flowerpaste. The fruit is actually quite large, however, I have made my version slightly smaller to make it easier to use on cakes. Moisten the hook with water and insert it into the ball of flowerpaste. Work the flowerpaste into more of an oval shape and then slightly flatten both sides of the shape, pinching a gentle ridge around the edges. Pinch a little of the flowerpaste at the base of the fruit down onto the wire and work it between your finger and thumb to create an elongated thickened stem. Gently bend the stem. Allow to dry a little before dusting.

Monstera

Monstera deliciosa is a creeping vine native to the tropical rainforests of southern Mexico and south of Panama. Often known as the Swiss cheese plant because of the large holes in the plant's leaves, it has other fun common names connected with part of the plant's edible fibre and also its size: fruit salad plant, window leaf and my favourite, delicious monster!

LEAF

1 Roll out a large piece of well-kneaded mid-green flowerpaste, leaving a long, thick ridge for the wire. Cut out the leaf shape using one of the monstera leaf cutters or refer to the templates on page 252 and use the plain-edge cutting wheel to cut out the shapes.

2 Insert a suitable gauge of white wire moistened with fresh egg white into the thick ridge of the leaf to support about half to two-thirds of the length of the leaf. Next, place the leaf against the non-stick board with the ridged side (the back) of the leaf uppermost. Use the smooth ceramic tool to roll, thin and broaden each of the leaf sections a little.

3 Place the leaf onto the foam pad and soften the edges using the large metal ball tool. Pick up the leaf and pinch it from behind, starting at the base and working through to the tip to create a central vein and a little movement too.

4 Use a pair of angled smooth tweezers to pinch a raised central ridge vein down the leaf.

MATERIALS

Mid-green flowerpaste
22-, 20- and 18-gauge white wires
Fresh egg white
Woodland, forest, foliage, vine, aubergine and moss petal dusts
Edible spray varnish
Nile green floristry tape

COLOURING

5 It is best to dust the leaves while they are still pliable so that a good depth of colour is achieved easily without damaging the fairly fragile sections of the form. Dust in layers of woodland, forest, foliage, moss and a touch of vine petal dusts using a large flat dusting brush. Add tinges of aubergine if desired to the tip and side edges of the leaf to break up the space a little. Leave to dry and then glaze using edible spray varnish. Although the leaves are fairly shiny, it is best to build up the shine with a couple of fine layers of glaze rather than one heavy one.

6 Tape and thicken the stem using a few layers of half-width nile green floristry tape.

EQUIPMENT

Non-stick rolling pin
Monstera leaf cutters (AD)
Plain-edge cutting wheel
Non-stick board
Smooth ceramic tool
Foam pad
Large metal ball tool
Angled smooth tweezers
Large dusting brushes

Frangipani

Frangipani (*Plumeria*) is one of the best-loved tropical plants. The flowers may be white, yellow, pink, apricot or red. The plant is named after a 12th-century Italian, famous for creating a perfume from the flowers, which were a favourite of European noble ladies, including Catherine de Medici.

MATERIALS

White and mid-green flowerpaste

28-, 26-, 24- and 22-gauge white wires

Fresh egg white

Nile green floristry tape

Daffodil, sunflower, plum, coral, edelweiss, aubergine, forest and foliage petal dusts

Edible spray varnish

EQUIPMENT

Simple leaf cutters (TT)

Non-stick rolling pin

Plain-edge cutting wheel

Foam pad

Metal ball tool

Very large rose petal veiner (SKGI)

Dresden tool

Smooth ceramic tool

Dusting brushes

Mandevilla leaf veiner (SKGI)

PETALS

1 Choose one of the simple leaf cutters (there are eight sizes in total). The size and shape of the flower varies between varieties. I prefer to squash the cutter to make a slightly narrower shape. Roll out some well-kneaded white flowerpaste, leaving a thick ridge for the wire. These flowers are fairly fleshy so don't roll the flowerpaste too thinly. Cut out the petal shape using your cutter or refer to the frangipani petal template on page 252 and use the plain-edge cutting wheel to cut out the shape.

2 Insert a 28- or 26-gauge white wire moistened with fresh egg white into the thick ridge so that it supports about a third of the length of the petal. The gauge will depend on the size of the flower you are making. Place the petal on the foam pad and soften the edge using the ball tool.

3 Texture the petal using the very large rose petal veiner. Remove from the veiner and place back onto the foam pad with the wire pointing towards you. Use the broad end of the dresden tool on the inner edge of the right-hand side of the petal to apply pressure, stroking the flowerpaste with the tool so that it creates a curled edge. Pinch the petal from the base to the tip and curve back slightly. Repeat to make five petals.

4 Quickly tape the five petals together using half-width nile green floristry tape to create a tight, spiralled shape. Use the smooth ceramic tool and your fingers to reshape the curled edge if needed.

COLOURING

5 Mix together daffodil and sunflower petal dusts. Add some colour at the base of each petal. Next, mix together plum and coral petal dusts with a touch of edelweiss. Dust the petals from the edge towards the centre. Add colour to the backs, too. There is also often a stronger aubergine-coloured sterol at the back of each petal. Allow to dry and then steam to set the colour.

LEAVES

6 Roll out some mid-green flowerpaste, leaving a thick ridge for the wire. Cut out the leaf using the plain-edge cutting wheel. Insert a 26-, 24- or 22-gauge white wire, moistened with fresh egg white, into the leaf. Soften the edge and vein using the mandevilla leaf veiner. Pinch from the base to the tip to accentuate the central vein.

7 Dust in layers with forest and foliage petal dusts. Add a tinge of aubergine. Allow to dry. Spray with edible spray varnish.

Ladder fern

There are many varieties of fern (*Nephrolepsis*). This is one of the quickest to make, however, it is fairly fragile, so care must be taken when using it in complicated arrangements and bouquets to avoid breakage.

FERN FROND

1 Roll out some well-kneaded mid-green flowerpaste onto the non-stick board. Remove the flowerpaste from the board and place over the sword fern cutter. Smooth over the flowerpaste against the cutter using your palm and then roll over the top with the non-stick rolling pin. This usually gives a cleaner cut than cutting out the shape in the conventional way against the board.

2 Carefully remove the flowerpaste from the cutter using the fine end of the dresden tool. This is a very fragile shape and the flowerpaste often gets stuck in the cutter, so a little care and patience is needed. Place the leaf onto the non-stick board and then double-frill the edges of each section of the leaf using the broad end of the dresden tool. Pull the tool against the flowerpaste onto the non-stick board at close intervals to create a tight, slightly untidy, frilled effect.

3 Place the leaf onto the foam pad and use the fine end of the dresden tool to draw a central vein down each section.

4 Tape over a length of 24-gauge white wire with quarter-width nile green floristry tape. Paint fresh egg white onto the length of the wire and then quickly insert the wire down the length of the fern. Press it in place and then flip the leaf over. Use angled tweezers to pinch the flowerpaste against the wire to secure the two together. Turn the leaf back over and pinch each section between your finger and thumb to give more movement. Leave to dry slightly before colouring.

COLOURING

5 The leaves vary in depth of colour and new growth would be a much paler, brighter green. Dust in layers with vine, foliage and forest petal dusts until you have the desired effect. Curve the length of the leaf at this stage too. Allow to dry and then spray with edible spray varnish.

Red passionflower

There are around 500 species of passionflower and some wonderful hybrid forms too. I have based the flower pictured here on *Passiflora vitafolia*, which is a native of the rainforests of South America. The flowers are pollinated by hummingbirds and butterflies with long tongues as the complicated stamen structure can make it difficult for bees to get close to the nectar. It is this section of the flower that is the most time-consuming aspect of the flower to make.

MATERIALS

33-, 30-, 28-, 26-, 24-, 22-, 20-gauge white wires

Pale green, white, pale coral and mid-green flowerpaste

White and nile green floristry tape

Vine, sunflower, ruby, coral, African violet forest, aubergine, foliage and edelweiss white petal dusts

Isopropyl alcohol

Fresh egg white

Edible spray varnish or quarter-glaze

EQUIPMENT

Wire cutters

Plain-edge cutting wheel

Scalpel

Dusting brushes

Fine paintbrushes

Non-stick rolling pin

Grooved board

Jasmine leaf or single petal daisy cutter

Metal ball tool

Stargazer B petal veiner

Dresden tool

Briar rose leaf veiner

Hop leaf cutter (TT)

Non-stick board

Very large hydrangea leaf veiner (SKGI)

PISTIL

1 Cut three short lengths of 30-gauge white wire. Roll a small ball of pale green flowerpaste and insert a wire into it. Work the flowerpaste down the wire, leaving a rounded bead at the tip and a slender neck. Curve the shape into a lazy 'S' shape. Repeat to make three identical sections. Use the plain-edge cutting wheel to indent the underside of the bead shape on each section. Tape the three sections together using quarter-width white floristry tape.

2 Below the pistil is the ovary, which after pollination of the flower, develops into the fruit. At this flower stage the ovary is fairly small. Attach a small piece of pale green flowerpaste to the base of the pistil and form it into an oval shape.

STAMENS

3 Cut five short lengths of 33-gauge white wire. Blend a small amount of pale green flowerpaste onto a wire to create the short length of filament. Flatten the flowerpaste slightly. Repeat to make five filaments. Allow to dry a little. Next, form the

anther, shaping a small ball of pale green flowerpaste into a sausage shape. Moisten the tip of the filament and insert it into the anther to form a 'T'-shaped stamen. Use the plain-edge cutting wheel or scalpel to mark a single line along the top length of the anther. Repeat to make five stamens. Curve the length of the filaments slightly before taping them around the ovary using quarter-width white floristry tape. Allow to dry.

4 Next, work a small amount of pale green flowerpaste down the wire below the stamens to cover about 2.5 cm (1 in) of the wire, creating a fine platform.

5 Dust this section, plus the stamen filaments, the ovary and the underside of the pistil sections with a mixture of vine and edelweiss white petal dusts. Dust the stamen anthers with sunflower petal dust. Use ruby and coral petal dusts to colour the upper surface of the three pistil sections.

6 Dilute a small amount of ruby and coral petal dusts with isopropyl alcohol and add tiny spots to the filaments and platform using a fine paintbrush.

7 Add a ball of white flowerpaste at the base of the platform and form it into a teardrop shape. Use the plain-edge cutting wheel to create a series of lines in the teardrop to represent the closed filaments at the base. Allow to dry.

8 Next, create the finer filaments, rolling several fine strands of white flowerpaste, trying to taper them into a fine point. Attach these filaments around the base using fresh egg white. You might need to hang the section upside down at this stage to allow the filaments to firm up and hold their shape. Curve the tips as you work. You will probably need between 25 and 30 of these fine sections.

9 Dust the base of the filaments with a mixture of coral and ruby petal dusts. Dilute some African violet petal dust with isopropyl alcohol and paint the tips of the filaments (this does vary between varieties – some have almost black tips, while others are pure white, and some have completely red filaments).

PETALS

10 Roll out a small amount of pale coral flowerpaste, leaving a thick ridge for the wire – you might prefer to use a grooved board for this. Cut out the petal shape using the jasmine leaf cutter or single petal daisy cutter, or use a sharp scalpel and the template on page 252. Insert a 28-gauge white wire moistened with fresh egg white into the broader end of the shape so that the wire supports about a third of the length of the petal.

135

11 Soften the edge of the petal using the metal ball tool and then vein using the double-sided stargazer B petal veiner. Remove the petal from the veiner and gently pinch it from the base through to the tip to accentuate the central vein and give the shape some movement. Repeat to make five inner petals and then repeat the process with the five outer petals, but trim them slightly to create a finer shape.

12 Dust the petals with a mixture of coral and ruby petal dusts. Add extra depth to the edges with ruby petal dust. Use slightly less colour on the back of each petal. Tape the five broader petals around the base of the filaments using half-width nile green floristry tape and then position the slimmer petals slightly behind them to fill in the gaps. It is good if the

flowerpaste is still pliable at this stage as it will allow you to reshape and curve the petals into shape.

13 Behind the petals there is a fleshy section. Create this by adding a ball of well-kneaded coral-coloured flowerpaste flattened tightly behind the petals. Use the plain-edge cutting wheel to divide this into ten sections.

BRACTS

14 There are three leaf-like bracts behind the flower. Roll out some pale green flowerpaste and cut out three small bract shapes using a small simple leaf cutter. Use the broad end of the dresden tool to work the edges of the bracts pulling them out at intervals to create a slightly serrated edge. Next, vein them using a briar rose leaf veiner. Pinch each bract from the base through to the tip and attach to the back of the flower using fresh egg white. Allow to dry a little, then dust with a mixture of foliage and vine green petal dust. Tinge the edges with a mixture of ruby and aubergine petal dust.

BUDS

15 Form a ball of well kneaded coral-coloured flowerpaste into a slender teardrop shape. Bend a hook in the end of a 22-gauge white wire, moisten it with fresh egg white and insert into the broad base of the shape.

16 Next, divide the surface of the bud to create five outer petals using a combination of flat angled tweezers and and your finger and thumb to pinch them into flanges/ridges. Pinch the edges of each section until they are quite fine on the edges. Twist the petals around the bud slightly to create a more spiralled formation.

17 Use a smooth ceramic tool or small celstick to mark and indent a waistline near the base of the bud to echo the rounded back of the flower. Dust as for the flower petals and then add the three bracts as described in step 14.

LEAVES

18 Roll out some mid-green flowerpaste, leaving a thick ridge down the centre for the wire. Cut out the leaf shape using the hop leaf cutter or refer to the template on page 252. Depending on the size of the leaf, insert a 26-, 24- or 22-gauge white wire moistened with fresh egg white into the thick ridge to support about half the length of the leaf.

19 Place the leaf ridge-side up against the non-stick board and work the edges slightly to create a gently serrated edge using the broad end of the dresden tool. Use the tool to pull out the edges against the board.

20 Vein using the very large double-sided hydrangea leaf veiner. Remove leaf and pinch each section from base to tip to accentuate the central vein. Repeat to make leaves in graduating sizes. Tape over each leaf stem with quarter-width nile green floristry tape.

21 Dust with layers of forest, foliage and vine petal dusts. Add a tinge of aubergine mixed with ruby to the edges. Allow to dry, then spray lightly with edible spray varnish or dip into a quarter-glaze.

FRUIT

22 Bend an open hook in the end of a length of 22-gauge white wire. Moisten the hook with fresh egg white and insert into a ball of pale green well-kneaded flowerpaste. Next, form the ball into more of an oval/egg shape. Pinch the base of the shape against the wire to secure it in place. Work some of the paste down against the wire to create a fleshier stem. Curve the stem slightly.

23 Dust with a mixture of forest, foliage and edelweiss white petal dusts. Add gentle tinges of aubergine to the tip and the base. Add white markings to the surface of the fruit using a mixture of isopropyl alcohol and edelweiss petal dust with a slight touch of foliage green just to take the extreme whiteness away a little. Use a fine paintbrush to add the random markings over the fruit. Allow to dry and spray very lightly with edible spray varnish.

24 Create the impression of dead petals to add at the base of the fruit using a few pieces of white floristry tape cut into pointed petal shapes. Stretch each of the tape petals and pinch them at the tips and at the base and then tape onto the stem of the fruit using half-width nile green floristry tape. Dust with a light mixture of cream and white petal dust. Add tinges of aubergine.

ASSEMBLY

25 Take a length of 20-gauge white wire and add a small leaf at the top using half-width nile green floristry tape. Continue to add leaves down the stem alternating their position and increasing a little in size too. Add tendrils at leaf axils. These are simply lengths of 33-gauge wire taped over with quarter-width nile green tape and curled and spiralled a little around a fine paintbrush handle. Continue adding leaves gradually introducing the buds and eventually the flowers again adding them at leaf axils. Add extra 20-gauge wire for added support and length.

Devil's ivy

These wonderful silver-spotted, long, heart-shaped leaves are great to trail and add detail at the same time to bouquets and arrangements. There are about 400 species of philodendron with the shape, size and colour varying quite substantially between each one.

MATERIALS

Mid-green flowerpaste
26-, 24-, 22- and 20-gauge white wires
Fresh egg white
Foliage, forest, edelweiss and aubergine petal dusts
Myrtle bridal satin dust
Isopropyl alcohol
Nile green floristry tape
Edible spray varnish

EQUIPMENT

Non-stick rolling pin
Heart-shaped leaf cutters
Plain-edge cutting wheel
Foam pad
Large metal ball tool
Dimpled foam or crumpled kitchen paper
Dusting brushes
Fine paintbrushes

1 Roll out some mid-green flowerpaste not too thinly, leaving a thicker area at the centre to hold the wire. Cut out the leaf shape using one of the heart-shaped leaf cutters or refer to the devil's ivy template on page 251 and use the plain-edge cutting wheel to cut out the shape.

2 Insert a 26-, 24- or 22-gauge white wire moistened with fresh egg white into the thick ridge to support about half the length of the leaf. Place the leaf onto the foam pad or onto your palm and soften the edge using a rolling action with the large metal ball tool.

3 Pinch the leaf from the base to the tip to create a central vein and give the leaf some movement at the same time. Allow to dry over some dimpled foam or crumpled kitchen paper to help give the leaf a little support and shape. Repeat to make leaves in graduating sizes.

COLOURING AND ASSEMBLY

4 Dust the leaves with a mixture of foliage, forest and edelweiss petal dusts. Dilute some myrtle bridal satin dust with isopropyl alcohol and paint a series of irregular-sized dots and then use the brush to catch the edge of the leaf to create a border around the outside. Add tinges of aubergine to the edges of each leaf.

5 Tape over each stem with half-width nile green floristry tape. Start taping a trailing stem together, starting with a small leaf on the end of a 22- or 20-gauge white wire using half-width nile green floristry tape. Add the other leaves so that they alternate down the stem, then gradually work with full-width floristry tape to create fleshier stems as the leaves increase in size. Bend the length of the main stem to create an attractive bend and curve. Spray lightly with edible spray varnish.

Blue Egyptian water lily

This beautiful purple-blue water lily is a native to the river Nile and other areas of East Africa. The flowers have been used since ancient times to produce perfumes and have also been used in aromatherapy. Recent studies have shown that *Nymphaea caerulea* has mild psycho-active properties. It may have been used in ancient Egypt and by certain South American cultures as a sacrament. In modern culture, the flowers are often used to create a tea and to flavour wine and Martini cocktails.

MATERIALS

33-, 26-, 24-, 22- and 20-gauge white wires
Pale yellow, white and mid-green flowerpaste
Fresh egg white
Sunflower, plum, African violet, vine, white, foliage, forest and aubergine petal dusts
Nile green floristry tape
Isopropyl alcohol
Edible spray varnish

EQUIPMENT

Fine-nose pliers
Non-stick rolling pin
Medium and large metal ball tool
Dusting brushes
Wire cutters
Non-stick board
Medium paintbrush
Sage leaf cutters (TT852, 855)
Foam pad
Stargazer B or wide amaryllis petal veiner (SKGI)
Dimpled foam or kitchen ring former (p11)
Plain-edge cutting wheel
Large circle cutter
Fine scissors
Very large nasturtium leaf veiner (SKGI)

CENTRE

1 The main wire for the centre needs to be formed into a ski stick shape. Bend an open hook in the end of a 22-gauge white wire using fine-nose pliers. Next, press the hook against the main length of wire. Now hold the hook at the centre using fine-nose pliers and bend it to form a halo or ski stick shape.

2 Roll a ball of well-kneaded pale yellow flowerpaste. Moisten the hooked wire with fresh egg white and push it into the base of the ball shape. Pinch the flowerpaste firmly around the hook and form the base into a slightly pointed shape.

3 Use the medium metal ball tool to hollow out the upper surface of the shape. Leave to firm up a little before dusting with sunflower petal dust.

STAMENS

4 Cut several short lengths of 33-gauge white wire using wire cutters. Attach a tiny ball of pale yellow flowerpaste onto one of the wires and blend it against the wire using your finger and thumb to coat about 2.5 cm (1 in) of the wire. Work the tip into a fine point. Next, flatten the shape against the non-stick board using the flat side of one of the petal veiners.

5 Pick the shape off the board and pinch it from the base through to the tip to give a little more shape. Curve the tip to represent the anther. Repeat to make about 25 to 30 stamens for each flower.

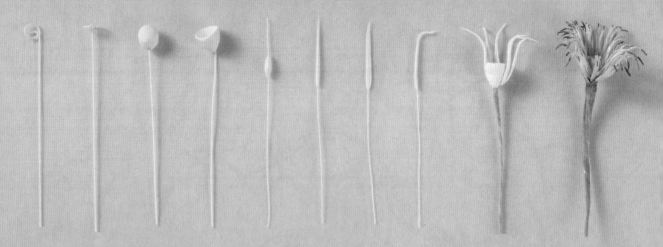

ASSEMBLY AND COLOURING

6 It is best to tape the stamens around the dried centre before they have a chance to dry so that a little reshaping to the anthers can be done easily. Tape the stamens tightly at first around the sides of the dried centre using half-width nile green floristry tape.

7 Dust the stamens with sunflower petal dust. You might prefer to do this prior to taping them onto the centre. Next, dilute some plum and African violet petal dusts mixed with isopropyl alcohol. Use a medium paintbrush to apply the colour to the tips of each of the stamens. Allow to dry and then glaze with edible spray varnish. Place to one side until required.

PETALS

8 Roll out some well-kneaded white flowerpaste, leaving a tapered thick ridge for the wire – this is quite a large-petalled flower so don't roll the flowerpaste too fine. Cut out a petal shape using the smallest of the sage leaf cutters or refer to the water lily template on page 250.

9 Insert a 26-gauge white wire moistened with fresh egg white into the thick ridge of the petal to support about a third to half

the length of the petal. Pinch the flowerpaste slightly at the base down onto the wire to create a slightly more elongated shape.

10 Place the petal onto the foam pad or onto your palm and soften the edges using the metal ball tool, using a rolling and not a rubbing action. Try not to frill the edges you are just trying to remove the harsh cut edge from the petal.

11 Texture the surface of the petal using the double-sided stargazer B or wide amaryllis petal veiner. The latter has stronger veins so it will depend on the effect you prefer. Remove the petal from the veiner and pinch it gently from the base to the tip to create a subtle central vein. Hollow the length of the petal gently to encourage a curved shape. Place the petal onto dimpled foam or into a homemade paper ring former. Repeat to make five petals the same size.

12 Next, increase the size of the cutter to make ten larger petals. Repeat the above process using a 26- or perhaps even a 24-gauge white wire to support each petal.

13 Dust each petal back and front from the edges towards the base with African violet petal dust. Leave the base of each petal slightly paler. Dust the base of each petal with a light mixture of vine and white petal dusts.

14 Dust the back outer five petals with a mixture of foliage and forest petal dusts to create a broad streak of colour down the centre of each.

15 Tape the five smaller petals around the stamen centre using half-width nile green floristry tape. If the petals are still pliable, then this will enable you to bend and reshape them slightly if needed. Next, tape five slightly larger petals to fit in the gaps left by the first five petals. Finally, add the remaining five petals to complete the flower. Allow the flower to dry and then hold over a jet of steam from the kettle or use a clothes steamer to set the colour and leave a slight shine – be careful not to hold the flower in the steam for too long as this will result in a very shiny finish or worse still a sticky mess!

BUDS

16 Take a large ball of well-kneaded white flowerpaste and form it into a large cone shape. Tape over a 20-gauge white wire with half-width nile green floristry tape and bend a large hook in the end using fine-nose pliers. Moisten the hook with fresh egg white and insert it into the broad end of the cone of flowerpaste. Divide the surface of the cone into five sections using the plain-edge cutting wheel to represent the outer petals of the bud. Gently pinch each petal down the centre using your finger and thumb to create a subtle ridged effect.

17 To make a larger bud, repeat the above process adding five softened and veined unwired small petals over the cone using a little fresh egg white to secure them in place. Allow to dry and then dust as for the outer petals of the flower.

LILY PAD/LEAF

18 Roll out some well-kneaded mid-green flowerpaste, leaving a thick ridge for the wire. Cut out the leaf shape using the large circle cutter.

19 Use a pair of fine scissors to cut out a slender 'V'-shape from the base of the leaf. Insert a 22- or 20-gauge white wire moistened with fresh egg white into the thick ridge to support quite a bit of the length of the leaf.

20 Soften the edges using the large metal ball tool and then vein using the very large nasturtium leaf veiner, pressing firmly to create strong veins on the leaf. Remove the leaf from the veiner, then allow it to firm up a bit, drying it on a piece of dimpled foam or in a kitchen paper ring.

21 Dust the back and edges of the leaf with a mixture of plum and aubergine petal dusts. Dust the upper surface with forest and then lots of foliage petal dusts. Allow to dry and then glaze lightly with edible spray varnish. Bend the wire at the back of the leaf to create the plant's characteristic floating lily pads. Tape over the wire several times with half-width nile green floristry tape.

141

Tuberose

The tuberose (*Polianthes tuberose*) is thought to have originated in Mexico, although it is grown and used extensively in other countries. I have given instructions for both single and double forms.

MATERIALS

Small, white seed-head stamens
Hi-tack non-toxic craft glue
28-, 26-, 24- and 18-gauge
white wires
Sunflower, daffodil, vine, moss, plum, edelweiss
and foliage petal dusts
White and pale green flowerpaste
Fresh egg white
Nile green floristry tape
Plastic food bag

EQUIPMENT

Wire cutters
Dusting brushes
Non-stick rolling pin
Six-petal pointed blossom cutters (OP N1, 2, 3)
Foam pad
Medium and small metal ball tools
Plain-edge cutting wheel or dresden tool
Non-stick board
Smooth ceramic tool or celstick
Dried sweetcorn husk veiner

STAMENS

1 Take three small, white seed-head stamens and glue them together from the centre, working the glue towards the tips at either end. Try not to use too much glue as this will take too long to dry and create too much bulk. Allow the glue to dry and then cut the stamens in half. Trim them so that they are quite short. Apply a little more glue and attach to the end of a 24-gauge white wire. Allow to dry. Dust the tips with a mixture of sunflower and daffodil petal dusts. Dust the base of the stamens with vine petal dust.

FIRST AND SECOND LAYER OF PETALS FOR THE DOUBLE FLOWER

2 Roll out some well-kneaded white flowerpaste, leaving a raised pimple at the centre. Cut out a flower shape using the smallest six-petal pointed blossom cutter. Place the shape onto a foam pad and soften the edges using the medium metal ball tool. Next, hollow the length of each petal using the small ball tool.

3 Add fine veins to each petal using the small end of the plain-edge cutting wheel or the fine end of the dresden tool.

4 Moisten the base of the stamens with fresh egg white and thread the wire through the centre of the flower shape. Pinch the pimple behind the flower to secure it in

place and push the petals upwards to create a tight centre. Allow to dry. Repeat the process to create the second layer of petals, but this time using the slightly larger six-petal pointed blossom cutter. Attach the shape onto the back of the first layer, positioning the petals over joins in the first layer. Allow to dry.

THIRD LAYER FOR THE DOUBLE FLOWER (OR METHOD FOR THE SINGLE FORM)

5 These instructions apply to the outer layer of the double tuberose, as well as being the complete method for the single variety. Form a ball of well-kneaded white

flowerpaste into a long sausage. Pinch out one end of the shape to form a wizard's hat shape. Place the flat part of the 'hat' against the non-stick board and roll out the 'brim' using the smooth ceramic tool or celstick, remembering the flower is quite fleshy.

6 Cut out the flower shape using the largest of the six-petal pointed blossom cutters. Rub your thumb over the edge to get rid of any rough edges.

7 Remove the flower from the cutter and place it face-down on the foam pad. Soften the edges of each petal gently. Use the metal ball tool to hollow the upper side of each petal for an opening flower and the back of each petal for a fully open flower. Add a few fine veins to each petal as before.

8 Open up the centre of the flower using the pointed end of the celstick or smooth ceramic tool. Moisten the back of the wired flower with fresh egg white and thread the wire through the centre of the outer flower so that the petals fill the spaces in the previous layer. Pinch the tips of the petals slightly and curl some or all of them back. If you are making the single form, thread the wired stamens through the centre instead.

9 Thin down the back of the flower between your finger and thumb, and pinch off any excess flowerpaste if needed. Use the plain-edge cutting wheel to mark six lines on the back of the flower, following the indent in between each petal. Add some finer lines in-between these divisions too. Curve the back gracefully.

BUDS

10 Form a ball of well-kneaded white flowerpaste into a cone shape. Insert a hooked 28- or 26-gauge white wire moistened with fresh egg white into the broad end. The gauge of wire will depend on the size of the bud you are making.

11 Work the flowerpaste at the base of the bud to create a more slender neck shape. Divide the upper section of the bud into three sections to represent the outer petals. Next, pinch each section gently between your finger and thumb to create a subtle ridge.

12 Use the plain-edge cutting wheel to divide and vein the surface of the bud as for the flower. Repeat to make buds in graduating sizes, remembering that they are in pairs down the stem.

BRACTS

13 To each pair of buds and flowers there is a single bract attached where they join the main stem. They can be created quickly with nile green floristry tape cut into a pointed bract shape or with flowerpaste. Roll out some pale green flowerpaste, leaving a ridge down the centre.

Use the plain-edge cutting wheel to cut out freehand pointed arrow-shaped bracts in graduating sizes.

14 Soften the edges and then texture using the dried sweetcorn husk veiner. Cut out as many bracts as required and cover with a plastic food bag to stop them drying out.

ASSEMBLY AND COLOURING

15 Tape two small buds onto the end of an 18-gauge white wire using half-width nile green floristry tape. Thicken the stem with a strip of kitchen paper wrapped around the wire and taped over with nile green floristry tape. Attach a small bract at the base of the buds using a little fresh egg white to secure it. Add the next two buds plus a bract. Continue this method until you have added all the buds and flowers in pairs down the stem.

16 Dust the backs of the flower and buds with vine petal dust and then add a little more depth using a mixture of daffodil and moss on top. Use this colour on the tips of the smaller buds too. Mix together plum and edelweiss petal dusts. Tinge the buds gently and add a little to the back of each flower too. Dust the bracts with a mixture of vine, moss and a touch of foliage. Allow to dry and then hold over a jet of steam to set the colour and leave a slightly waxy finish.

Sacred lotus

There several forms of lotus (*Nelumbo*), with the flower varying in size and form, although the colour is always in varying shades of pink or white, or in the case of the American lotus, yellow. The lotus is the national flower of India where it is linked with mythology and prayer. The dried seed-heads of the flower are used as decorations and in flower arranging. The dried stamens are used in China to make a fragrant herbal tea and food is often served on the leaves. Even the seeds are edible, eaten raw or dried and cooked like popcorn, or they can be boiled and turned into a paste with sugar and used in pastries, such as mooncakes or as a flavouring for rice pudding. The roots are also sliced and pickled or can be cooked into crisp decorative chips.

POD/OVARY

1 I find it easier to make this section of the flower with cold porcelain so that I can use non-toxic glue to bond the stamens around the pod. Bend a large hook in the end of an 18-gauge white wire using fine-nose pliers. Roll a ball of pale green cold porcelain and then form it into a cone shape. Moisten the hooked wire with water and insert it into the fine end of the cone.

2 Work the cold porcelain down onto the wire to elongate the cone slightly. Next, flatten the top of the shape and pinch around the sides to create a sharper edge.

3 Use fine plain-edged angled tweezers to pinch a slight ridge around the circumference of the shape. Next, use the pointed end of the smooth ceramic tool to create several indents in the upper surface of the pod.

4 Roll lots of tiny balls of pale green cold porcelain and drop one into each of the holes on the pod. Use the needle tool or a strong wire to indent the centre of each of the balls.

EQUIPMENT

Fine-nose pliers

Fine plain-edged angled tweezers

Smooth ceramic tool

Needle tool or strong wire

Dusting brushes

Large scissors

Non-stick rolling pin

Large cymbidium orchid cutter (TT) or use the lotus petal template on p 250

Plain-edge cutting wheel

Foam pad

Large metal ball tool

Wide amaryllis petal veiner (SKGI)

Kitchen paper ring former (p11)

Sage leaf cutters (TT852, 855) or use the lotus petal template on p 250

Wide diamond jubilee rose petal cutters (TT776, 777)

Very large nasturtium leaf veiner (SKGI)

MATERIALS

26-, 24-, 22-, 20- and 18- gauge white wires

Pale green cold porcelain

Vine, foliage, aubergine, sunflower, edelweiss, plum, African violet and forest petal dusts

White seed-head stamens

Non-toxic craft glue

White and mid-green flowerpaste

Fresh egg white

Nile green floristry tape

Edible spray varnish

5 Dust the pod as desired. The colour varies between varieties – it can be creamy, yellow, bright green or a darker, almost blue-green colour with aubergine tinges too. Here I have used vine and foliage green and then tinged gently with aubergine petal dust.

STAMENS

6 You will need one-and-a-half to two bunches of white seed-head stamens for each flower. Divide the stamens into several smaller groups and line up their tips. Bond each group together with a little non-toxic craft glue at the centre. Squeeze the glue with your finger and thumb to create a neat line of glue at the centre. Flatten the stamens as you work. Allow the glue to set and then cut the stamens in half using a large pair of scissors.

7 Trim the stamens a little shorter if needed – you will be able to tell if you try one group against the pod to see if they are going to be too long. Apply a little more non-toxic craft glue to each group in turn and add them around the pod. Hold each group firmly against the pod to the count of ten. This should allow the glue to become tacky and hold the stamens in place. Try not to use too much glue as this

will take too long to dry and result in the stamens dropping off. Once you have created a nice full stamen centre leave it to dry before colouring.

8 Use the tweezers to pull and curl the stamens out a little, creating a more realistic effect. Use sunflower petal dust to colour the anther tips of the stamens. Use vine petal dust on the filament lengths of the stamens.

PETALS

9 The number and size of petals varies on each flower. Start with the largest petals as these will take the longest to dry. Roll out some well-kneaded white flowerpaste, leaving a thick ridge for the wire. Use the large cymbidium orchid cutter to cut out the petal shape or refer to the template on page 250 and use the plain-edge cutting wheel to cut out the shape.

10 Insert a 24-gauge white wire moistened with fresh egg white into the thick ridge to support about a third to half the length of the petal. Pinch the flowerpaste slightly at the base down onto the wire to elongate it.

11 Place the petal on your palm or the foam pad and soften the edges using the large metal ball tool and a rolling action to take away the cut edge. Try not to frill the edges.

12 Place the petal into the double-sided wide amaryllis petal veiner and press the two sides together to texture the petal. Remove the petal from the veiner and hollow out the length of the petal using the large metal ball tool or your fingers and thumb.

13 Rest the petal in a kitchen paper ring former until it is a little firmer and holding its shape well. Repeat to make several wired petals in varying sizes, using the sage leaf cutters for the smaller petals.

COLOURING AND ASSEMBLY

14 Dust the base of each of the petals with a light mixture of vine and edelweiss petal dusts. Next, mix together plum petal dust with a touch of African violet and dust the petals from the edges, fading towards the base on both sides of each petal.

15 Tape the petals around the stamen centre using half-width nile green floristry tape, starting with the smaller petals and then increasing the size using the largest petals last. Use the side of a pair of scissors to polish the stem and disguise the lines created by the floristry tape. If the petals are still pliable as you assemble the flower, then this will enable you to reshape them, giving a more realistic finish. Allow to dry and then hold the flower over a jet of steam from a kettle or clothes steamer – this will set the colour to give a more waxy finish to the flower.

BUDS

16 Roll a large ball of well-kneaded white flowerpaste. Form the ball into a coin shape and then insert a hooked wire moistened with fresh egg white into the broad end of the bud. Neaten the join between the bud and the wire using your finger and thumb to blend the flowerpaste.

17 Use the plain-edge cutting wheel to divide the length of the bud into three sections. Roll out some more white flowerpaste and cut out six petal shapes using the smallest sage cutter or the template on page 140. Soften the edges and vein as for the wired petals.

18 Attach the petals onto the sides of the bud using fresh egg white. Pinch the base and the tips as you add each one to create a more pointed finish. To create larger buds, add some extra wired petals. Colour the bud in the same way as the flower.

Peony

I love using peonies on my cakes. They are such large showy flowers and not many are required to fill space and create instant impact. The peony illustrated here is based on a flower I bought from my local florist, which was almost but not quite the variety 'bowl of beauty'. I loved its creamy-white fringed petals at the centre of the flower. This section is fairly time-consuming to make, however, it could be made gradually over a period of days, adding the petals a few at a time. The peony originates from China where it has been cultivated for over one thousand years.

MATERIALS

Pale green, white, pale pink, and mid-green flowerpaste

33-, 30-, 28-, 26-, 24- and 22-gauge white wires

Nile green floristry tape

Vine, plum, sunflower, daffodil, edelweiss, African violet, foliage, aubergine and forest petal dusts

Fresh egg white

Edible spray varnish

EQUIPMENT

Non-stick rolling pin

Fine-nose pliers

Dusting brushes

Non-stick board

Single peony leaf veiner (SKGI)

Scissors and fine scissors

Large metal ball tool

Ceramic silk veining tool

Dresden tool

Golden jubilee rose cutters (TT)

Kitchen paper ring former (p11)

Standard rose petal cutters (TT278-280) or use the peony petal template on p 252

Grooved board

Plain-edge cutting wheel

Cattleya orchid wing petal cutters (TT)

OVARY

1 This part of the flower can have two, three, four or sometimes more sections to it. I prefer three or four in my interpretation of the flower. Roll a small ball of well-kneaded pale green flowerpaste. Form the ball into a fine cone shape. Bend a hook in the end of a 28-gauge white wire using fine-nose pliers. Moisten the hook with water and insert it into the base of the cone, pushing it deep into the shape to give a good support. Thin the tip of the cone into a very fine point.

2 Next, pinch a gentle ridge down one side of the shape using your finger and thumb. Curl the fine tip over onto the ridged side. Repeat to make three or four equal-sized sections.

3 Tape the sections together while they are still pliable so that they sit closely together using quarter-width nile green floristry tape. Allow to dry.

4 Dust the ovary lightly with vine petal dust. Tinge the tips with plum.

FRINGED PETALS

5 These are made using a freehand technique to give more of a random formation, which is required for this style of flower. Cut several lengths of 33-gauge white wire into quarters. Insert a dry wire into a small ball of white flowerpaste and work the paste down the wire to create an elongated carrot shape with the tip being left slightly broader.

6 Place the shape onto the non-stick board and flatten it using the flat side of a leaf/petal veiner. Remove the shape from the board, trim it with scissors if the shape is too distorted and then soften the edges using the large metal ball tool.

7 Place the shape back onto the non-stick board and texture the surface using the ceramic silk veining tool to roll gently over both sides. Try not to apply too much pressure as this will make the petals too wide. Next, use the broad end of the dresden tool to flatten and pull out the edge at the very tip of the petal. This will create a tight frilled effect as well as thinning the flowerpaste, making it easier to create the fringed effect.

8 Use the fine end of the dresden tool to cut into the thinned section to create the fringe, or alternatively, use a pair of fine scissors to cut slender 'V'-shapes into the edge.

9 Pinch the petal from the base to the tip to create movement and a gentle central vein. Repeat to make a large quantity of petals – about 40 to 50. Remember, these can be built up gradually. I usually tape groups of these petals around the ovary as I am working so that I can assess just how many more petals I am going to need to complete this section. Reshape the petals as you work too.

10 Dust the petals from the base using a mixture of sunflower, daffodil and edelweiss petal dusts. Fade the colour towards the mid section. Tinge the tips of the petal very gently with plum petal dust – this is optional and will depend on the variety you are copying.

OUTER PETALS

11 Squash the golden jubilee rose cutter to create a longer slender petal shape. Roll out some well-kneaded pale pink flowerpaste, leaving a thick ridge for the wire. Cut out a petal shape using the squashed cutter or refer to the peony petal template on page 252. Insert a hooked wire moistened with fresh egg white into the thick ridge to support about a third of the petal's length. The hook is to stop the petals spinning around at the taping-up stage, though you might prefer not to create a hook.

12 Pinch the flowerpaste at the base down onto the wire. Place the petal onto the non-stick board and thin out the shape slightly using the non-stick rolling pin. Next, use the ceramic silk veining tool to roll the petal at intervals in a fan formation, creating a series of fine veins over the petal. Turn the petal over and repeat on the back. Use the same tool to create a gentle frill to the edge of the petal.

13 Hollow the centre of the petal using your fingers and thumb. Dry the petal in a homemade kitchen paper ring former. Repeat to make ten outer petals. The number varies but ten is a good starting point.

COLOURING AND ASSEMBLY

14 Mix together plum, edelweiss and a touch of African violet. Use a flat dusting brush to colour the petals from the base fading out towards the edges and then dust from the edges in towards the base. Repeat on the back of each petal.

15 Tape the petals around the fringed petal centre using half-width nile green floristry tape. It helps if the petals are still slightly pliable at this stage so that you can reshape them to create a more realistic effect.

CALYX

16 There are three rounded sepals and two or three long leaf-like sepals that make up the calyx. The rounded sepals can be cut out using the three sizes of the standard rose petal cutter set or they can be made using a freehand technique, as illustrated here. Insert a 30- or 28-gauge

white wire into a ball of pale green flowerpaste. Work the base of the ball down onto the wire to form a cone shape. Flatten the shape against the non-stick board using the flat side of the single peony leaf veiner.

17 Next place the shape onto your palm and thin the edges using the metal ball tool. Hollow the shape too using the same tool. Pinch a slight point into the top edge. Repeat to make three sizes of sepal.

18 The longer leaf-like sepals are also made freehand. Roll a ball of pale green flowerpaste onto a 28-gauge white wire, blending the flowerpaste against the wire to form it into a long, slender leaf

shape pointed at both ends. Again, flatten the shape with the flat side of a leaf/petal veiner. Soften the edges and then pinch the shape from the base to the tip to create a central vein.

19 Dust each of the sepals with a mixture of foliage and vine petal dusts. Tinge the edges and tips with a mixture of aubergine and plum petal dusts. Spray lightly with edible spray varnish.

20 Use half-width nile green floristry tape to secure the three rounded sepals to the back of the flower with the hollowed-out side against the petals. Next,

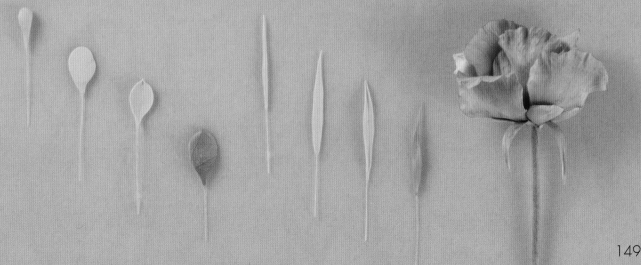

add the longer leaf-like sepals in between the rounded sepals. These should fall away from the other sections of the calyx.

LEAVES

21 Roll out some well-kneaded mid-green flowerpaste, leaving a thick ridge for the wire – a grooved board can be used for this purpose.

22 Use the plain-edge cutting wheel to cut out a freehand leaf shape or use one of the cattleya orchid wing petal cutters if you prefer (these will need to be squashed slightly to create a longer, more slender shape).

23 Insert a 26- or 24-gauge white wire moistened with fresh egg white into the thick ridge of the leaf to support about half its length. Place the leaf onto the foam pad or the palm of your hand and soften the edges with the metal ball tool.

24 Place the leaf into the double-sided peony leaf veiner and press firmly to texture the leaf. Remove the leaf from the veiner and pinch it from the base through to the tip to accentuate the central vein. Repeat to make two smaller leaves to set on either side of the larger central leaf.

COLOURING

25 Dust the leaves in layers, starting with a very light dusting of forest petal dust. Over-dust heavily with foliage and then add some vine. Tinge the edges very slightly with aubergine petal dust. The backs of the leaves should be much paler in colour. Allow to dry and then spray lightly with edible spray varnish.

26 Tape the leaves together into sets of three using half-width nile green floristry tape.

150

Heart's desire orchid

I first saw these pretty orchids during a visit to an early-morning flower market in São Paulo, Brazil. At the time I was not sure what type of orchid it was and it was only after consulting several of my orchid books that I found that they are actually part of the Laelia orchid family, which is native to South America.

MATERIALS
White and green flowerpaste
22-, 24-, 26- and 28-gauge white wires
Plum, edelweiss white, African violet,
    aubergine, daffodil, foliage, forest
    and vine green petal dusts
White and nile green floristry tape
Edible spray varnish (Fabilo)
Cyclamen liquid colour (SKGI)

EQUIPMENT
Wire cutters
Smooth ceramic tool
Rolling pin
Non-stick board
Heart's desire orchid cutters (AD)
    or see templates on page 253
Sharp scalpel
Metal ball tool
Stargazer B petal veiner (SKGI)
Fine tweezers
Small ball tool
Dresden tool
Dusting brushes
Grooved board
Plain-edge cutting wheel (PME)
Large tulip leaf veiner (SKGI)

COLUMN

1 Form a small ball of well-kneaded white flowerpaste into a cone shape. Cut a short length of 26-gauge white wire, moisten and insert it into the fine end of the cone so that it supports most of the length. Line up the wired cone against the rounded end of a ceramic tool so that it is slightly higher than the tip. Press the paste against the tool to hollow out the underside of the column. Thin out the side edges slightly too. Leave to dry overnight if time allows.

LIP/LABELLUM

2 Roll out some white paste leaving a fine central ridge – this is not to be wired but gives extra support to the shape. Cut out the lip/labellum shape using either the cutter or the template on page 253 and a sharp scalpel. Soften the edge of the petal with the metal ball tool.

3 Vein using the double-sided stargazer B petal veiner. Use fine tweezers to pinch two small ridges at the base of the petal. Use a small ball tool to hollow out the two side sections of the petal.

151

4 Moisten the base and two bottom side edges of the column and position the hollowed side down against the lip/labellum. Carefully press the two side sections of the petal onto the column. Flick back the edges of these side sections and curl the tip of the lip too. You should have a gap between the lip petal and the underside of the column – if this is not the case then simply open up the centre using the broad end of the dresden tool. Leave to firm up slightly before colouring.

5 Dust very gently with a light mixture of African violet, plum and edelweiss petal dusts. Increase the plum colouring at the tip of the lip. Add a dark patch of aubergine into the throat. Add a slight yellow tinge beyond the aubergine deep into the throat with a little daffodil petal dust. Paint a series of five lines over the dark dusted area using cyclamen liquid colour and a fine paintbrush.

LATERAL PETALS

6 Roll out some white paste leaving a fine ridge for the wire (you can use a grooved board for this). Cut out the petal shape using the widest of the three outer petals shapes. Insert a short length of moistened 28-gauge white wire into the thick ridge of the petal to support about half the length.

7 Soften the edge of the petal and then texture with the stargazer B petal veiner. Pinch the petal from the base to the tip to create a very gentle central vein and curve to the petal. Repeat to make two matching petals.

DORSAL AND LATERAL SEPALS

8 Repeat the process described in steps 6 and 7 to create the dorsal sepal using the longer of the two narrow cutters, and two lateral sepals using the shorter of the cutters or use the templates on page 253 and a sharp scalpel.

COLOURING AND ASSEMBLY

9 Gently dust the petals and outer sepals back and front, from both the base and the tip, with the light mixture of African violet, edelweiss and plum used earlier on the lip.

10 Using quarter-width white floristry tape, attach the two lateral petals onto either side of the lip/labellum. Next, position the dorsal sepal behind, covering the gap between the two petals. Tuck the two lateral sepals into the underside of the orchid and tape over the stem to create a neat finish. It helps at this stage if the petals/sepals are still pliable so that you can create a more realistic, relaxed flower shape.

11 Attach a ball of well-kneaded white paste onto the stem behind the flower and work it into a fine neck shape. Blend the join between the ball of paste and the petals using the broad end of the dresden tool. Curve the stem slightly and dust with the flower colour plus a tinge of vine green and white from the base of the neck.

BUDS

12 Cut lengths of 26-gauge white wire into thirds. Form a ball of well-kneaded white paste into a cone shape and insert the wire into the broad end of the cone. Work the paste down the stem to create the long neck shape of the flower.

13 Gently squeeze the tip of the bud between two fingers and your thumb to create a three-sided angular shape. Divide each side with the plain-edge cutting wheel – this represents the three outer sepals of the flower. Curve the neck gently. Repeat to make several buds

Spider chrysanthemum

Chrysanthemum are cultivated and grown the world over and have become very popular as cut flowers. This form of chrysanthemum originates from the Orient. These are very effective flowers to make in sugar or cold porcelain, but they are really very time-consuming. It is best to build up the many petals over a period of days rather than trying to complete the flower in a day.

MATERIALS

Pale vine green and mid-green flowerpaste
35-, 33-, 30-, 28-, 26- and 22-gauge white wires
Vine green, moss, forest, foliage and aubergine petal dusts
Nile green floristry tape
Edible spray varnish (Fabilo)

EQUIPMENT

Fine-nose pliers
Sharp scalpel or plain-edge cutting wheel
Smooth ceramic tool or paintbrush
Fine curved scissors
Dusting brushes
Wire cutters
Cocktail sticks or fine celstick
Daisy cutters in assorted sizes
Rolling pin
Non-stick board
Chrysanthemum leaf cutter (Jem)
Chrysanthemum leaf veiner (SKGI)

CENTRE

1 Roll a ball of well-kneaded pale vine green flowerpaste. Bend an open hook in the end of a 22-gauge wire using fine-nose pliers. Moisten the hook and pull it through the ball of paste. Blend the ball and pinch it onto the wire to secure it in place.

2 Texture the surface of the ball using a sharp scalpel or plain-edge cutting wheel to mark a series of fine lines radiating from the centre to represent the inner petals. Indent the centre slightly using the rounded end of the ceramic tool or a paintbrush handle.

3 Use a pair of fine curved scissors to snip at the indented section of the centre and also to snip some petals around the edge of the ball. Leave to dry overnight.

4 Dust with vine green and a little moss green petal dust.

OUTER PETALS

5 Cut lengths of 35-, 33-, 30- or 28-gauge wire, depending on the size of petals you are working on. This is not an exercise of exact numbers. You simply keep making and taping the petals around the centre, starting with very fine petals and gradually increasing them in size. It is best to tape the petals onto the centre while they are still wet so that you can reshape to create a more realistic flower shape. Work a small ball of paste onto each wire working the paste towards the tip. Smooth down the sides between the fleshy part of your hands.

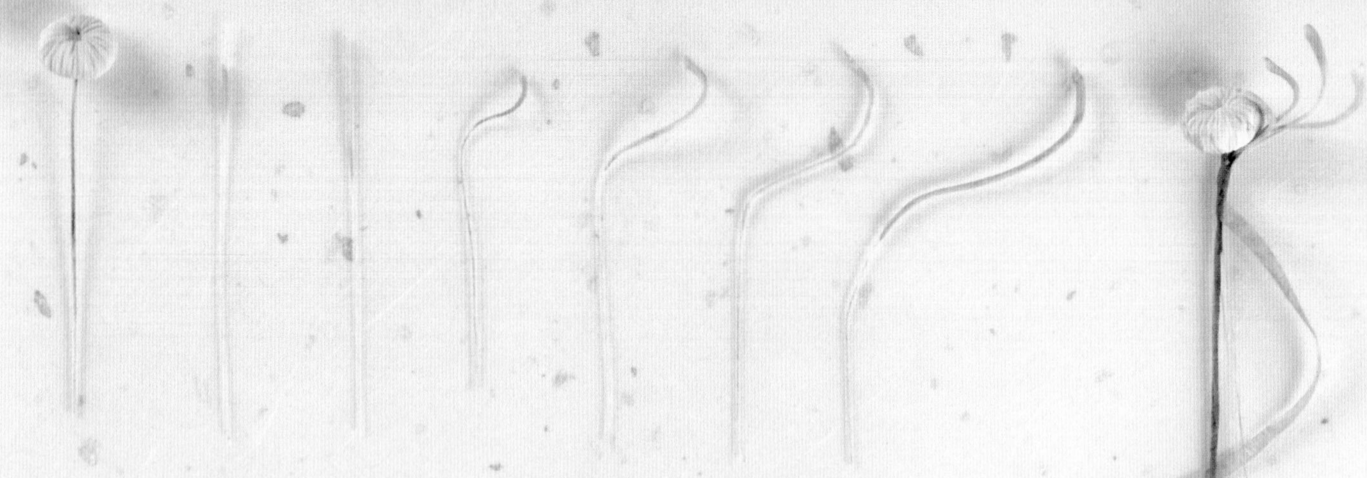

6 Hollow out the tip using a cocktail stick, fine celstick or the point of the ceramic tool. Curve the length of the petal prior to taping onto the dried centre with quarter- or half-width nile green floristry tape. Once you have several petals around the centre you can start to reshape them. Continue making and adding petals, gradually increasing in size as you build up each layer.

7 Dust with vine green and touches of moss green. Spray lightly with edible spray varnish or steam to set the colour and give a gentle shine.

CALYX

8 I am tempted to omit the calyx if the flower is to be displayed in a tight arrangement or spray. However, if you are creating a flower for a competition or an arrangement where the back will be visible it is best to add a calyx. Cut out a few layers of shapes using a daisy cutter or attach lots of individual fine green sepals to the back of the flower.
Dust with foliage green.

LEAVES

9 Roll out some mid-green flowerpaste leaving a thick ridge for the wire. Cut out the leaf shape using a chrysanthemum leaf cutter. Insert a 26-gauge wire into the thick ridge so that it supports about half the length of the leaf.

10 Soften the edges of the leaf and then texture using the chrysanthemum leaf veiner. Pinch the leaf to accentuate the central vein.

11 Hollow out the back of the leaf slightly and then allow to dry a little before dusting. Dust in layers with forest, foliage and very lightly with aubergine. The backs of the leaves are much paler than the upper surface. Spray lightly with edible spray varnish or steam to set the colour. Chrysanthemum leaves are generally not shiny, however sometimes sugar leaves need a tad of artistic licence.

Lily of the valley

I love making lily of the valley (Convallaria). This design was developed by my friend, Tombi Peck. She based the idea on one of Fabergé's Pearl lily of the valley designs. It is 20 years since she first showed me this flower but I have never tired of it.

MATERIALS
24- and 35-gauge white wires
White flowerpaste
Nile green floristry tape
Vine green and foliage petal dusts

EQUIPMENT
Wire cutters
Fine-nose pliers
Rolling pin
Non-stick board
Tiny five-petal plunger blossom cutter (PME)
Smooth ceramic tool (HP)
Dusting brush

BUDS

1 Cut several short lengths of 35-gauge white wire – you will need a lot of wire for the flowers and buds. Bend a hook in the end of each length of wire using fine-nose pliers. Roll lots of balls of white flowerpaste in graduating sizes. Insert a hooked wire into each and reshape if needed.

FLOWERS

2 Roll out a small amount of white flowerpaste and cut out a flower shape using the blossom cutter. Next, roll a ball of white paste and place the blossom shape onto the ball – if both pieces of paste are still fresh they will stick together without the need for fresh egg white.

3 Embed the blossom into the ball of paste using the pointed end of the ceramic tool, which should also help to create a hollowed out finish.

4 Moisten a hooked wire and thread it through the centre of the flower. Repeat to make five–seven flowers for each stem. Leave to dry.

ASSEMBLY AND COLOURING

5 Tape a tiny bud onto the end of a 24-gauge wire using quarter-width nile green floristry tape. Continue to add the buds, graduating the size as you add them to the stem. I usually use between five–nine buds per stem and then add between three and seven flowers.

6 Using fine-nose pliers curl the stem of each flower and bud so that their heads curve downwards.

7 Dust the main stem and each of the shorter ones with vine green petal dust. Add some of the colour to the smaller buds, gradually decreasing as you approach the flowers. Tinge the base of the main stem with foliage green petal dust.

Stephanotis

Sometimes known as the Madagascan jasmine, which is where the plant originates. Stephanotis floribunda is highly scented, and in the language of flowers, it is supposed to represent happiness in marriage, making it an ideal flower for bridal work!

MATERIALS

White and pale green flowerpaste
24- and 26-gauge white wires
Vine, daffodil, foliage and edelweiss petal dusts
Edible spray varnish

EQUIPMENT

Non-stick board
Smooth ceramic tool (HP)
Extra large stephanotis cutter (TT) or Nasturtium calyx cutter (TT448)
Dresden tool (J)
Flat dusting brushes
Small stephanotis cutter (TT568)
Sharp scalpel

FLOWERS

1 Form a ball of white paste into a sausage shape and pinch out one end to form a pedestal. Place the flat section against the board and roll out the base using the ceramic tool. Lift the shape up and place this rolled-out section on top of the extra large stephanotis or nasturtium calyx cutter.

2 Use the ceramic tool to roll over the paste against the edge of the cutter to cut out the shape. Rub your thumb over the edges to remove any fuzzy bits. Remove the shape from the cutter and place the flat part back against the board. Use the ceramic tool to broaden and elongate each of the petals slightly.

3 Open up the centre of the flower using the pointed end of the ceramic tool. Rest the flower against a finger and hollow out the centre of each petal using the broad end of the dresden tool.

4 Bend a hook in the end of a 24-gauge wire and pull through the centre of the flower. Work the back of the flower between your finger and thumb to create an arched slender back that broadens towards the base. Pinch off any excess paste at the base.

5 Dust the base with a light mixture of vine, daffodil and edelweiss petal dust. Add a tinge of colour at the flower centre too.

6 Roll out some pale green paste and cut out a calyx using the smallest stephanotis cutter. Soften the edges and attach to the base of the flower. Keep this shape fairly flat. Dust with vine and foliage green. Spray very lightly with edible spray varnish or steam to create a waxy finish.

BUDS

7 Hook and moisten a 24- or 26-gauge white wire depending upon the size of bud you are making. Form a cone shape of paste and insert the wire into the broad base. Work the paste as for the back of the flower to create its characteristic long neck. Divide the tip into five sections with a sharp scalpel. Twist very slightly if desired. Add a calyx as for the flower.

Gardenia

There are about 250 species of gardenia! The flowers are mostly white and cream but there are yellow and orange forms too. They are native to tropical and subtropical regions of Africa, Asia, Australasia and Oceania. Gardenias are used for button-holes, corsages and bridal bouquets, favoured because of their exquisite but heady scent.

MATERIALS

White and mid-green flowerpaste

22-, 24-, 26-, 28-, 30-, 33 and 35-gauge white wires

Vine, moss, forest, foliage, edelweiss and sunflower petal dusts

Nile green and white floristry tape

White seed-head stamens

Non-toxic hi-tack craft glue (Impex)

Clear alcohol

Three-quarter glaze or edible spray varnish (Fabilo)

EQUIPMENT

Fine-nose pliers

Flat-edge tweezers

Dusting brushes

Wire cutters

Cupped Christmas rose veiner (SKGI) or anemone petal veiner (ALDV)

Rolling pin

Non-stick board

Christmas rose (TT282, 283, 284) or Australian rose cutters (TT349-352) or gardenia cutters (AD) or see the Australian rose templates on page 254

Sharp scalpel

Foam pad

Dresden tool

Grooved board

Plain-edge cutting wheel (PME)

Ball tool

Gardenia leaf veiner (SKGI)

BUDS

1 Form a ball of well-kneaded white flowerpaste into a cone shape and insert a moistened, hooked 24- or 22-gauge wire into it. (The size of the wire will depend upon how big the bud is.) Work the base of the cone down onto the wire to create a slender neck.

2 Using flat-edge tweezers pinch six flange-like petals from around the upper section of the bud. Go back and thin the edges with your finger and thumb. Next, hold the petals and persuade them to spiral – the direction will depend upon the exact variety but try to make sure that the buds and flowers follow the same direction.

3 Dust with vine green and edelweiss petal dust – try to get some colour into the grooves of the petals.

CALYX

4 Cut six short lengths of 35- or 33-gauge wire. Attach a tiny ball of green paste to a wire and work it to blend a long slender sepal shape. Flatten the shape using the smooth side of a petal veiner. Pinch a ridge down the length between your finger and thumb and then curve slightly towards the tip. Repeat to make six sepals. Dust with foliage green petal dust.

5 Tape the six sepals around the base of the bud using half-width nile green floristry tape.

TIGHT CENTRE

6 You now need to decide if you are going to make a gardenia with a tight, spiralled centre or one that has matured to open up and reveal its centre. I have included instructions for both (next page). Bend a hook in the end of a 24-gauge wire using fine-nose pliers. Form a small cone shape of white paste and insert the moistened, hooked wire into the base. Leave to dry.

8 Place the petals onto a foam pad and work on the inside edge on the left-hand side of each petal using the broad end of the dresden tool to encourage the petal to curl.

9 Moisten the dried cone or the petals with egg white and place the petals one by one onto the centre. Overlap them and tuck the last petal in to create a tight spiral. Curl back the edges if required.

OPEN CENTRE

10 Here are the instructions for the centre of a more mature flower. Use a 26-gauge wire to create the pistil. Blend a tiny amount of pale green paste onto the end to form a slender bud shape. Pinch a few ridges and then spiral the tip. Allow to dry.

11 Tape six seed-head stamen tips around the pistil using quarter-width nile green tape or simply attach them using hi-tack craft glue. Dust the tips with sunflower petal dust. Sometimes the stamens are more creamy in colour and as the flower fades they turn a more brown/aubergine colour.

12 Create six wired petals using the small cutter used for the tight centre method. Roll out the paste to leave a thick ridge for a fine wire and then cut out the petal shape. Insert a moistened short length of 30-gauge wire into the ridge. Pinch the base of the petal down onto the wire to secure it in place. Soften the edges and vein as before. You may also want to create the curled edge as above too – this very much depends upon the style of

gardenia you are making. Cup the centre very slightly. Repeat to make six petals.

13 Tape the six petals in a spiral form around the stamens using quarter-width white floristry tape.

OUTER PETALS

14 The number of outer petals varies. To make a half-open gardenia I use six petals using either the same size cutter as previously or more often I use the next size up in the set (or use the gardenia petal templates on page 252). To make a more open flower I make yet another six petals using the largest petal cutter. Use a 30- or a 28-gauge white wire for a larger petal - soften, vein, wire and curl the left-hand edge as created previously.

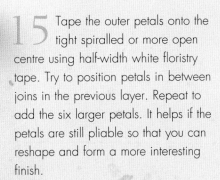

15 Tape the outer petals onto the tight spiralled or more open centre using half-width white floristry tape. Try to position petals in between joins in the previous layer. Repeat to add the six larger petals. It helps if the petals are still pliable so that you can reshape and form a more interesting finish.

16 Add a ball of white paste to the back of the flower and work it down the wire to form a slender neck. Some gardenias have very long necks while others are fairly short. Blend the paste into the base of the petals using the broad end of the dresden tool and a touch of clear alcohol – try not to get the petals too wet as they will dissolve. Create and add six sepals as for the bud and tape to the base of the flower with half-width nile green tape.

COLOURING

17 Mix together vine green and edelweiss petal dusts. Add strong green colouring to the slender neck and under the curl of each of the outer petals. A little of the soft colour can be used at the centre of the flower too. As the flowers fade they turn more creamy yellow in colour, in fact some varieties are yellow. If this is the case then you can mix together some sunflower and edelweiss to colour all the petals to the depth required. Allow the flower to dry and then steam gently to create a waxy finish.

LEAVES

18 Roll out some well-kneaded mid-green flowerpaste leaving a thick ridge for the wire – a grooved board can be used successfully for this job. Cut out a basic ovate-shaped leaf using the plain-edge cutting wheel.

19 Insert a moistened 28-, 26- or 24-gauge wire depending on the size of the leaf. The wire should support about half the length of the leaf. Place the leaf onto a foam pad or in your palm and soften the edges, working half on the paste and half on your hand, with a metal ball tool.

20 Texture the leaf using the double-sided gardenia leaf veiner. Remove the leaf from the veiner and then, if you wish, hollow out the back of the leaf very slightly (this does vary between varieties). Pinch the leaf from the base through to the tip to accentuate the central vein.

21 Dust in layers with forest, moss, foliage and vine green. The smaller new growth foliage tends to be a much brighter green than the larger leaves. The backs of the leaves are paler than the top. Tape over each leaf stem with half-width nile green tape.

22 Leave to dry and then dip into a three-quarter glaze or spray with edible spray varnish to create fairly glossy foliage.

Golden gardenia

This is an African single form of gardenia that is much quicker and simpler to make than the more common varieties. The flowers occur in white, cream and yellow, working through to orange colouring.

MATERIALS
24-, 26- and 28-gauge wires
Pale green and pale yellow flowerpaste
Seed-head stamens
White and nile green floristry tape
Sunflower, edelweiss, vine, forest, foliage, daffodil and aubergine petal dusts

EQUIPMENT
Curved gardenia petal cutters or Australian rose petal cutters
Rolling pin
Non-stick board
Cupped Christmas rose or stargazer B petal veiner (SKGI) or anemone petal veiner (ALDV)
Gardenia leaf veiner (SKGI)
Dusting brushes
Dresden tool

PISTIL AND STAMEN

1 These are made in the same way as the open gardenia centre (see steps 10 and 11 on the previous spread). Colour the tips of the stamens with sunflower and a little aubergine petal dust.

PETALS

2 There can be between 5 and 12 petals on this form of gardenia. The size of flower varies quite a bit too. Roll out some pale yellow flowerpaste, leaving a thick ridge for the wire.

3 Insert a short length of 28-gauge white wire into about a third of the ridge. Soften the edges and vein using one of the petal veiners listed above. Repeat to make the required number of petals. Curl the back of the petal with the dresden tool as described for the gardenia (see step 8).

4 Tape the petals around the stamens and pistil using half-width white floristry tape. Add a ball of yellow paste and work it into a slender neck on the back of the flower.

COLOURING

5 Dust the petals and the back of the flower to your requirements – here I have used a mixture of edelweiss, a touch of daffodil and quite a bit of sunflower petal dusts. Add tinges of vine green/foliage to the base of the neck. Add a calyx as described for the gardenia (see step 4).

BUDS

6 The buds are much longer and very slender. Bend a hook in the end of a 24-gauge wire. Attach a cone of pale yellow paste and thin down the base to create the long neck shape. Pinch several petals from the broader upper section and spiral as described for the gardenia (see steps 1 and 2). Dust as for the flower and add the calyx.
The leaves are made in the same way as on Gardenia (steps 18 to 22).

Trailing succulent

Senecio radicans has a wonderful trailing nature that works well with sprays, bouquets and arrangements. On occasion I have been known to make these when travelling as a passenger on long car journeys as they require very little effort or equipment. There is another Senecio that I am fond of making too – its common name is string of pearls. In my classes the succulents have been nicknamed 'the flirts' as they are addictive to make!

MATERIALS
33- or 35-gauge white wires
Pale green flowerpaste
Nile green floristry tape
Forest, foliage, vine, edelweiss and aubergine petal dusts
Edible spray varnish (Fabilo)

EQUIPMENT
Wire cutters
Fine-nose pliers
Plain-edge cutting wheel (PME) or sharp scalpel
Large dusting brush

LEAVES
1 Cut several short lengths of 35- or 33-gauge white wire – the finer the better. Roll small balls of flowerpaste, gradually increasing the size, and then form them into slender cone shapes. Insert a moistened wire into the ball and work the base of the cone into a slight point at the base, onto the wire. Curve the tip slightly using fine-nose pliers.

2 Mark a central vein down the curved upperside of the leaf using a plain-edge cutting wheel or a sharp scalpel – this vein is known as the leaf's window! Repeat to make loads of leaves in varying sizes.

ASSEMBLY
3 The leaves may be dusted prior to assembling the long trails but I prefer to tape them and then dust as they are much easier to control that way. Use a 33-gauge 'leader wire' and tape the leaves onto it using quarter-width nile green tape. Start with the smallest leaves. Leave a little of each individual wire on show and make sure that their 'windows' are facing towards the light.

COLOURING
4 Use a mixture of foliage, a touch of forest and edelweiss to dust the leaves. Add touches of vine green and aubergine if desired. Glaze lightly with edible spray varnish.

Smilax

Smilax occurs in several forms. It is a fairly quick foliage to produce, making it ideal to use when lots of greenery is required for a wedding cake.

3 Place the leaf against the board and flatten using the flat side of the stargazer B veiner. This should give you a larger, thinner leaf shape. You might need to trim the edges with sharp scissors to create a neater shape – but with practice you will find that you manage to form more consistent leaves.

4 Place the leaf into the stargazer B veiner to texture. Remove from the veiner and pinch the leaf at the base and at the tip to accentuate a central vein.

COLOURING AND ASSEMBLY

5 Dust the leaf lightly with forest green and overdust heavily with foliage and vine green. Spray with edible spray varnish – these leaves should be quite glossy so you might need to apply a couple of light coats to create the desired effect.

6 Tape into sets of three using half-width nile green floristry tape and then continue to tape the leaves onto a longer, stronger wire.

MATERIALS
28-, 30- and 33 gauge white wires
Green flowerpaste
Forest, foliage and vine green petal dust
Edible spray varnish (Fabilo)
Nile green floristry tape

EQUIPMENT
Wire cutters
Non-stick board
Stargazer B petal veiner (or similar)
Sharp scissors
Flat dusting brushes

CLADODES

1 These look like the leaves of the plant but they are actually modified flattened stems that produce tiny white flowers often followed by red berries. In the remainder of the text they will be referred to as leaves! Cut short lengths of 33-, 30- or 28-gauge white wire – the size of the wire depends upon the size of leaf you plan to make.

2 Roll a ball of green flowerpaste and then form it into a slender carrot shape. Insert a wire into the broad end of the carrot. Work the paste onto the wire and into a smooth shape rolling it between your palms.

Cotinus

Cotinus provides the flower maker with a very simple yet extremely effective foliage as the leaves of the plant can be a bright fresh green, often tinged with red and also brown and purple, which is great for adding depth to a bouquet or arrangement.

MATERIALS
Pale green flowerpaste
22-, 26-, 28- and 30- gauge wires
Aubergine, African violet, nutkin
  brown and foliage petal dusts
Nile green floristry tape
Edible spray varnish (Fabilo)

EQUIPMENT
Rolling pin
Non-stick board
Rose petal cutters (TT 276-280) or
  bougainvillea cutters (J)
Medium ball tool
Rose leaf or poinsettia leaf veiners
  (SKGI)

LEAVES

1 Roll out some pale green flowerpaste leaving a thick ridge for the wire. Cut out a leaf shape using one of the rose petal or bougainvillea cutters.

2 Insert a moistened wire – the gauge will depend upon the size of the leaf, 26-gauge for a larger leaf, 28-gauge for a medium and 30-gauge for a small leaf.

3 Soften the edge of the leaf using a medium-sized ball tool. Place in a poinsettia or rose leaf veiner to texture. Pinch the leaf from the base to the tip to accentuate the central vein. Repeat to make the required number of varying-sized leaves.

COLOURING

4 To create depth of colour in the leaves it is best to dust them while the paste is still pliable. Dust with layers of aubergine, African violet and nutkin brown petal dust. It is important to leave the backs of the leaves mostly green although a little of the colour catching the veins can be very effective.

5 Tape over each stem with quarter-width nile green tape and then tape the leaves into fairly tight snug groups using half-width tape. Add these small groups onto a 22-gauge wire to form longer stems if required. Dust the stems with the same colours as the foliage. The leaves are not very shiny so it should be enough to spray very lightly with edible glaze spray varnish (see page 12).

Ginger lily

This ginger lily (Hedychium gardneranum) is native to the Himalayas. The flowers are smaller with longer stamens than the more common white ginger lily. These wonderfully scented flowers are often available as cut flowers. Although the stems are usually massed with flowers I find them easier to incorporate into sprays and arrangements with fewer flowers. There are white, cream, yellow, orange, pink and coral varieties too.

MATERIALS
20-, 22-, 26-, 28-, 30- and 33-gauge white
   wires
Pale creamy yellow and green flowerpaste
Sunflower, daffodil, ruby, coral, foliage,
   aubergine and vine green petal dusts
Isopropyl alcohol
White and nile green floristry tape

EQUIPMENT
Wire cutters
Dusting brushes
Rolling pin
Non-stick board
Simple leaf cutter (TT229, 230) or see
   the templates on page 254
Stargazer B petal veiner (SKGI)
Curved scissors
Small celstick or smooth ceramic tool
Silk veining tool (HP)
Plain-edge cutting wheel (PME)

PISTIL

1 The pistil is actually a combination of pistil (stigma and style) combined with a fertile stamen (anther and filament). Use a third of a length of a 33-gauge white wire. Attach a ball of pale yellow paste about 4–5 cm (1½–2 in) from the end of the wire and firmly and quickly work the paste to the tip to create a fine smooth coating. Curve the length of the paste into a graceful curve.

2 Form a fine sausage of paste and make sure it is slightly pointed at both ends. Attach to the tip of the coated wire. Allow to dry before colouring. (I often find very fine things like this are easier and stronger if made with cold porcelain, which would allow you to use non-toxic hi-tack glue to hold the paste onto the end of the wire.) Dust the length of the pistil with coral and ruby petal dust. Dilute a little ruby dust with isopropyl alcohol and paint the sausage tip.

PETALS

3 To make life more confusing, what look like the three large petals to this flower are in fact stamenoids – petal-like infertile stamens! To make the instructions simpler to follow I will refer to them as petals. To make the two smaller petals, roll out some pale yellow flowerpaste leaving a thick ridge for the wire. Cut out a petal shape using one of the two sizes of simple leaf cutters – this will depend upon how big you want to make the flower. Insert a moistened 30- or 28-gauge white wire into the ridge from the pointed end of the petal. Work the base of the petal to elongate it slightly.

4 Soften the edges with a ball tool and then texture using the stargazer B petal veiner. Pinch the petal to accentuate the central vein. Curve the petal back slightly. Repeat to make two petals.

5 To make the larger heart-shaped petal roll out some yellow paste to leave a thick ridge. Cut out the petal shape using the simple leaf cutter and insert a 28-gauge wire about half way into the petal. Twist the base to elongate the shape and secure the petal firmly to the wire.

6 Cut the top of the petal into a heart shape using curved scissors. Place the paste back onto the board and broaden each half of the petal using a celstick or smooth ceramic tool.

7 Vein the petal using the stargazer B petal veiner and then place the petal onto your index finger and work the top edges using the silk veining tool to texture and frill the edge slightly. Pinch the central vein and curve the petal back slightly.

NARROW PETALS

8 There are three fine appendages to the flower – these look like bracts but are actually the true petals. These are made using 33-gauge wire. Roll a tiny ball of paste onto the wire and work into a fine elongated petal. Flatten the shape to thin it and then texture with the stargazer B veiner. Pinch from the base to the tip. Repeat to make three – although often these drop off the real flower and one, two or none of them will be present!

COLOURING AND ASSEMBLY

9 Dust all the petals from the base to the tip with a mixture of sunflower and daffodil petal dusts. Add colour from the edges towards the base. Add a tinge of coral at the base of each petal.

10 Tape the heart-shaped petal onto the pistil using quarter-width white floristry tape. Add the two side petals next, followed by the three narrow petals at the base.

11 Blend a ball of yellow paste behind the flower to create the neck. Dust to match the petals.

BUDS

12 Use 28- and 26-gauge white wires for the various sizes of buds. Form a cone shape of yellow paste and insert the wire into the base. Work the paste down the wire to create an elongated bud shape.

13 Pinch three flanges from the tip of the bud to represent the three outer petals. Twist the petals around the tip of the bud to create a spiral look. Dust with daffodil and sunflower petal dusts.

BRACT

14 There is a bract at the base of each bud and flower that conceals the ovary of the flower. I usually only create the bract shape. Roll out some green flowerpaste and cut out a pointed arrowhead shape using the plain-edge cutting wheel. Texture the surface of the bract using the stargazer B veiner and then wrap it around the base of the flower or bud.

15 Dust with vine green and a touch of foliage. Add ruby or aubergine to the edges.

16 Tape the buds to the end of a 20- or 22-gauge wire using half-width nile green tape. Spiral the buds around the stem, gradually introducing the flowers.

Sandersonia

This plant is native to South Africa but it is grown commercially in many countries for the cut-flower market. The plant is related to the more familiar gloriosa lily and is equally as poisonous, so care must be taken when handling fresh specimen flowers. The flowers can be yellow or orange in colour.

EQUIPMENT
Scissors
Wire cutters
Flat dusting brush
Rolling pin
Non-stick board
Sandersonia flower cutter (AD) or see the
    template on page 254 and sharp scalpel or
    plain-edge cutting wheel
Medium metal ball tool
Dresden tool (JEM) or porcupine quill
Celstick
Sandersonia leaf cutters (AD) or see the
    templates on page 254 and sharp scalpel
    or plain-edge cutting wheel
Lily leaf veiner

MATERIALS
White seed-head stamens
Non-toxic hi-tack craft glue (Impex)
22-, 24-, 26- and 28-gauge white wires
Daffodil, sunflower, coral, vine and foliage
    petal dusts
Creamy yellow and mid-green flowerpaste
Fresh egg white
Edible spray varnish (Fabilo)
Nile green floristry tape

STAMENS

1 Take three stamens and fold them in half. Bond the fold in the stamens with a small amount of non-toxic hi-tack craft glue. Squeeze the glue into the stamens to flatten them slightly and secure together. Allow to set and trim off the excess from the glued sections.

2 Cut a half length of 24-gauge wire. Apply a little more glue onto the base of the stamens and attach onto the end of the wire. Firmly squeeze the stamens and wire together to secure firmly. Allow to dry. Dust the stamens with vine green and the tips with sunflower petal dust.

3 Add a small ball of green flowerpaste at the base of the stamens to represent the ovary. Allow to dry.

FLOWER

4 Roll out some creamy yellow flowerpaste – not too thinly. Cut out the flower shape using the sandersonia flower cutter or use the template on page 254 and cut out using a scalpel or plain-edge cutting wheel.

5 Soften the edges of the petals using a medium ball tool. Hollow each section of the shape using a rolling action with the ball tool.

6 Turn the shape over and draw a line to separate each petal using the fine end of the dresden tool or a porcupine quill.

7 Carefully pinch each section at the base to make sharp points and create a gathered effect.

8 Moisten one side of the shape and wrap the two edges together. Place the shape onto a celstick and blend the join by pressing the paste against the celstick with your thumb.

9 Apply a little more egg white to the gathered points of the shape and carefully squeeze the six sections together to form the bell shape of the flower.

10 Pull the stamens through the centre of the flower and pinch the flower firmly against the wire. Allow to dry before dusting with daffodil and sunflower petal dusts mixed together. Tinge with vine green and foliage. A light dusting of coral may also be used to create a warmer colouring.

LEAVES

11 Roll out some mid-green flowerpaste leaving a thick ridge. Cut out the leaf using one of the sandersonia leaf cutters or use the template on page 254 and cut out using a scalpel or plain-edge cutting wheel.

12 Insert a 26- or 28-gauge wire into the thick ridge – the gauge will depend upon the size of the leaf.

13 Soften the edges with a ball tool. Vein using a lily leaf veiner or create freehand veins using the small wheel of the plain-edge cutting wheel.

14 Pinch the leaf from the base to the tip to accentuate the central vein. Curve into shape.

15 Dust in layers with foliage and vine green. Glaze lightly with edible spray varnish.

ASSEMBLY

16 Tape a few leaves tightly to the end of a 22-gauge wire using half-width nile green floristry tape. Continue to work down the stem, adding buds and gradually flowers.

Beetleweed

This heart-shaped leaf (Galax urceolata), often used by florists for arrangements and bridal bouquets, is quite leathery in texture. The leaf can be used flat in an arrangement or curled to form interesting spiral effects.

MATERIALS
Mid-green flowerpaste
22-, 24- and 26-gauge white wires
Kitchen paper
Fresh egg white
Foliage, forest, vine green and aubergine petal dusts
Edible spray varnish (Fabilo)
Nile green floristry tape

EQUIPMENT
Rolling pin
Non-stick board
Beetleweed leaf cutter set (AD) or see templates on page 253
Dresden tool
Very large nasturtium leaf veiner (SKGI) or beetleweed leaf veiner (SC)
Large ball tool
Flat dusting brush

CUTTING AND WIRING
1 Roll out some well-kneaded mid-green flowerpaste, leaving a thick ridge for the wire. Cut out the leaf shape using your chosen size of beetleweed cutter or refer to the templates on page 253.

2 Insert a moistened 22-, 24- or 26-gauge wire into the central ridge – the gauge will depend upon the size of the leaf. The leaf needs a fair amount of support especially if it is to curl into a spiral shape.

TEXTURING AND SHAPING
3 Use the broad end of the dresden tool to work the edges of the leaf to break up the regimental serrations to create a more interesting effect.

4 Texture the leaf using the double side nasturtium or beetleweed leaf veiner.

5 If needed, soften the edge using a large ball tool. Pinch the leaf to accentuate the central vein and create 'movement'. Allow to dry supported by some crumpled kitchen paper or roll the leaf up to create a curved, spiral effect. Use little egg white to help hold the shape, along with a sharp pinch at the base to prevent it unravelling. Repeat to make the required number of leaves.

COLOURING AND ASSEMBLY
6 Allow to firm up a little before dusting. Tinge the edges with aubergine petal dust. Use vine green, foliage and a touch of forest green in layers to colour the main body. Dust the back of the leaf lightly using any green colour left on the brush.

7 Allow to dry and then glaze using edible spray varnish. Tape over each stem using half-width nile green floristry tape.

Crescent spray

This style of spray is very useful for filling space and also for following a curve on a cake. It was the first shaped spray I was taught when I started making sugar flowers.

FLOWERS

9 stephanotis flowers (see page 156)
7 stephanotis buds (see page 156)
2 fully open yellow gardenias
  (see page 157-9)
1 full gardenia (see pages 157-9)
3 half gardenias (see pages 157-9)
1 gardenia bud (see page 157)
7 stems of smilax (see page 163)
6 stems of lily of the valley (see page 155)
7 stems of wire vine (see page 71)

EQUIPMENT

22- and 24-gauge wires
Wire cutters
Fine-nose pliers
Nile green floristry tape

PREPARATION

1 Strengthen any stems that require extra support or length using an appropriate gauge wire and half-width nile green floristry tape.

ASSEMBLY

2 You need to form two 'arms' for this spray. Create a line/arm using two stephanotis buds and three flowers. Add the elements to a 22-gauge wire with half-width nile green tape. Alternate the buds and flowers down the wire. Repeat to create a mirror image and then bend both stems to a 90-degree angle and tape them together. This forms the base of the spray and also the handle that will be inserted into the posy pick. Trim off any excess wires as you work to cut down on some of the bulk.

3 Add another shorter stem of stephanotis to create the width of the spray. This helps to balance out the overall shape.

4 Place the largest gardenia flower in the centre of the spray to create the focal point. This flower should stand higher than any of the others in the spray. Continue to add the remaining gardenia flowers and buds around the focal flower to fill out more of the shape of the spray. Use the small flowers towards the edges.

2

3

4

5 Add the ruscus foliage around the edges of the spray and use the gardenia leaves behind the focal flower and some around the base of the spray too. These will help to hide any 'holes' in the display.

6 Use the lily of the valley stems to soften the edges of the spray. Group the flowers and use them at opposite ends of the display.

7 Add the trailing stems of wire vine to create a more relaxed feel to the spray. Trim off any excess wires and tape over the handle of the spray with full-width nile green tape to neaten it.

Rangoon creeper

The Rangoon creeper (Quisqualis indica) is from Tropical Asia – it is also known by the hilarious common name of Drunken Sailor! I came across the plant at the botanical gardens in Christchurch, New Zealand. It is a crazy vine massed with flowers that start off very pale and gradually turn to a peach then coral through to red.

MATERIALS
Fine white stamens
Non-toxic hi-tack craft glue (Impex)
35-, 33-, 30-, 28-, 26-, 24- and 22-gauge
   white wires
Primrose, coral, red, ruby, white, vine green,
   foliage and aubergine petal dusts
Pale apricot and pale green flowerpaste
White and nile green floristry tape
Edible spray varnish (Fabilo)

EQUIPMENT
Sharp scissors
Wire cutters
Dusting brushes
Non-stick board
Cupped Christmas rose petal veiner (SKGI)
Medium ball tall
Foam pad
Fine curved scissors
Rolling pin
Plain-edge cutting wheel (PME)
Mandevilla leaf veiner (SKGI)

STAMENS

1 Fold three fine white stamens in half and line up the tips. Remove one tip to leave five stamens. Glue the group together at the bend with hi-tack glue. Leave for a few minutes to dry and then trim off the excess to leave a short group of stamens. Cut a short length of 33-gauge wire and apply a tiny amount of glue to the end. Press the glued wire onto the stamens and pinch them firmly together. Leave to dry and then dust the tips with primrose petal dust.

PETALS

2 Roll a tiny ball of pale apricot flowerpaste and then form it into a cone shape. Insert a short length of 35- or 33-gauge white wire into the base. Work the base of the cone between your finger and thumb to elongate the shape.

3 Place the wired shape onto the non-stick board and flatten it with the smooth side of the Christmas rose petal veiner. At first you might need to trim the shape of the petal slightly but you will gradually start to create more consistent shapes. Soften the edge of the petal using a medium-sized ball tool. Texture the petal using the double-sided Christmas rose veiner.

4 Place the petal on your palm or a foam pad and gently hollow out the back of the petal. Pinch the petal at the base and slightly at the tip to create a little movement. Repeat to make five petals.

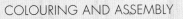

COLOURING AND ASSEMBLY

5 The petals can be dusted before or after you assemble the flower – I prefer to tape it together first around the stamens using quarter-width white floristry tape.

6 Dust it as a whole as I find it easier to balance out the colour between petals. Use layers of coral, red and ruby petal dusts to create the depth of colour required. For paler flowers add a touch of white petal dust to the coral. Keep the backs of the petals undusted or very, very pale.

7 Work a ball of very pale green paste at the back of the flower to create a long, slender-necked calyx. Use fine curved scissors to snip a five-sepal calyx, aiming to get a sepal in between a petal. Curve the neck slightly. Dust the calyx very gently with vine green petal dust.

BUDS

8 Cut lengths of 33-, 30- and 28-gauge white wire for the buds (the size of the wire will depend on the size bud you are making). Form a small cone of pale green paste and insert a dry wire into the broad end. Work the base of the bud down onto the wire to create a long, slender neck. Smooth the neck between the fleshy part of your hands. Curve the neck slightly. Snip a quick calyx as for the flower.

9 Dust lightly with vine green. Add a tinge of red to the tip but be careful not to create too much colour – remember the backs of the petals are pale so the bud needs to match.

LEAVES

10 The leaves grow in pairs. Roll out some pale green paste, leaving a thick ridge for the wire. Cut out the leaf using the plain-edge cutting wheel. Insert a 28-, 26- or 24-gauge wire into the thick ridge. Soften the edges and vein using the mandevilla leaf veiner. Pinch the leaf from the base to the tip to accentuate the central vein. Repeat to make the leaves in pairs of graduating sizes.

11 Dust the edges lightly with a mixture of ruby and aubergine. Use layers of foliage and vine green to colour the upper surface of the leaf. Keep the backs a much paler green. Spray lightly with edible spray varnish.

12 Form a trailing stem using a 22-gauge wire. Tape two very small leaves together at the tip of the wire using half-width nile green tape. Leave a gap and then introduce a group of small buds accompanied by a pair of leaves. Continue in this way until you have created the required length.

Silver trail posy

Although in theory a posy of flowers is fairly easy to assemble, you will find that you use quite a lot of flowers to complete a project of this sort. A balanced result is needed to help form the characteristic posy shape. I have updated the style slightly by adding a cage and trails of fine crimped metallic wires that catch the light.

FLOWERS

1 green-tinged large full rose
  (see pages 34-6)
6 hydrangea florets (see pages 57-9)
3 Christmas orchids (see pages 96-8)
3 masdevallia orchids (see page 187)
3 blue butterfly bush flowers
  (see page 201)
8 beetleweed leaves (see page 169)

EQUIPMENT

Nile green floristry tape
24- and 28-gauge wires
Double-sided pink/green satin ribbon
Fine-nose pliers
Wire cutters
Fine silver, pale green and turquoise metallic
  crimped reel wires
Pale aqua beaded wires

PREPARATION

1 Use half-width nile green tape and 24-gauge wire to strengthen or lengthen any of the flower stems that need it.

2 This posy is built on a series of figure-of-eight ribbon loops – these are optional but can prove useful for filling in gaps in a posy or even at the heart of a crescent-shaped spray. Simply form figure-of-eight double loops. The double-sided ribbon works well for this purpose. Bend a length of 28-gauge wire at the centre of the loops and twist it together to hold the ribbon in place. Repeat this process as required and then layer up the loops to form a circle of ribbons on which the posy can be built.

ASSEMBLY

3 Use the full rose as the centre and focal point of the posy – this flower should stand higher than any others. Tape into place using half-width nile green tape.

4 Start to encircle the rose with the hydrangea florets. Trim away excess bulk wires from the handle of the spray as you work.

5 Continue to work around the posy adding the Christmas and masdevallia orchids, alternating them as you build the arrangement.

6 Create a little more interest by adding cool notes of blue clerodendron flowers evenly around the posy.

7 Use the beetleweed leaves as the final layer of the posy to create a more compact feel and to frame the display. Finally, weave around the flowers with silver, pale green and turquoise crimped wires and curls of aqua-coloured beaded wire. Add trails of crimped wire to soften the whole display.

Vincent orchid

This pretty orchid is based on the *Isochilus* orchid.
However, when making this in class I decided
that the curved formation reminded me of the
headbands that cake designer Kerry Vincent wears
– and so I have nicknamed this the Vincent orchid!

COLUMN AND LIP (LABELLUM)

1 Cut a short length of 33-gauge white wire. Attach a tiny ball of pink flowerpaste to the end and work it down the wire leaving it slightly bulbous at the tip. Hollow out the underside using the rounded end of the celstick or smooth ceramic tool. Curve and leave to dry.

2 To make the lip, attach another piece of pink flowerpaste to a 33-gauge white wire and work the paste to create a fine tapered petal. Flatten it and vein with the stargazer B petal veiner. Pinch and curve the shape and then tape it onto the base of the column with quarter-width nile green floristry tape.

WING/LATERAL PETALS AND LATERAL SEPALS

3 The two wing petals are made as for the lip/labellum described above. Tape them onto the side of the column using quarter-width nile green floristry tape. These three petals form the framework on which the outer three sepals are added. These three are unwired but form the same shape as the petals. Attach to the orchid using fresh egg white. Curl back the tips of the petals and sepals. The flower looks almost like a bluebell in shape.

4 The buds are long, slender pieces of pink flowerpaste worked onto the end of a 30- or 28-gauge white wire. Divide into three to represent the outer sepals.

5 Tape the buds and flowers onto a 24-gauge white wire with nile green floristry tape to form a curved stem. Start with the smallest buds, gradually increasing in size and then add the flowers. Dust with plum and African violet petal dusts.

LEAVES

6 These are made almost like ruscus leaves. Blend a teardrop piece of holly/ivy flowerpaste onto a 30-, 28- or 26-gauge white wire and form it into a fine point. Flatten and vein using the stargazer B petal veiner. Pinch from the base to the tip. Repeat to make numerous leaves. Dust with foliage and vine petal dusts. Add tinges of aubergine to the edges. Spray lightly with edible spray varnish. Tape onto the flowering stem using half-width nile green floristry tape, starting with the smallest leaves and graduating in size down the stem. Curve the stem as you work.

MATERIALS

33-, 30-, 28-, 26- and 24-gauge white wires
Pink and holly/ivy flowerpaste
Nile green floristry tape
Fresh egg white
Plum, African violet, foliage, vine and aubergine petal dusts
Edible spray varnish

EQUIPMENT

Wire cutters
Celstick or smooth ceramic tool (HP)
Stargazer B petal veiner
Dusting brushes

Pachyveria succulent

These cultivated fleshy succulents are a cross hybridisation between *Pachyphytum* and *Echeveria*. Succulents are great to make as no cutters or veiners are required and there is a good excuse for working the paste on the thicker side too!

MATERIALS

Pale holly/ivy flowerpaste

33-, 30-, 28-, 26-gauge white wires

Fresh egg white

White floristry tape

Forest, foliage, edelweiss, plum and aubergine petal dusts

Edible spray varnish

EQUIPMENT

Medium metal ball tool (CC)

Dusting brushes

1 Roll a ball of pale holly/ivy flowerpaste. Form it into a teardrop shape and insert a wire moistened with fresh egg white – the gauge will depend on the size of leaf you are making. Work the paste at the base of the cone down onto the wire to form a 'neck'. Flatten the shape a little, leaving a thicker area at the centre.

2 Hollow the whole leaf slightly using the medium metal ball tool. The pressure of the tool against the wire will create a central vein. Pinch the tip into a sharp point. Repeat to make numerous leaves in varying sizes.

3 Tape the leaves together to form a rosette shape using quarter-width white floristry tape, starting with the smallest leaves snuggled tightly together. Gradually increase the size of the leaves as you work and use half-width white floristry tape for the larger leaves.

4 Dust the rosette leaves and stem as a whole using a mixture of forest, foliage and edelweiss. Tinge the tips and edges as desired – I tend to use a mixture of plum and aubergine petal dusts. Glaze lightly with edible spray varnish or steam gently to remove the dusted finish.

Japanese painted fern

I first came across these Japanese ferns (*Athyrium niponicum*) with painted faces in a seed/plant catalogue. Several of these unusual ferns were pictured but it was this purple-tinged variety that grabbed my attention the most. I love using foliage, and these decorative, colourful forms are ideal for adding interest to sprays and arrangements.

1 Make sure the very pale green flowerpaste is very well kneaded. Using the celstick, roll out the paste onto a fine grooved board or roll the paste leaving a fine ridge for the wire. The paste needs to be rolled very fine to allow you to retrieve it easily from the fern cutters. Cut out the fern sections using the three sizes of Australian fern cutters; beware the smallest cutter can be very tricky! The leaves grow almost in pairs of the same size down the stem. Insert a 33- or 30-gauge white wire into each leaf, depending on the size of the leaf. Alternatively, roll out the flowerpaste thinly, cut out the leaves and attach the wire covered with a thin layer of paste to patch onto the back.

2 Work the edges of each leaf using the broad end of the Dresden tool to create an almost feathered effect. Pinch a central vein from the base to the tip. Curve slightly. Repeat to make lots of leaves.

COLOURING AND ASSEMBLY

3 Dust from the edges of each leaf with a mixture of African violet and plum petal dusts. Use a light dusting of moss and foliage and a touch of white bridal satin on the front of the leaves — try not to let the green dominate the foliage. Dilute some plum petal dust with isopropyl alcohol and paint fine veins onto the front and back of each leaf, concentrating mainly on the central vein.

4 Tape the leaves onto a 26-gauge white wire using quarter-width nile green floristry tape, starting with a medium-size leaf at the very end followed by the smallest leaves in pairs down the stem and then gradually working through the other sizes to create the required length of fern. Introduce a 22-gauge white wire to the stem if a very large length is required. Dust the main stem with plum, African violet and a light dusting of aubergine too. Spray very lightly with edible spray varnish or steam to set the colour.

MATERIALS

Very pale green flowerpaste
33-, 30-, 26- and 22-gauge white wires
African violet, plum, moss, foliage, white bridal satin and aubergine petal dusts
Isopropyl alcohol
Nile green floristry tape
Edible spray varnish

EQUIPMENT

Celstick
Fine grooved board
Australian fern cutter set (APOC)
Dresden tool
Dusting brushes
Fine paintbrush

Rose hips

Rose hips, with their wonderful shape, size and colour variations, make them a very welcome decorative fruit addition to floral displays and cake designs.

STAMENS AND CALYX

1 Part two fingers and then wrap 120-gauge lace maker's thread around them several times – the number will depend on the size/type of hip you are making. Remove the loop from your fingers and twist into a figure of eight shape and then fold in half to produce a smaller loop. Bend a length of 24-gauge white wire through the centre of the loop and tape over tightly with half-width nile green floristry tape. Repeat this process at the opposite side of the loop to create two sets of stamens. Cut through the centre using scissors. Trim shorter as required.

2 Fluff up the tips of the stamens by rubbing the thread against an emery board. Dust with nutkin and a touch of black petal dusts. To create a more decayed finish, simply hold the stamens over a naked flame to singe the tips very slightly.

3 To make the calyx, follow the steps for the rose calyx (see steps 12 to 15, pages 34–5) to make five sepals. Tape the sepals around the thread using half-width nile green floristry tape. Dust each sepal with a light mixture of foliage and vine green petal dusts. Catch the tips and edges with a mixture of ruby and aubergine. The inside of each sepal benefits from a light dusting of white petal dust.

HIP

4 Roll a ball of pale green flowerpaste to the desired size and shape. Pull the wired calyx/stamens through the ball using a very small amount of fresh egg white to secure them together.

5 Dust the hip before the paste starts to dry. Here I have used tangerine, ruby, vine green and tinges of foliage green petal dusts. Allow to dry and then spray in layers with edible spray varnish until you achieve the desired glossy finish. Follow steps 16 to 18 on page 35 to make the rose leaves.

MATERIALS
120-gauge lace maker's thread (APOC)
24-gauge white wire
Nile green floristry tape
Nutkin, black, foliage, vine, ruby, aubergine white and tangerine petal dusts
Pale green flowerpaste
Fresh egg white
Edible spray varnish

EQUIPMENT
Scissors
Emery board
Dusting brushes
Rose leaf cutters (Jem)
Large briar rose leaf veiner (SKGI)

Perfumed perfection bouquet

A fairly traditional bouquet shape using very unconventional flowers and foliage. That is the beauty of making flowers in sugar or cold porcelain – artistic licence allows the creator to use whatever components they fancy.

MATERIALS AND EQUIPMENT

22- and 20-gauge white wires
Nile green floristry tape
Fine-nose pliers
Wire cutters or floristry scissors

FLOWERS AND FOLIAGE

5 trailing stems of decorative yam foliage (p 21)
3 white perfume flowers (p 18)
7 ylang-ylang flowers (p 22)
15 ylang-ylang leaves (p 23)
5 groups of ylang-ylang berries (p 23)
5 perfume flower leaves (p 20)

PREPARATION

1 Strengthen any of the flower and foliage stems that require extra support or length by taping 22- or 20-gauge white wires into the main stems using half-width nile green floristry tape. The gauge of the wire will depend on the weight of each item.

ASSEMBLY/CONSTRUCTION

2 Take two lengths of decorative yam foliage, one longer than the other, and bend the end of their stems to a 90-degree angle using fine-nose pliers. Tape the two stems together using half-width nile green floristry tape.

3 Next, add and tape in the three white perfume flowers to create the focal area of the bouquet. Use wire cutters or floristry scissors

to trim off any excess bulk created by the wires. Add a third shorter stem of decorative yam foliage to the left-hand side of the bouquet to balance and create the width of the display.

4 Use the ylang-ylang flowers and leaves to fill in the gaps in the bouquet, using a couple of flowers to exend colour to the bottom length of the bouquet.

5 Use the five groups of ylang-ylang berries to add more interest, positioning the smaller groups at the edges of the display.

6 Finally, add the large perfume flower leaves around the focal area to fill in the remaining gaps.

Moon and sun bouquet

A very dramatic and stunning combination of white and blue crane flowers, spotted scorpion orchids, monstera foliage, eucalyptus and succulent foliage are used here to maximum effect in these complementing bouquets.

MATERIAL AND EQUIPMENT

Wire cutters or large sharp scissors

22- and 18-gauge white wires

Nile green floristry tape

Pewter tankard (optional)

Decorative paper-covered wire

FLOWERS

2 crane flowers plus one set of petals/stamen (p 44)

7 monstera leaves, in assorted sizes (p 49)

2 flapjack kalanchoe (p 89)

3 spotted scorpion orchids (p 68)

2 pale green scorpion orchids (p 68)

2 groups of gum nuts, plus foliage (p 70)

5 umbrella tree stalks (p 71)

5 gingko leaves (p 48)

PREPARATION

1 First of all strengthen/lengthen any of the flower or foliage stems that require it by taping onto extra 22- or 18-gauge white wires using half-width nile green floristry tape.

ASSEMBLY

2 Take one crane flower and then tape three monstera leaves around its neck using full-width nile green floristry tape.

3 Next, add a flapjack kalanchoe rosette where the crane flower stem and the monstera leaves join. Use the single set of crane flower petals to the left-hand side of the display to balance out the display.

4 Tape in two spotted scorpion orchids to the left-hand side of the display, then add the pale green scorpion orchid diagonally opposite to balance the shape and colour.

5 Add a group of gum nuts and their foliage and a few umbrella stalks to the edges of the bouquet to soften them. Place the bouquet into a pewter tankard supported by a ball of tangled decorative paper-covered wire.

6 Tape together the second crane flower with the remaining flowers and foliage into an informal group using full-width nile green floristry tape to secure them. Rest the spray at the base of the tankard to complete the design.

Magical sensation spray

I love working with dark, rich red flowers. Here, a dark red rose forms the focal point, with the wonderfully vibrant striped scorpion orchids and dark red-tinged anthuriums adding an instant tropical sensation. The spiky groups of red umbrella tree stalks add an extra touch of drama, creating almost a firework effect at the edges of the spray.

MATERIALS

22-gauge white wires

Nile green floristry tape

EQUIPMENT

Wire cutters

Decorative vase (optional)

FLOWERS

1 dark red rose (p 100)

3 scorpion orchids (p 68)

2 flamingo flowers (p 29)

1 regular anthurium (p 28)

5 sprigs of ylang-ylang berries (p 23)

3 senecio leaves (p 113)

3 groups of gum nuts plus foliage (p 70)

7 umbrella tree stalks (p 71)

PREPARATION

1 Add extra length or strength to any of the components by taping them onto 22-gauge white wire using half-width nile green floristry tape.

ASSEMBLY

2 Take the dark red rose and place the three striped scorpion orchids around it. Tape their stems together using half-width nile green floristry tape. Angle their faces in different directions – there is nothing worse than having them all pointing the same way. Trim off any excess wires using wire cutters.

3 Next, tape the two red-tinged flamingo anthuriums plus one regular anthurium opposite each other on either side of the rose to fill some space in between the orchids. Add the sprigs of ylang-ylang berries to add extra length to the spray. The piece at the tip of the spray should be longer than the piece at the back. Remember that when forming sprays, a good guideline is to divide the length into thirds: two-thirds from the tip of the spray to the focal point and the remaining third from the focal point to the top of the spray.

4 Use the senecio leaves and the gum nuts and their foliage to fill in the remaining gaps around the edges of the spray.

5 Finally add the umbrella tree stalks around the edges of the spray. Display the spray on a cake or as pictured here in a suitable container. Add a few umbrella stalks at the base of the display.

Tranquil waters spray

A gentle colour combination of a single blue water lily, white tuberoses and soft-green assorted foliage help to create a very tranquil feel to this pretty spray of flowers.

MATERIALS

22- and 20-guage white wires
Nile green floristry tape

EQUIPMENT

Fine-nose pliers
Decorative silver paper-covered wire
Wire cutters or florist's scissors

FLOWERS

3 trailing stems of piper (p 136)
1 blue Egyptian water lily, plus foliage (p 77)
1 group of King tillandsia leaves (page 103)
3 trailing stems of devil's ivy (p 76)
5 gingko leaves (p 48)
3 stems of tuberose (p 80)

PREPARATION

1 Elongate and strengthen any of the stems that require it by taping them onto 22- or 20-gauge white wires using half-width nile green floristry tape.

ASSEMBLY

2 Tape the three trailing stems of piper foliage behind the blue water lily using half-width nile green floristry tape. Curve the stems to create a relaxed 'S'-shaped spray.

3 Continue adding more foliage around the water lily, starting with a group of tillandsia foliage to the left-hand side of the spray. Add a few trails of devil's ivy and then fill in the gaps with the gingko leaves.

4 Next, add two stems of tuberoses and curve their stems to follow the line of the relaxed 'S'-shape of the spray. Add the third shorter stem to the left-hand side of the spray to balance the form a little more.

5 Finally, add loops and curled trails of decorative silver paper-covered wire, taping them tightly in place with half-width nile green floristry tape. Trim off any excess wire using wire cutters or florist's scissors as you go. Use fine-nose pliers to bend and reposition any of the flowers and leaves to create a more relaxed end result.

Masdevallia orchid

There are many types of masdevallia orchid native to central and South America. The one shown here is a very simple form that is quick, easy and very effective to use on a cake.

LATERAL SEPALS

1 The three petal-like shapes are actually the flower's dorsal and lateral sepals, with the labellum and lateral petals being very tiny at the centre of the flower. They are so tiny that I decided to leave them out and concentrate on the three outer sepals, which makes the process a much quicker one. The three sepals are all made using the same method. You need to make two larger lateral sepals and a much smaller dorsal sepal. Work a ball of well-kneaded white flowerpaste onto a fine wire. Work the paste so that it is broad at the base and very fine at the tip. The wire should support the whole length of the petal.

2 Place the petal against the non-stick board and flatten it using the smooth side of the stargazer B petal veiner – this will thin out the petal and create a much broader shape. With practice the shapes will start to conform to that required, although from time to time you will need to trim the shape with a sharp pair of fine scissors.

3 Soften the edges and then place into the double-sided stargazer B petal veiner to texture. Pinch from the base to the tip to accentuate the central vein. Repeat to make a mirror image pair of lateral sepals. Tape them together with quarter-width white floristry tape.

4 Repeat the process with a 33-gauge wire and less paste to create the dorsal sepal. Tape it tightly onto the lateral sepals and curl the tip.

5 Add a small amount of paste to the back of the flower to create a neck. Blend the paste into the back of the petals using the broad end of the dresden tool. Draw fine lines onto the neck with the plain-edge cutting wheel. Tape over the main stem with quarter-width nile green tape.

COLOURING

6 These orchids can be white, cream, yellow, orange, pink or red, and variations in between, too. I have used layers of plum, African violet and a touch of aubergine to create the flowers shown here.

MATERIALS

White flowerpaste
24-, 30- and 33-gauge white wires
White and nile green floristry tape
Plum, African violet and aubergine petal dusts
Edible spray varnish (Fabilo)

EQUIPMENT

Non-stick board
Stargazer B petal veiner (SKGI)
Sharp fine scissors
Dresden tool
Plain-edge cutting wheel (PME)
Dusting brushes

Flapjack kalanchoe

These wonderful succulents belong to the *Kalanchoe* family. There are over 125 species in this family, with many of them producing pretty flowers. Other common names include desert cabbage and paddle plant. I love how fleshy the leaves of the Flapjack kalanchoe are. They fill space and provide interest and character to flower arrangements. They are made freehand and with no veiners, so they are quick to make and perfect for the novice sugarcrafter.

LEAVES

1 Roll a ball of well-kneaded pale green flowerpaste. Form it into a cone shape and insert a 26-, 24- or 22-gauge white wire moistened with fresh egg white into the finer end of the cone. The exact wire gauge you use will depend on the size of leaf you are making.

2 Next, flatten the shape using your fingers and thumb, pinching a thinned-out ridge along the top end of the leaf, which will help create more of a fan-shaped formation.

3 Press the leaf between your palms to pick up some palm-print veined texture to the leaf. Pinch the leaf at the base and curve and bend the top edge slightly to give a little more movement. Use a large metal ball tool to hollow out the centre of each leaf slightly. Repeat to make numerous leaves in graduating sizes.

ASSEMBLY AND COLOURING

4 Tape two of the smaller leaves together using Nile green floristry tape before the flowerpaste dries out and they can snuggle tightly together. Continue adding leaves around two central leaves using half-width nile green floristry tape until the required size of succulent is created.

5 Dust the base of each leaf on the back and front with a mixture of foliage, woodland and edelweiss petal dusts. Catch the top edges with a mixture of plum, ruby and coral petal dusts. Over-dust with aubergine. Allow to dry and then spray lightly with edible spray varnish.

MATERIALS

Pale green flowerpaste
26-, 24- and 22-gauge white wires
Fresh egg white
Nile green floristry tape
Foliage, woodland, edelweiss, plum, ruby, coral and aubergine petal dusts
Edible spray varnish

EQUIPMENT

Non-stick rolling pin
Large metal ball tool
Large flat dusting brushes

Senecio

I came across this succulent recently in a garden centre – its name struck me as fun – *Senecio* 'Kilimanjaro'. However, its size and simplicity to make also appealed to me. Succulents are wonderful to make, being fairly quick and providing a bulk that fills an arrangement quickly and effectively.

MATERIALS

30-, 28- and 26-gauge white wires
Pale green flowerpaste
Fresh egg white
Nile green floristry tape
Forest, foliage, white, edelweiss and aubergine petal dusts
Edible spray varnish

EQUIPMENT

Wire cutters
Plain-edge cutting wheel
Dusting brushes
Fine-nose pliers

LEAVES

1 Cut several short lengths of 30-, 28- or 26-gauge white wires, depending on the size of leaves you are making. Next, take a piece of well-kneaded pale green flowerpaste and form it into a ball. Insert a wire moistened with fresh egg white into the ball and then carefully work the flowerpaste down the wire to create the length of the leaf. Smooth the leaf between your palms.

2 Use the plain-edge cutting wheel to mark a single line down the leaf to represent the central vein. Repeat to make leaves in varying sizes.

ASSEMBLY

3 The leaves may be dusted before assembly – I prefer to assemble and then colour them as they are easier to handle this way. Use a 26-gauge white wire as a leader wire to start taping a few smaller leaves around the end using half-width nile green floristry tape. Continue adding leaves around the wire, gradually increasing in size as you work. If the leaves are still pliable this will allow you to reshape them a little to give a more realistic effect.

COLOURING

4 Mix together forest, foliage and white (edelweiss in mats) petal dusts. Use a large dusting brush to apply colour all over the leaves and the main stem. Add tinges of aubergine petal dust here and there if desired to help break up the space. Allow to dry and then spray lightly with edible spray varnish.

Anthurium

These exotic heart-shaped flowers originate from the rain forests of Columbia, although they are now cultivated in most flower-growing areas of the world. They are often known as 'painter's palette' flowers and exist in a vast selection of colour combinations.

MATERIALS

Fresh anthuruim flower

White flowerpaste

24- and 22-gauge white wires

Fresh egg white

Cornflower

Sunflower, daffodil, edelweiss, plum, coral, vine, moss-green aubergine and ruby petal dusts

Edible spray varnish

Nile green floristry tape

EQUIPMENT

Homemade spadix veiner (see opposite)

Non-stick rolling pin

Dusting brushes

Plain-edge cutting wheel

Foam pad

Large metal ball tool

Flamingo anthurium spathe veiner (Aldaval)

Dimple foam

Cotton wool

Fine paintbrush

SPADIX

1 First of all you need to buy a fresh anthurium flower to make a mould of the pointed textured spadix. Try to find a flower that has plenty of raised dots on the surface of the spadix. Use a silicone moulding paste (see page 7 for more information on making a mould). Form a ball of well-kneaded white flowerpaste and insert a 22-gauge white wire moistened with fresh egg white into it. Work the paste down the wire to create the required length and thickness – this does vary quite a bit between the various types of anthurium. Place the spadix into the silicone mould. Squeeze the sides of the mould against the soft flowerpaste to texture the surface, then remove from the mould. Allow to set a little and decide if you want a straight spadix or a slightly curved one. This will depend on the variety you are making. Allow to dry.

SPATHE

2 Roll out some white flowerpaste (or your chosen colour) fairly thickly leaving a thicker ridge for the wire. Remember this is quite a waxy flower and the veiner has strong veins that will cut through the paste if it is too thin. Insert a 22-gauge white wire moistened with fresh egg white into the thick ridge to

support about half the length. Dust the flowerpaste with cornflour and carefully position it into the double-sided anthurium spathe veiner. Press the two sides of the veiner firmly into the paste to texture it.

3 Remove the shape from the mould and carefully cut out around the edge with the plain-edge cutting wheel or a pair of sharp scissors. Pinch the paste down the centre and then dry on some dimpled foam with pads of cotton wool or kitchen paper to support the shape.

COLOURING

4 The colouring will depend on the variety you are making. The spadix shown has been dusted at the base with a mixture of coral and plum petal dusts and a mix of vine and moss green at the tip. Colour the spathe as desired. Here, vine green and edelweiss petal dusts have been used with an over dust of vine and moss green to catch the edges and ridges of the spathe. The darker forms have been coloured to various degrees with coral and plum and an overdusting of aubergine. Spray with edible spray varnish to give a glossy finish. Tape the spadix onto the spathe with half-width nile green floristry tape.

Flamingo flower

Anthurium scherzeranum is native to Guatemala and Costa Rica. They have a gentle shape and veining, and once again, the colour range is vast. Its common name comes from the curly formation of the spadix.

MATERIALS

White flowerpaste

24- and 22-gauge white wires

Sunflower, daffodil, edelweiss, plum, coral, vine, aubergine and ruby petal dusts

Fresh egg white

Isopropyl alcohol

Nile green floristry tape

Edible spray varnish

EQUIPMENT

Nutmeg grater or homemade spadix veiner (see opposite)

Dusting brushes

Non-stick rolling pin

Plain-edge cutting wheel

Foam pad

Large metal ball tool

Flamingo anthurium spathe veiner (Aldaval)

Dimple foam

Cotton wool

Fine paintbrush

SPADIX

1 Attach a ball of well-kneaded white flowerpaste to the end of a 24-gauge white wire. Work the flowerpaste down the wire to create a slender spadix. Texture it using either a nutmeg grater or a homemade spadix veiner. Allow to firm up a little before curling into a flamingo neck shape.

2 Dust as desired. The paler pink flower pictured has the spadix dusted with a light mixture of sunflower, daffodil and edelweiss petal dusts. The two darker flowers were dusted at the base fading towards the tip with a mixture of plum, coral and edelweiss petal dusts. Use a little of the colour from the tip towards the base too, leaving a paler area mid-way.

SPATHE

3 Roll out some well-kneaded white or pale-coloured flowerpaste, leaving a thick ridge for the wire. Use the template on page 141 and the plain-edge cutting wheel to cut out the spathe, or simply cut out freehand. Insert a 24- or 22-gauge white wire moistened with fresh egg white into the thick ridge to support about a third to half the length.

4 Place the wired spathe onto the foam pad and soften the edges, working half on the flowerpaste and half on the foam pad with a large metal ball tool. Use a rolling action to thin the edge, but do not frill. Texture the spathe using the double-sided flamingo anthurium spathe veiner. Press firmly to give a stronger veining. Remove and hollow out the back slightly using your fingers and thumb. Curve the shape as desired. Pinch from the base through to the tip to accentuate the central vein. Leave to dry, supported with dimpled foam and cotton wool.

COLOURING

5 The flowers pictured were dusted using a mixture of plum, coral and edelweiss petal dusts. Working from the base fading out towards the middle, catch the edges and increase the colour at the tip. Introduce a light mixture of vine and edelweiss, or use aubergine petal dust to create a very dark spathe colour. The darkest of the three flowers has extra depth of colour, added by painting the spathe with a mixture of isopropyl alcohol and aubergine, and also veins added using a diluted mixture of ruby petal dust and isopropyl alcohol. Tape the spadix onto the spathe using half-width nile green floristry tape. Allow to dry and then spray a few times lightly with edible spray varnish.

Zinnia

Originally from Mexico, the zinnia is grown worldwide. Their bright and brash colour combinations are wonderful to reproduce in sugar and cold porcelain. There are many varieties of zinnias, with some forming double flowers. I have kept my version as a simple single variety. The centre of the zinnia is very time consuming to make as it is made up of tiny individual flowers.

MATERIALS

Yellow and green cold porcelain
22-, 26-, 28- and 30-gauge white wires
Green sisal
Non-toxic hi-tack glue (Impex)
Sunflower, vine, foliage, coral, tangerine,
   plum, ruby and aubergine petal dusts
White and green flowerpaste
Nile green floristry tape
Fresh egg white

EQUIPMENT

Celstick or ceramic silk veining tool
Fine sharp scissors
Fine-nose pliers
Dusting brushes
Rolling pin
Non-stick board
Single petal daisy cutter
Plain-edge cutting wheel (PME)
Small ball tool
Wire cutters
8-petal daisy cutter
Heart-shaped rose petal cutter (AD) or
   see templates on page 141
Mock orange leaf veiner (SKGI)

CENTRE

1 Although the centre can be made with flowerpaste I prefer to make it with cold porcelain as the individual flowers are very fiddly to make and are also quite fragile. Roll a tiny ball of yellow cold porcelain and then form it into a cone shape.

2 Open up the broad end of the cone using the pointed end of a celstick or ceramic tool. Using fine sharp scissors, cut the edge to create five petals.

3 Pinch each petal between your finger and thumb to create five pointed petal shapes. Flatten each petal in turn between your finger and thumb. Repeat to make numerous flowers and leave to dry.

4 Bend a hook in the end of a 22-gauge wire using fine-nose pliers. Attach a ball of green cold porcelain paste onto it. Shred some green sisal (available from art shops and florists). Lightly apply non-toxic hi-tack glue over the ball and roll it in the sisal to texture it. Leave to dry. Dust with vine green and foliage petal dusts.

5 Attach the dried tiny flowers onto the sisal-coated centre using a tiny amount of non-toxic hi-tack glue to hold them in place. Dust the flowers with sunflower petal dust.

OUTER PETALS

6 The number of petals varies between varieties – usually from eight upwards. Roll out some white paste leaving a thick ridge for the wire. Cut out a petal shape using the single petal daisy cutter.

7 Insert a 30- or 28-gauge white wire into the base of the thick ridge on the petal. Hold the petal firmly between your finger and thumb so that the wire does not pierce through the petal.

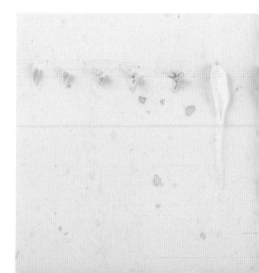

8 Using a fine pair of scissors, cut a slight indent from the tip of the petal. Use the plain-edge cutting wheel to draw a few veins onto the petal. Turn the petal over and hollow out the underside slightly using a small ball tool. Pinch the petal from the base to the tip to accentuate the central vein. Repeat to make the required number of petals.

COLOURING AND ASSEMBLY

9 Dust the upper surface of the petal with the desired colour of petal dust. Here I have used a mixture of plum, tangerine and coral petal dust. Try to keep the undersides much paler.

10 Tape the petals around the centre using half-width nile green floristry tape. Trim off excess wires as you work to cut down on some of the bulk behind the flower.

CALYX

11 Roll a ball of green flowerpaste and form it into a long teardrop shape. Pinch out the broad end so that the shape looks like a wizard's hat. Thin out the brim using a celstick or ceramic tool. Cut out the calyx shape using the 8-petal daisy cutter. Soften each petal and then draw a line down each to create central veins. Open up the centre of the calyx using the pointed end of a celstick.

12 Roll out some more green paste and cut out another calyx shape using the 8-petal daisy cutter. Soften and vein as before and then place on top of the first calyx, making sure that the sepals are positioned to cover a join in the first layer.

13 Carefully thread the calyx onto the back of the flower using a little fresh egg white to secure it in place. Work the neck of the calyx to refine it slightly. Trim off the excess.

14 Dust with foliage and vine green petal dusts. Add tinges of aubergine to the edges.

FOLIAGE

15 Roll out some green paste leaving a ridge for the wire. Cut out the leaf shape using the heart-shaped rose petal cutter or the heart-shaped rose petal templates on page 141. Insert a moistened 28- or 26-gauge white wire into the thick ridge. Soften the edges and then vein using the mock orange leaf veiner. Repeat to make leaves in pairs.

16 Dust with foliage and vine green. Add a tinge of ruby/aubergine to the edges. Tape in pairs down the flower stems. Dust the stem as for the leaves.

Butterfly flower bouquet

Exotic orange butterfly flowers have huge impact in this eye-catching bouquet combined with Joseph's coat foliage and *Zantedeschia* berries. The display is completed with the addition of a tropical fantasy butterfly.

MATERIALS AND EQUIPMENT

22-gauge white wires

Nile green floristry tape

Green, yellow and orange paper-covered decorative wires

Wire cutters

Yew wood vase (optional)

FLOWERS

3 orange butterfly flowers and 5 leaves (p 34–36)

7 Joseph's coat leaves (p 38)

3 stems of *Zantedeschia* berries (p 37)

1 fantasy butterfly (p 92)

PREPARATION

1 Strengthen the flower or foliage stems by taping 22-gauge white wire onto the main stems using half-width nile green floristry tape. Take a few lengths of green, yellow and orange paper-covered decorative wires and plait them together – not too neatly or tightly.

ASSEMBLY

2 Tape together the three orange butterfly flowers into a group using the largest/prettiest flower as the focal point. Add a few of its own foliage to fill in the gaps.

3 Use the Joseph's coat leaves to surround and frame the flowers. Trim off any excess bulk wire from the handle at the back of the bouquet using wire cutters. Tape over with half-width nile green floristry tape.

4 Use the *zantedeschia* berries spaced around the flowers to extend the shape of the bouquet and add further interest.

5 Finally, add the length of plaited paper-covered decorative wires to trail at the base of the bouquet. Use a few more loops of wire at the back of the bouquet too. Tape over the handle of the bouquet with full-width nile green floristry tape. Thread the wire of the butterfly into the bouquet and tape it onto the handle. Curve its wire to blend with the plaited wires. Display in a suitable container.

Cosmos

There are about 26 species in the Cosmos family. The family originates from Mexico although the plants have naturalized themselves in many other parts of the world. Commonly the flowers are white, pink or lavender but there are also red, orange, yellow and dark chocolate-coloured varieties. For the brave at heart there are also semi-double and double forms!

MATERIALS
White seed-head stamens
Non-toxic hi-tack craft glue (Impex)
White or pale pink, and pale green flowerpaste
22-, 26-, 28-, 30-, 33- and 35-gauge white wires
Plum, aubergine, African violet, foliage and vine green petal dusts
Nile green floristry tape

EQUIPMENT
Fine sharp scissors
Australian rose petal set (TT349-352)
Rolling pin
Non-stick board
Dresden tool (J)
Ball tool
Small cosmos petal veiner (SKGI)
Dusting brushes
Plain-edge cutting wheel
Wire cutters

Bond each group at the centre using non-toxic hi-tack glue. Squeeze the glue into the length of the stamens to create an even line but make sure the tips and a little of the length is left unglued to create a natural finish in the final centre. Allow the glue to set a little and then cut the stamens in half and trim off the excess to create fairly short stamens that are held together by a fine line of glue.

PETALS

2 You may need to adjust the shape of the rose petal cutter by squashing it to make a narrow petal (see templates on page 140). Roll out some white or pale pink flowerpaste, leaving a thick ridge for the wire.

3 Cut out the petal shape using the largest of the Australian rose petal cutters. Moisten a 28-gauge white wire and insert into about a third to half the length of the thick ridge in the petal. Pinch the base to secure it to the wire.

4 Place the petal topside down and work the top edge into three or four rough points using the broad end of the dresden tool. Soften the side edges of the petal using a ball tool.

5 Vein the petal using the double-sided cosmos petal veiner. Remove from the veiner and curl the edges backwards or forwards slightly, depending on the look you want – gradually unfurling or open and sunning itself! Make eight petals.

CENTRE

1 The centre can be made with solid flowerpaste but I prefer to use seed-head stamens to give a more freestyle feel to the flower. You will need to use about a quarter to half bunch of seed-head stamens to create the centre. Divide the stamens into smaller groups and line up the tips so that they are roughly the same height in each group.

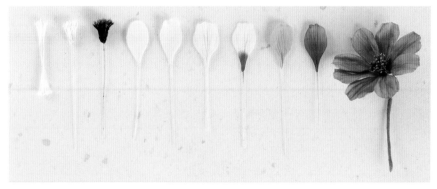

COLOURING

6 For a white flower dust a patch of plum petal dust on both sides at the base of each petal. For a pink flower use plum dust and perhaps add a tinge of aubergine or African violet at the base. The back is much paler than the front.

ASSEMBLY

7 Tape the eight petals around the stamens using quarter-width nile green floristry tape. Keep the petals quite high up against the stamens, adding a 22-gauge wire to elongate the stem. If the petals are still soft at this stage you will be able to add movement to the flower or decide if you want to close the petals in tighter to represent a just-opening flower. Leave to dry and then steam to set the colour.

CALYX

8 There are two layers of calyces. I prefer to make each sepal individually but you can also use an eight-petal daisy cutter if you prefer. Form eight small, fine, teardrop shapes of green paste and then flatten each of them. Mark a single line down the length of each and attach this side against each petal.

9 The second layer can be made with paste but these are finer and longer than the first calyx so you might prefer to use eight twisted lengths of quarter-width nile green floristry tape instead. Whichever you decide on, position these sepals in between those of the first layer. Dust with vine green and foliage. Tinges of aubergine can work wonders too.

BUDS

10 Roll a ball of green paste and insert a hooked, moistened 26-gauge wire into the base. Pinch the ball to secure it to the wire. Use a plain-edge cutting wheel or sharp scalpel to divide the surface into eight sections. Indent each section using the broad end of the dresden tool. This represents the first layer of sepals. Dust with foliage, vine and aubergine petal dusts. Add an outer calyx as for the flower.

LEAVES

11 These leaves can be made with floristry tape or rolled sections of flowerpaste – the latter is very fragile but very effective. If you decide you are brave enough to tackle the paste version then you will need short lengths of 35- or 33-gauge wire. Work a tiny amount of green paste onto the end of a wire, forming a fine strand with a fine end. Roll a separate fine strand of paste and fold in half and then attach at the base of the central wired strand.

12 Flatten the sections slightly and, if you feel confident, cut into each section with a fine pair of scissors to create a more frond-like finish. Repeat this process to make several leaf sections and then tape together using quarter-width nile green floristry tape.

13 Dust very carefully with foliage, vine and tinges of aubergine petal dusts. The tape version is constructed in a similar way but using twisted strands of quarter-width floristry tape instead.

14 Tape the buds and flowers together, adding sets of foliage in various sizes every time you join a bud or flower onto the main stem. Add a stronger wire for support if needed. Dust the main stem with foliage and vine green. Add a little aubergine to one side of the stem – this is usually where the sunlight hits the plant.

Fantasy butterflies

A few years ago my friend and very talented cake decorator John Quai Hoi introduced me to his wired sugar butterflies. I have been hooked on making them ever since! You might decide to copy the wing designs of real butterflies but I find them more fun made with a fantasy approach.

MATERIALS

35-, 33-, 28- and 26-gauge white wires
White flowerpaste
Fresh egg white
Seed-head stamens
Non-stick rolling pin
Cornflour bag (p 11)
White or nile green floristry tape
Vine, African violet, plum and aubergine petal dusts
Isopropyl alcohol
Hi-tack non-toxic craft glue (optional)
Non-toxic disco glitters (EA) (optional)

EQUIPMENT

Fine-nose pliers
Scalpel or plain-edge cutting wheel
Non-stick rolling pin
Butterfly cutters (Jem) or templates on p 227
Metal ball tool
Hibiscus petal veiner (SKGI) or anemone petal veiner (Aldval)
Dusting brushes
Fine paintbrushes

THE BODY

1 The body can be made as an all-in-one shape and divided into sections using a scalpel or you can make it as I do in three sections joined together. Using fine-nose pliers, bend a hook in the end of a 26-gauge white wire. Roll a ball of white flowerpaste for the centre of the body (thorax) and insert the wire moistened with fresh egg white into it. Pinch it firmly to secure the two together. Next, roll a smaller ball of white flowerpaste for the head and stick it onto one side of the body with fresh egg white. Divide this section in half using the scalpel or plain edge-cutting wheel to create two eyes. Form a carrot shape and attach at the other side of the body to represent the abdomen.

2 Curl a short length of 35- or 33-gauge white wire to represent the tongue (proboscis) and insert into the head area, through the body and into the tail – this should help to give more support to the whole shape.

3 Cut one seed-head stamen in half to give two lengths to represent the antennae. Trim both a little shorter if desired and insert one into each eye. Leave to dry.

WINGS

The butterfly cutters that I prefer contain the four wing sections in one plastic piece – it drives me nuts. So I have taken a large pair of scissors to my set and cut them in half – I find this much easier to deal with now!

4 Roll out some well-kneaded white flowerpaste, leaving a fine ridge for the wire. Cut out the larger wing section using the wing cutter. Carefully remove the shape from the cutter and insert a 28-gauge white wire moistened with fresh egg white into the thick ridge to support about half the length of the wing.

5 Soften the edge with the metal ball tool and then texture the wing using the double-sided hibiscus or anemone petal veiner. Dust the wing with cornflour prior to veining to prevent it sticking to the veiner and take care not to press too hard so that you don't cut through the paste.

6 Pinch the wing from the base to the tip to give a little movement. Repeat to make the opposite wing section plus the two smaller lower wings. Leave to firm a little before assembling and colouring.

ASSEMBLY AND COLOURING

7 Tape the larger forewings onto either side of the body using white or nile green floristry tape. Position and tape the smaller hind wings slightly behind the forewings.

8 As these are fantasy butterflies, you can colour them as you desire or even just leave them white. I have used layers of vine green at the base of the wings and a mixture of African violet and plum on the edges.

9 Dilute some aubergine petal dust with isopropyl alcohol and paint over the body, antennae and proboscis using a fine paintbrush. Add detail spots and catch the extreme tips with this diluted colour too. Allow to dry.

10 If you feel like a bit of glitz, then simply apply a thin layer of non-toxic craft glue to the tips of the wings and the antennae and dip into disco glitter – please note that although these glitters are non-toxic they are not a food item! Therefore I would only recommend that you use the glitter to decorate items that are not intended to be eaten.

Butterflies and flowers

Stencilled butterflies echo and complement the more dominant butterfly flowers of the trailing bouquet on this small birthday cake design.

MATERIALS

15 cm (6 in) curved heart-shaped fruitcake placed on a thin cake board of the same size

23 cm (9 in) round cake drum

450 g (1 lb) white almond paste

450g (1 lb) white sugarpaste

Fine and broad orange satin ribbon

Clear alcohol (Cointreau or kirsch)

Non-toxic glue stick

Small amount of white flowerpaste

Vine, white, tangerine, coral and aubergine petal dusts

EQUIPMENT

Straight-edged sugarpaste smoother

Non-stick rolling pin

Non-stick board

Butterfly stencil (J)

Dusting brushes

Scalpel

Fine paintbrush

Non-slip mat

Perspex tilting cake stand (Cc)

FLOWERS

Butterfly flower bouquet (p 194)

PREPARATION

1 Cover the cake and cake drum as described on pages 16–17. Position the cake on top of the coated drum and use the straight-edge sugarpaste smoother to blend the join between the cake and board. Allow to dry for a few days.

2 Attach a band of fine orange satin ribbon to the base of the cake, using a small amount of sugarpaste softened with clear alcohol to hold it in place. Secure a band of broad orange satin ribbon to the cake drum's edge using non-toxic glue.

STENCIL DESIGN

3 Roll out a little well-kneaded white flowerpaste thinly onto the non-stick board. Peel the flowerpaste off the board and flip it over so that the sticky side is uppermost. Place the butterfly stencil on top of the sticky flowerpaste to hold it in place. Next, use petal dusts to colour in the various sections of the butterfly design. Use a mixture of vine and white petal dusts at the base of each wing. Use tangerine and coral petal dusts mixed together for the outer area of each wing.

4 Remove the stencil from flowerpaste. Use the scalpel to cut out around the dusted butterfly design. Place to one side and repeat the process to create three stencilled butterflies. Attach onto the cake and drum using clear alcohol. Dilute some aubergine petal dust with clear alcohol and paint the body and antennae using a fine paintbrush and then add spots to the wings and detail to the tips of each wing section too.

5 Assemble the butterfly bouquet as described on page 194. Put a piece of non-slip mat onto the tilt of the Perspex cake stand and place the cake on top of it. Rest and position the butterfly bouquet at the base of the cake stand to complete the design.

200

Blue butterfly bush

The pretty blooms of Clerodendrum ugandense are wonderful as filler flowers on a cake where a blue element is needed. In the past I have made this flower as a single cut-out flower. However, it is much easier to wire each petal resulting in a stronger finished flower.

MATERIALS

Non-toxic hi-tack craft glue (Impex)
White seed-head stamens
28- and 33-gauge white wires
Ultramarine craft dust
African violet, deep purple and edelweiss petal dusts
White flowerpaste
Nile green floristry tape

EQUIPMENT

Scissors
Dusting brushes
Wire cutters
Non-stick board
Stargazer B petal veiner (optional)
Fine-nose pliers
Sharp scalpel
Small metal ball tool

STAMENS

1 Glue together five seed-head stamens with non-toxic hi-tack glue. Make one stamen stand longer than the others to represent the pistil. Cut off the tip of the pistil and when the glue has set cut off the tips from the base too. Glue onto a 33-gauge white wire. Pinch and leave to dry.

2 Curl the stamens. Dust the tips with a mixture of ultramarine craft dust and African violet petal dust. Dust the length of the stamens with the blue mixture mixed with a touch of edelweiss.

PETALS

3 Cut five short lengths of 33-gauge white wire. Attach a ball of well-kneaded white flowerpaste to the end of a wire and work it into a slight point at the tip and taper the base to form a slender neck. Place the shape onto the board and flatten it using the smooth side of the stargazer B petal veiner.

4 Vein the petal using the textured sides of the double-sided veiner and then hollow out the length of the petal using the small metal ball tool. Repeat to make four same-sized petals and one slightly longer petal.

5 Tape the five petals onto the stamens using quarter-width nile green floristry tape, with the longest petal positioned directly opposite the stamens so that they curve towards it.

6 Dust the petals using a mixture of edelweiss, African violet and ultramarine. For the longest petal use a stronger version, omitting the white petal dust.

BUDS

7 Cut short lengths of 28-gauge wires. Bend a hook in the end of each length. Attach a ball of paste to the end of each wire and roll the base slightly to form a neck. Divide the tip into five using a sharp scalpel. Dust with vine green and a little of the blue mixture, plus a touch of deep purple.

CAKES

Butterfly cake

A single butterfly used at the base of this pretty heart-shaped celebration cake helps to balance the overall design.

MATERIALS
25-cm (10-in) heart-shaped fruitcake
Apricot glaze
Icing sugar, sifted
1.25 kg (2 lb 10 oz) white almond paste
2 kg (4½ lb) champagne sugarpaste,
    to cover cake and boards
Clear alcohol (kirsch or Cointreau)
Silk-effect ivory paper, to trim the cake
Small amount of royal icing
Lemon yellow paper-covered wire
Edible gold leaf
Vine, foliage, daffodil, sunflower, edelweiss
    and black petal dusts
Flowerpaste
26- and 30-gauge white wires
Fine stamens
Nile green floristry tape
Decorative green ribbon, to trim the board
Non-toxic glue stick (Pritt) or corsage pins
Posy pick

EQUIPMENT
25-cm (10-in) heart-shaped thin cake board
Pastry brush
Rolling pin
Make-up sponge
Sugarpaste smoothers
35-cm (14-in) heart-shaped thin cake board
Leaf paper punch
Fine paintbrush
Butterfly cutter (Jem)
Anemone petal veiner (ALDV)
Fine-nose pliers
Sharp scalpel
Dusting brushes

FLOWERS
Crescent spray (see pages 170–1)

PREPARATION

1 Place the cake onto the same size board. Brush the cake with warmed apricot glaze and cover with white almond paste. If time allows leave the cake to dry overnight. Roll out the sugarpaste. Moisten the surface of the almond paste with clear alcohol using a make-up sponge. Cover the cake with sugarpaste using the sugarpaste smoothers to create a neat finish.

2 Lightly moisten and then cover the larger heart-shaped board with a layer of sugarpaste and trim off the excess. Transfer the cake to sit centrally on top of it. Blend the join between the base of the cake and the board using the straight-edged sugarpaste smoother. Leave the sugarpaste to firm up for a few hours or even overnight.

3 Secure a length of silk-effect paper ribbon to the sides of the cake using royal icing or softened sugarpaste/alcohol mix to hold it in place. Fasten the lemon yellow paper-covered wire around the base of the cake.

4 Cut out several gold leaf cut-outs using a leaf paper punch. Attach the gold cut-outs to the sides of the cake at intervals using a little clear alcohol. Dilute some foliage and vine green petal dusts and add delicate spotted trails to each cut-out design using a fine paintbrush.

BUTTERFLY

5 Use the butterfly cutter to cut out four wing sections from flowerpaste, leaving a thick ridge in each section. Wire each section onto a 30-gauge white wire. Soften the edges and vein with the anemone petal veiner. Pinch each section from the base to the tip and allow to firm up before painting.

6 To make the body, attach a ball of flowerpaste to a hooked 26-gauge wire. Add a smaller ball for its head and a carrot shape for the tail. Divide the head into two sections using a sharp scalpel and insert a stamen into each to represent the antennae. Texture the body to create a hairy effect using the scalpel. Leave to dry before painting with a diluted mixture of black petal dust and clear alcohol.

7 Tape the wing sections onto the body using quarter-width nile green floristry tape. Dust the wings with vine green and a mixture of daffodil and sunflower petal dusts. Add fine painted detail using the diluted black petal dust. Add white highlights to the tips. When complete, position the butterfly at the point of the cake.

ASSEMBLY

8 Attach a band of decorative green ribbon to the edge of the board using a non-toxic glue stick or corsage pins to hold it in place.

9 Assemble the crescent spray. Insert a posy pick into the cake and place the handle of the spray into it. Adjust and curve the trailing stems of wire vine to create a more relaxed finished display.

Cosmos cake

This pink, iced two-tier wedding cake is adorned with a refreshing combination of pink cosmos and vibrant zinnia blooms. The ornamental grasses help to soften the edges of the sprays and also add an almost rustic quality to the cake design – ideal for a more informal setting.

MATERIALS

13-cm (5-in) and 20-cm (8-in) round rich fruitcakes

Apricot glaze

1kg (2 lb) white almond paste

Icing sugar

1.4 kg (3 lb) white sugarpaste, to cover cake and board

Ruby paste food colour

Clear alcohol (Cointreau or kirsch)

Fine pink satin ribbon, to trim the cakes

Bright pink velvet ribbon, to trim the baseboard

Non-toxic glue stick

EQUIPMENT

13-cm (5-in) and 20-cm (8-in) round thin cake cards

Pastry brush

Rolling pin

Sugarpaste smoothers

Make-up sponge

35-cm (14-in) round cake drum

Floral embosser

Posy pick

FLOWERS

2 pink cosmos flowers, plus buds and foliage (see pages 196)

5 orange zinnias (see pages 192)

25 ornamental grasses (see page 66)

5 sprigs of cotinus foliage (see page 164)

PREPARATION

1 Place each cake onto the thin cake cards of the same size.
Brush both cakes with warmed apricot glaze. Roll out the almond paste on a light dusting of icing sugar. Polish the surface of the paste with a round-edged sugarpaste smoother to even out any unevenness in the rolled paste. Cover each cake in turn. Trim off the excess paste and polish the top of the cake with the round-edged smoother and the sides with the straight-edged smoother to achieve a neat finish. Allow to dry for a couple of days if time allows.

2 Colour the sugarpaste with a little ruby paste food colour. Knead the paste to distribute the colour evenly; be careful not to knead in too many air bubbles into the icing. Allow the paste to rest for a few hours.

3 Moisten the surface of the cake with clear alcohol using a make-up sponge. Roll out the sugarpaste and cover the cake as described above in step 1. An extra polished finish may be achieved by pressing a pad of sugarpaste into your palm and using it to work quickly over the surface. This will also help to soften any cracks in the icing, although cracked edges usually indicate that the sugarpaste has not been kneaded enough.

4 Cover the cake drum with the coloured sugarpaste. Trim off the excess and smooth as for the cake. Position the larger cake centrally on top of the coated board. Use the straight-edged smoother to create a tight, neat join at the base of the cake. Place the smaller cake on top and repeat to create a neat join.

5 Emboss a floral design at intervals around the board edge. Allow the coating to dry for about a day or two if you have time. Attach a fine band of pink ribbon around the base of the two cakes using a small amount of softened sugarpaste/clear alcohol to secure the ribbon in place. Attach a band of bright pink velvet ribbon to the board edge using the non-toxic glue stick.

FLOWERS

6 Wire together two informal sprays, one large and one small. Insert a plastic posy pick into the top tier and then place the handle of the spray into it. Rearrange the grasses if needed to create a more relaxed design. Add the small corsage at the base of the cake.

18th birthday

A cake design suitable for a shoe-loving woman of any age! The feathered texture of the unusual nigella flowers complements the peacock feathers perfectly. The shoe, feathers and side design have been embossed into the sugarpaste coating while the paste was still soft and then painted over with melted coloured cocoa butter.

MATERIALS

25 cm (10 in) round rich fruitcake placed on a thin cake board of the same size

1.25 kg (2 lb 10 oz) white almond paste

2 kg (4½ lb) champagne sugarpaste

Tracing or greaseproof paper

Blue dragées

Mug and saucer

Cocoa butter, grated

White, plum, forest, foliage, vine, white bridal satin, cornflower and African violet petals dusts

Edible gold leaf-covered flowerpaste

Gold braid

Royal icing

Blue organza ribbon

Pins or non-toxic craft glue stick (Pritt)

Gold and pink paper-covered wires

Pink crimped wire

Assorted beads

EQUIPMENT

35 cm (14 in) round thick cake drum

Scriber or pen that has run dry

Plain-edge cutting wheel

Stitch effect wheel (PME)

Small circle cutter set

No.4, No.3 and No.2 piping tubes

Paintbrushes

FLOWERS

2 nigella flowers, plus foliage (p 22–3)

EMBOSSING

1 Cover the cake and cake drum as described on p 16–7. Trace the shoe template on p 259 onto tracing or greaseproof paper and then scribe it onto the surface of the cake using a scriber or a pen that has run dry. Mark the main lines of the feathers using the plain-edge cutting wheel, and the finer lines using the stitch effect wheel. Add the eye markings to the feathers using a series of small circle cutters. Add embossed dots to the sole of the shoe and in amongst the feathers using various sizes of piping tubes. Embed a single blue dragée into the centre of each peacock eye detail.

2 Emboss the side design onto the cake using a series of circle cutters followed by dotted detail and flower embossing with No.4, No.3 and No.2 piping tubes. Again, attach a single dragée into the centre of the flower design. At this stage you might prefer to leave the sugarpaste to dry before painting in the details. I was impatient when I created this cake and so decided to paint directly onto the wet sugarpaste!

COLOURED COCOA PAINTING

3 Melt some grated cocoa butter onto a dish above a mug filled with just-boiled water. Mix in small amounts of petal dusts as they are required to create the painting medium. I have used white and plum for the main colour of the shoe. Allow each layer to set before darkening the mixture to add shaded and defined areas to the design. Paint in the feather lines and trailing vine around the shoe using the various greens mixed with white bridal satin petal dust. Paint over the blue dragées with cornflower blue, African violet and white bridal satin mixed together.

4 Add some dried broken pieces of gold leaf-covered flowerpaste to the heal and front of the shoe (see p 19 for more information).

5 Paint over the embossed side designs to pick up the same colouring as used in the shoe design. The cocoa-painted designs will dry but be careful not to store the cake in a hot room or touch the design too heavily as the design can melt again.

6 Attach a band of gold braid around the base of the cake using a dab of royal icing or softened sugarpaste to hold it in place at the back. Secure two bands of blue organza ribbon to the cake drum's edge using pins or non-toxic craft glue.

7 Tape two corsages using the nigella flowers, gold and pink paper-covered wires and pink crimped wire with beads. Position one spray on top of the cake and the other at the base.

Ruby birthday

This colourful two-tiered cake was designed for a 40th birthday celebration – with the butterfly symbolising just how quickly the years fly by! The bold use of a ruby-coloured peony also makes the design suitable for a ruby anniversary cake or even for a small wedding cake – with the addition of another symbolic butterfly of course!

MATERIALS

Non-toxic glue stick (Pritt) or double-sided stick tape

15-cm (6-in) and 20-cm (8-in) round rich fruitcakes placed on thin cake boards of the same size

1 kg (2 lb) white almond paste

1.4 kg (3 lb) white sugarpaste coloured with bluegrass paste food colour

Fine aqua satin ribbon

Royal icing

Broad colourful floral ribbon

Pins or non-toxic craft glue stick (Pritt)

Tracing or greaseproof paper

Mug and saucer

Cocoa butter, grated

White, plum, aubergine, foliage, vine, bluegrass and sunflower petal dusts

Blue, pink and yellow paper-covered wires

Nile green floristry tape

Large food-grade plastic posy pick

EQUIPMENT

Two 30-cm (12-in) round cake drums

Scriber or a pen that has run dry

Fine paintbrushes

FLOWERS

1 peony, plus foliage (p 45–7)

5 sprigs of pink brunia (p 44)

7 trails of hearts entangled (p 26)

1 fantasy butterfly (p198–9)

PREPARATION

1 Double up the cake drums and stick them together using non-toxic craft glue or doubled-sided sticky tape. Cover the cakes and cake drum as described on p 16–7.

2 Next, position the larger cake on top of the cake drum and then place the smaller cake on top of it. Attach a band of fine aqua satin ribbon around the base of the cakes, using a dab of royal icing or softened sugarpaste to hold it in place. Secure a band of broad floral ribbon to the doubled-up cake drums' edge using pins or non-toxic craft glue.

COCOA PAINTING

3 The side design can be painted freehand or you may prefer to trace the floral design from the template on p 190 onto tracing or greaseproof paper and then scribe the design onto the side of the cakes using a scriber or a pen that has run dry. Melt some grated cocoa butter onto a dish above a mug filled with just-boiled water. Be careful not to apply too much heat as this will make the medium too runny to paint with; equally, if the heat is not sufficient it will be too thick to paint with.

4 Add small amounts of petal dust in turn to execute the floral design using fine paintbrushes. The addition of a touch of white petal dust will create a more opaque painting medium. Use plum to colour the peony flower and buds. Add depth and finer details by adding a touch of aubergine to the plum. Use foliage and vine petal dusts mixed together to paint the foliage, adding more foliage to define the leaf shapes and to add shading. Use bluegrass to paint dotted flowers and flowing lines through the design. Finally, add sunflower yellow petals into the design to soften the edges. Allow the design to dry and if desired, etch away some fine detail lines in the petal and leaf formations.

5 Use the peony as the focal point, surrounded by its foliage and sprigs of brunia. Add trails of coloured paper-covered wires and hearts entangled foliage, holding the flowers together with nile green floristry tape. Add a single wired fantasy butterfly to the bouquet and then insert into a large posy pick pushed into the top tier. Re-arrange any of the elements as required.

80th birthday

This brightly coloured rose and lavender display was designed as a feminine 80th birthday cake. However, it could be used to celebrate any other milestone age or even as a single-tiered wedding cake. The piped leaf side design is very easy to execute and creates an unusual, yet very effective, finish to the design.

MATERIALS

23 cm (9 in) round rich fruitcake placed on a thin cake board of the same size

1 kg (2 lb 3 oz) white almond paste

1.5 kg (3 lb 5 oz) white sugarpaste coloured with gooseberry paste food colour

Lavender braid

Royal icing

Lavender velvet ribbon

Pins or non-toxic craft glue stick (Pritt)

Gooseberry paste food colour

Pearlised dragées

African violet, white bridal satin, plum and gold petal dusts

Clear alcohol (Cointreau or kirsch)

Nile green floristry tape

Food-grade plastic posy pick

EQUIPMENT

33 cm (13 in) round thick cake drum

Piping bag fitted with a leaf tube

Piping bag fitted with a No.1 plain tube

Fine paintbrush

FLOWERS

10 pink roses of varying sizes (p 30–3)

7 epigenium orchids (p 54–6)

12 green beetleweed leaves (p 169)

15 sprigs of French lavender (p 73–4)

7 trails of hearts entangled (p 26)

PREPARATION

1 Cover the cake and cake drum as described on p 16–7. Transfer the cake onto the cake drum and allow to dry at least overnight before piping the side design. Attach a band of lavender braid around the base of the cake, using a dab of royal icing or softened sugarpaste to hold it in place. Secure a band of lavender velvet ribbon to the cake drum's edge using pins or non-toxic craft glue.

PIPED LEAF SIDE DESIGN

2 Colour some royal icing with gooseberry paste food colour to match the depth of colour used in the sugarpaste coating. Fill a piping bag fitted with a leaf tube with a small amount of green royal icing. Pipe a series of leaves onto the side of the cake – you will need to wiggle the bag and tube a little as you pipe to create a little movement to the piped leaves. Allow to dry before continuing.

3 Next, fill a piping bag fitted with a No.1 plain tube with green royal icing. Carefully pipe a dot of royal icing above each leaf to secure a single dragée onto each one. Use the same tube to pipe a leaf shape onto either side of the dragée. If the larger leaf shape is dry enough you can now continue to pipe tiny dots onto the edge of

each leaf. Allow to dry before painting the dragées with a diluted mixture of African violet, white bridal satin and clear alcohol. Use this colouring and a fine paintbrush to highlight the piped dots on the edges of the leaves too. Dilute a small amount of plum petal dust and add extra painted leaf detail above the dragées and use a tiny amount of diluted gold petal dust at the very tip of each of the ornate piped leaves.

4 Assemble the larger posy using the largest rose as the focal flower. Add the other flowers and foliage around this central flower to create a rounded posy-style shape using half-width nile green floristry tape to hold them in place. Soften the edges of the posy using the hearts entangled foliage to twine around the display. Insert the handle of the posy into the posy pick and insert this into the cake. Tape together a smaller spray, again using a rose as the focal point and add the remaining sprigs of flowers and foliage to create a slightly tapered display. Rest this spray at the base of the cake to complete the design.

Pearl anniversary

This pretty two-tiered 30th pearl anniversary cake features pearlised sugar dragées and a bouquet of pretty green and pink orchids. This cake could also serve as a wedding cake.

MATERIALS

15 cm (6 in) curved heart dummy cake
25 cm (10 in) curved heart rich fruitcake placed on a thin cake board of the same size
Silver cake board paper
1.25 kg (2 lb 10 oz) white almond paste
1.4 kg (3 lb) white sugarpaste coloured with gooseberry green paste food colour
Green floral ribbon
Royal icing
Large corsage pins
Gold organza material
Pearl dragées in various sizes (APOC)
Edible gold/silver leaf-covered flowerpaste
White bridal satin, plum, African violet and green lustre petal dusts
Clear alcohol (Cointreau or kirsch)
Green paper-covered wire
Nile green floristry tape
Gold wire

EQUIPMENT

Tall tilting cake stand (CC)
Piping bag fitted with a No.1 piping tube
Fine paintbrush
Tall glass bottle

FLOWERS

3 stems of Vincent orchids (p 176)
5 moth orchids (p 60–2)
5 epigenium orchids (p 54–6)
3 pachyveria succulents (p 177)
10 trails of hearts entangled (p 26)

I prefer to use a dummy cake for the extreme tilt of the top tier as it is lighter than a real cake. The bottom tier is a real fruitcake and is displayed at less of a tilt. Cake boards for this shape are not commercially available so it is a case of finding a kind soul to cut the boards for you and then cover them with silver cake board paper. Cover both the dummy cake and the fruitcake as described on p 16 (but leave off the white almond paste covering on the dummy cake).

1 Attach a band of green floral ribbon around the base of each cake, using a dab of royal icing or softened sugarpaste to hold it in place. Alternatively, wet the ribbon, remove the excess water and then wrap it around the cake – this makes the ribbon sticky and adheres the two together. The ribbon eventually dries to an even colour.

2 Position the smaller dummy cake onto the tilting cake stand using large corsage pins to hold it in place. Wrap some gold organza material around the stand and pin this into the base of the cake too.

3 Attach the various sizes of pearl dragées in groups around the curve of each cake, using small piped dots of royal icing to secure them. The flakes of gold and silver leaf are simply leftover pieces of gold and silver leaf-coated flowerpaste from other

projects (see p 19 for more information) that were broken up to leave shards that are ideal for adding interest to a design. Attach these too with royal icing.

4 Dilute some white bridal satin, plum and African violet petal dusts with clear alcohol and paint over some of the dragées. Do the same with the green lustre petal dust and then add painted dotted lines to connect the dragées groups together.

5 Form the outline of the bouquet by plaiting several lengths of green paper-covered wire – try not to make the end result too neat. Curve the plaits into almost a heart shape. Add a tangled ball of green paper-covered wire at the centre of the heart shape: this will bulk up the focal area. Next, tape in the three stems of Vincent orchids, following the heart outline of the bouquet using half-width nile green floristry tape. Use the moth orchids at the centre of the display to create the focal point; these should stand slightly higher than any of the other flowers in the bouquet. Add the epigenium orchids to fill in around the moth orchids. Finally, add the pachyveria succulents, trails of hearts entangled and lengths of curled gold wire to complete the bouquet. Position the bouquet behind the cakes displayed in a glass bottle and draped with more gold organza.

Valentine sweet hearts

Gold hearts encrusted with red, purple and pink sugar crystals have been used on this Valentine's cake to complement the boldness of the red rose and sweet violet spray.

MATERIALS

20 cm (8 in) heart-shaped cake placed on a thin cake board of the same size
750 g (1½ lb) white almond paste
1 kg (2 lb) pale pink sugarpaste
Thin red velvet ribbon
Royal icing
Broad red velvet ribbon
Pins or non-toxic craft glue stick (Pritt)
Small amount of white flowerpaste
Edible gold leaf-covered flowerpaste
Red, pink and purple sugar crystals
Clear alcohol (Cointreau or kirsch)
Mug and saucer
Cocoa butter, grated
African violet, vine, white, ruby, aubergine and foliage petal dusts
Pale green flowerpaste
26- and 24-gauge white wires
Fresh egg white
Edible spray varnish
Nile green floristry tape
Food-grade plastic posy pick

EQUIPMENT

30 cm (12 in) round thick cake drum
Non-stick rolling pin
Non-stick board
Heart-shaped cutters (LS)
Fine paintbrush
Beetleweed leaf cutters (AD)
Dresden tool
Galex leaf veiner (SC) or (Aldaval)
Dusting brushes

FLOWERS

1 red rose (p 30–3)
5 red beetleweed leaves (see step 4)
7 sweet violets (p 24–5)
3 stems of Japanese painted fern (p 178)

1 Cover the cake and cake drum as described on p 16–7. Attach a thin band of red velvet ribbon around the base of the cake, using a dab of royal icing or softened sugarpaste to hold it in place at the back. Secure the broader red velvet ribbon to the cake drum's edge using pins or non-toxic craft glue.

SUGAR-ENCRUSTED HEARTS

2 Quickly sprinkle some coloured sugar crystals over some gold leaf-covered flowerpaste (see p 19 for more information) and then roll over them with the non-stick rolling pin to bond them onto the surface. Cut out several heart shapes in various sizes. Attach with clear alcohol to the top edge of the cake and around the cake drum too.

3 Melt some grated cocoa butter onto a dish above a mug filled with just-boiled water. Mix in some African violet, vine and white petal dusts and paint some fine dotted floral designs between the hearts using a fine paintbrush.

BEETLEWEED LEAVES

4 Use the basic leaf-making principle to create these leaves from pale green flowerpaste. Cut out the shape using the beetleweed cutters. Insert a 26- or 24-gauge white wire moistened with fresh egg white into the leaf. Work the edge using the broad end of the Dresden tool to create a more irregular effect to the serrated edge that the cutter gives. Soften the leaf and then vein using the galex leaf veiner. Pinch to accentuate the central vein. Dust in layers of ruby, aubergine and foliage. Allow to dry before spraying with edible spray varnish.

SPRAY ASSEMBLY

5 Using the rose as the focal point, tape together the flowers and the foliage using half-width nile green floristry tape. Insert the posy pick into the cake and then position the handle of the spray into it to complete the cake design.

Mothering Sunday

This charming cake uses the very simple technique of sugar-pressed flowers as its focal decoration. This style of flower-making is ideal for a novice cake decorator or as a fairly quick design for a cake.

MATERIALS

15 cm (6 in) round rich fruitcake placed on a thin cake board of the same size

450 g (12 oz) white almond paste

450 g (12 oz) champagne sugarpaste

Thin lavender ribbon

Royal icing

Foliage, white, vine, African violet, plum, aubergine, white bridal satin, daffodil, sunflower and plum petal dusts

Clear alcohol (Cointreau or kirsch)

Green, white and pale yellow flowerpaste

Black paste food colour

EQUIPMENT

23 cm (9 in) round decorative plate

Fine paintbrush

Non-stick board

Non-stick rolling pin

Set of 3 Australian fern cutters

Australian daisy leaf cutter

Plain-edge cutting wheel or Dresden tool

Dusting brushes

Daisy paper punch

Scalpel

Scriber

Rose petal cutters or pansy set (TT)

Ceramic silk veining tool

Cocktail stick

Clear sugarpaste smoother

SIDE DESIGN

1 Cover the cake as described on p 16. Place the coated cake onto the decorative plate. Attach a band of thin lavender ribbon around the base of the cake, using a dab or royal icing or softened sugarpaste to hold it in place. Tie and attach four small bows evenly spaced onto it.

2 Paint the design onto the sides of the cake using clear alcohol to dilute some foliage, white and vine petal dusts for the foliage section of the design, and then add the dotted flowers using a mixture of white, African violet and plum.

PRESSED LEAVES AND FLOWERS

3 The leaves are very simple to create – on a non-stick board, simply roll some green flowerpaste very thinly and cut out assorted shapes using a selection of fine cutters. Here I have used the Australian fern cutters and a fine daisy leaf cutter. Soften the edges, trying to keep each shape quite flat. Add very light central veins using the plain-edge cutting wheel or the fine end of the Dresden tool. Dust the fern leaves with foliage petal dust. Add tinges of African violet and aubergine to the edges. Dust the fine daisy leaves with foliage and over-dust with white bridal satin. Attach to the top of the cake using clear alcohol painted onto the back of each leaf. It is often best to position the items onto the cake without moistening so that you can create a good display prior to the final attachment. The daisies were cut out from thinly rolled white flowerpaste and a daisy paper punch. The petals were then split using a scalpel blade. The centre of the flowers is a simple ball of pale yellow flowerpaste flattened and textured using the scriber.

4 The pansies can be cut out using a set of pansy cutters which is basically made up from one heart-shaped lip cutter and two sizes of rose petal cutters, or you can use two sizes of rose petal cutters to cut out three large and two smaller petals from some thinly rolled white flowerpaste. Remove a 'V' shape cut from one of the larger petals to create the heart-shaped lip shape. Vein and broaden the lip petal using the ceramic silk veining tool, working on each half of the petal at a time to control an even shape. Frill and thin the edges further with a cocktail stick. Vein and frill the remaining large petals and the two small petals.

5 Overlap the two large petals, moistening to join them and then place the two smaller petals on top at each side followed by the large heart-shaped petal.

Engagement

I have used a painted heart design on this pretty heart-shaped cake to symbolise an engagement, echoed in the curled, almost ring-like, shapes of the beaded wires used in the floral spray along with roses – the flower most often used to demonstrate a couple's love for one other.

MATERIALS

20 cm (8 in) heart-shaped rich fruitcake placed on a thin cake board of the same size

750 g (1 lb 10 oz) white almond paste

1 kg (2 lb) white sugarpaste

Narrow pale pink ribbon

Royal icing

Broad pale pink ribbon

Pins or non-toxic craft glue stick (Pritt)

Tracing or greaseproof paper

Mug and saucer

Cocoa butter, grated

Foliage, vine, white, plum and aubergine petal dusts

Nile green floristry tape

Lilac beaded wires

Food-grade plastic posy pick

EQUIPMENT

30 cm (12 in) heart-shaped cake drum

Fine scriber or pen that has run dry

Paintbrushes

Wire cutters

Fine-nose pliers

FLOWERS

1 pink rose and 1 rosebud, plus foliage (p 30–3)

3 pachyveria succulents (p177)

3 single white chincherinchee flowers (p113)

7 dianthus flowers, plus buds and foliage (p 28–9)

3 green beetleweed leaves (p 169)

1 stem of Japanese painted fern (p178)

PREPARATION

1 Cover the cake and cake drum as described on p 16–7. Attach a band of narrow pale pink ribbon around the base of the cake, using a dab of royal icing or softened sugarpaste to hold it in place at the back. Secure the broader pale pink ribbon to the cake drum's edge using pins or non-toxic craft glue. Leave the cake to dry for a few days before painting the design onto the surface.

CAKE TOP DESIGN

2 Trace the dianthus flower template on p 248 onto tracing or greaseproof paper and scribe it onto the top of the cake using a fine scriber or a pen that has run dry.

3 Melt some grated cocoa butter onto a dish above a mug filled with just-boiled water. Mix in small amounts of petal dust to create the painting medium. Paint the design in layers, allowing each section to set before adding shading and detail. Add some painted dots at the opposite side of the cake, curving up onto the surface of the cake, alternating between a mixture of foliage, vine and white, and plum mixed with white to soften the colours. Add a dark detail at the centre of the dianthus flowers using aubergine petal dust mixed with melted cocoa butter.

SPRAY

4 Use the large rose as the focal point and, using half-width nile green floristry tape, tape the other flowers and foliage around it to create a tapered shape. Bind the flowers together to form a handle for the spray.

5 Cut lengths of lilac beaded wires, turning over each cut end with fine-nose pliers to prevent the beads from escaping. Curl the wires into shape and tape them into the spray to soften the edges of the shape. Insert a posy pick into the side of the cake. Bend the handle of the spray and insert it into the posy pick. Curl and bend the beaded wires to create an attractive shape to fit with the curves of the cake.

Rose and orchid wedding

Brush-embroidered royal-iced roses are used to complement the beautiful sprays of pink and orange roses and orchids on this two-tiered wedding cake.

1 Cover the cakes as described on p 16. Place the leaf shape sugarpaste-coated cake on top of the Perspex board and use the straight-edged sugarpaste smoother to create a good bond between the cake and the board. Attach a band of pink organza ribbon around the base of both cakes, using a dab of royal icing or softened sugarpaste to hold it in place. Leave to dry for a few days before executing the brush embroidery.

BRUSH EMBROIDERY DESIGN

2 This can be traced onto the surface of the coated cakes using the template on p 141 and a fine scriber or a pen that has run dry. Or you might prefer to pipe freestyle to complete the design.

3 You might prefer to add a teaspoon of piping gel to the royal icing to slow down the drying process: use 1 teaspoon of piping gel to 4 tablespoons of royal icing. Colour some of the royal icing pale pink and some to a pale green using rose and gooseberry paste food colours respectively. Fit two piping bags with No.1 tubes and fill with the coloured icings.

4 Using the piping bag filled with pink royal icing, start to pipe over the scribed lines of the rose petals. Apply quite a bit of pressure to give you enough royal icing to brush into a petal shape. Use a brush large enough to fit the design and dampen the bristles slightly with water – don't use too much water as this will swamp the design and dissolve the sugar; if you use too little water, the icing will end up with a dry finish. Brush the petal from the edge, leaving a raised border, and form petal veining as you work. Continue piping and brushing the petals until the rose is complete, following the direction of the veins in the petal.

5 Next, pipe in the rose leaves using the piping bag filled with pale green royal icing. Once again, use a damp paintbrush to create a veining process on each leaf. Leave to dry before painting.

6 Use clear alcohol to dilute the plum petal dust with a touch of white and then the tangerine mixed with plum to colour the rose petals. Add diluted sunflower and daffodil at the base of each petal. Use vine and foliage with a touch of white diluted to colour the leaves. Use a fine paintbrush to add fine painted vine leaves in between each of the roses.

Autumn wedding

This beautiful three-tiered wedding cake is adorned with silver leaf hand-painted flowers and floral displays of fiery brassada orchids, acer leaves and twigs of glossy orange ilex berries, creating a very opulent display perfect for an autumn wedding.

MATERIALS

15-cm (6-in), 18-cm (7-in) and 20-cm (8-in) round rich fruit cakes placed on thin cake boards of the same size

1.4 kg (3 lb) white almond paste

1.8 kg (4 lb) white sugarpaste coloured with tangerine paste food colour

Broad brown velvet ribbon

Non-toxic craft glue stick (Pritt)

Pale tangerine-coloured royal icing

White flowerpaste

Edible silver leaf-covered flowerpaste

Tangerine, aubergine and foliage petal dusts

Clear alcohol (Cointreau or kirsch)

Nile green floristry tape

3 food-grade plastic posy picks

EQUIPMENT

33 cm (13 in) round cake drum

Straight-edged sugarpaste smoother

Shallow Perspex separator

Piping bag fitted with a No.1 piping tube

Floral design paper punch

Fine paintbrushes

Fine-nose pliers

FLOWERS

6 brassada orchids (p 91 –3)

17 acer leaves (p111)

11 sprigs of ilex berries (p 110)

1 Cover the cakes and cake drum as described on p 16–7. Place the large cake on top of the coated cake drum and stack the middle tier on top. Blend the edge using the straight-edged sugarpaste smoother. Leave to dry. Secure a band of broad brown velvet ribbon to the cake drum's edge and the sides of the Perspex separator using non-toxic craft glue.

2 Pipe a snail trail around the base of the two bottom tiers using a piping bag fitted with a No.1 piping tube and filled with pale tangerine-coloured royal icing. Next, Place the shallow separator on top of the middle tier and then position the smallest cake on top.

SILVER LEAF SIDE DESIGN

3 Slide the silver leaf-covered flowerpaste (see p 19 for more information) into the decorative paper punch and stamp out the design. Repeat to create enough sections to decorate the sides of the cakes. Use royal icing to attach the sections around the base of the top tier so that each section hangs below the edge of the cake. Attach several pieces to the sides of the other tiers, as illustrated. Leave to dry.

4 Use tangerine petal dust diluted with a little clear alcohol to add detail paintwork to each flower of the design using a fine paintbrush. Continue in the same way, using diluted aubergine petal dust to paint the stems and add a calyx to each section. Paint fine vine leaves onto the surface of the cake using diluted foliage petal dust – this will help to soften the edges of the design.

SPRAY ASSEMBLY

5 Tape together three floral sprays using half-width nile green floristry tape. Insert three posy picks into the required positions and then insert the handle of the spray into them to complete the creation. Curve the stems of flowers and fruit to frame the side of the cake. Re-adjust the floral elements if required using fine-nose pliers.

White wedding

A bouquet of stephanotis flowers used en masse creates a very elegant and graceful display on this single-tier wedding cake. Once mastered, stephanotis can be produced fairly quickly, making them a useful addition to both the novice and more experienced flower maker's repertoire.

MATERIALS

25-cm (10-in) oval fruitcake
Apricot glaze
Icing sugar
1.25 kg (2 lb 10 oz) white almond paste
Clear alcohol (Cointreau or kirsch)
2 kg (4½ lb) white sugarpaste, to cover the cake and larger board
White royal icing
Gold pearl sugar dragées
White satin ribbon, to trim the board
Non-toxic glue stick (Pritt) or corsage pins
Nile green floristry tape

EQUIPMENT

25-cm (10-in) oval thin cake board
Pastry brush
Large non-stick rolling pin
Make-up sponge
Sugarpaste smoothers
38-cm (15-in) oval thin cake board
Sharp knife
Piping bag and no. 42 piping tube
Nile green floristry tape
Fine-nose pliers
Wire cutters
Pearl effect beads
Green crimped reel wire
Gold paper-covered reel wire

FLOWERS

40–50 stephanotis flowers (see page 156)
10 beetleweed leaves (see page 69)
2 groups of tillandsia foliage (see page 101)
9 stems of trailing succulent, two of which sprayed gold (see page 162)
5 stems of wire vine (see page 71)

PREPARATION

1 Place the cake on to the board of the same size. Brush the cake with warmed apricot glaze and cover with white almond paste. If time allows, leave the cake to dry overnight. Moisten the surface of the almond paste with clear alcohol using a make-up sponge. Cover the cake with sugarpaste and use the sugarpaste smoothers to create a neat finish.

2 Lightly moisten and then cover the larger oval board with sugarpaste. Trim off the excess with a sharp knife. Place the cake in the centre of the covered board. Blend the join between the base of the cake and the board using the straight-edged sugarpaste smoother. Leave the sugarpaste to firm up for a few hours or overnight.

3 Pipe a royal-icing shell border around the base of the cake using the piping bag fitted with a no. 42 piping tube. While the shells are still wet quickly add gold pearl dragées at intervals around the base. Allow to dry.

4 Attach a band of white satin ribbon to the edge of the board using a non-toxic glue stick (or corsage pins) to hold it in place.

ASSEMBLY

5 Gather and tape together the stephanotis flowers a few at a time to create the central posy shape and then encircle the flowers with beetleweed leaves. Next, add the tillandsia leaves into the posy, positioning them opposite each other and gradually add trails of succulents and wire vine, making sure you sweep some of the trailing stems around the top curve of the posy.

6 Weave a gold paper-covered wire nest around the posy section of the bouquet and also to create trails that tangle amongst the foliage. Introduce succulents that have been sprayed gold and also pull in lengths of wired pearl-like beads using green crimped wire to tangle as you work. Tape over the handle of the bouquet with full-width nile green tape. Wrap the handle of the bouquet either with gold paper-covered wire or ribbon.

Summer breeze

This beautiful three-tier wedding cake adorned with delicate sprays of gardenias, orchids, ruscus and gold curls would be ideal for summer nuptials – all that is missing is the exquisite scent of fresh gardenias! If you are decide to use sponge cakes or a combination of fruitcakes and sponge cakes you will need to dowel each layer of the cake. I usually use dummy cakes when creating a stacked cake as they are very heavy to lift.

MATERIALS
13-cm (5-in), 20-cm (8-in) and 28-cm (11in) round rich fruitcakes
Apricot glaze
Icing sugar
3 kg (6 lb) white almond paste
5 kg (10 lb) white sugarpaste, to cover baseboard and cakes
Clear alcohol (kirsch or Cointreau)
Gold organza ribbon, to trim the cakes
Green and gold braid, to double trim the cakes
Small amount of royal icing (optional)
Green velvet ribbon, to trim the baseboard
Non-toxic glue stick (Pritt) or corsage pins
Cocoa butter
Vine green and foliage petal dusts

EQUIPMENT
13-cm (5-in), 20-cm (8-in) and 28-cm (11-in) round thin cake cards
Pastry brush
Rolling pin
Sugarpaste smoothers
40-cm (16-in) round cake board
Make-up sponge
Saucer and mug
Fine paintbrush
3 posy picks

FLOWERS
5 large gardenias (see pages 157–60)
3 half gardenias (see pages 157–60)
3 gardenia buds (see pages 157–60)
15 sprigs of smilax (see page 163)
20 gardenia leaves (see pages 157–60)
6 eyelash orchids (see pages 38–39)

PREPARATION

1 Place the three cakes onto their matching thin cake cards. Brush the cakes with warmed apricot glaze and then cover each one with a layer of white almond paste. Use a curved smoother on the top of the cakes and a straight-edged smoother on the sides to create a neat join at the base of each cake. Leave to dry overnight.

2 Lightly moisten and cover the large baseboard with a layer of white sugarpaste.

3 Use a make-up sponge to apply a thin coat of clear alcohol onto the almond paste on each cake. Cover each cake with white sugarpaste. Use smoothers to create a neat finish. A pad of well-kneaded sugarpaste pressed in the palm of your hand will help to create a more polished finish.

4 Place the largest cake onto the baseboard. Use the straight-edged smoother to neaten and bond the edge of the cake with the board.

ASSEMBLY

5 Attach a band of gold organza ribbon around the base of each cake using royal icing or a small amount of softened sugarpaste. Double the impact with a layer of green and gold braid. Attach a band of green velvet ribbon to the board edge using non-toxic glue or corsage pins.

6 Melt a small amount of cocoa butter on a saucer over a mug of just boiled water. Mix in some vine and foliage green petal dusts to make a pale green paint. Use a fine paintbrush to add a trailing dotted design at intervals around the three tiers and to the baseboard.

SPRAY ASSEMBLY

7 These instructions are for the largest spray. Group together the large gardenia flowers using the largest, prettiest flower at the centre to create the focal point. Tape together using half-width nile green floristry tape. Add the half gardenia flowers and buds towards the edges of the spray. Next, add the smilax leaves around the flowers and create two extensions of this foliage to create an 'S' shape to the spray. Bulk out the spray with the gardenia foliage and finally add the eyelash orchids, taking care as the petals are very fragile. To complete the display, add trails of gold paper-covered wire. Insert the posy picks and sprays in the following positions: the large spray in the top cake, the medium spray in the top of the bottom tier and the small spray in the side at the base of the bottom tier.

Painter's paradise

This vibrant two-tier cake could be used as a wedding cake or birthday cake. The painted gingko leaf side design is fairly quick to create, complementing the gingko leaves in the display. The combination of the tropical, waxy-green anthuriums, with their resemblance to a painter's palette, and the vibrant pink frangipani flowers gives a contrast in texture and colour.

MATERIALS

12.5 cm (5 in) and 20 cm (8 in) round fruitcakes placed on thin cake boards of the same size

1.4 kg (3 lb 2 oz) white almond paste

1.8 kg (4 lb) white sugarpaste

30 cm (12 in) round cake drum

Clear alcohol (Cointreau or kirsch)

Fine and broad soft green satin ribbon

Non-toxic glue stick

Cocoa butter, grated

Mug and saucer

Vine, edelweiss, moss and foliage petal dusts

EQUIPMENT

Straight-edged sugarpaste smoother

Fine paintbrushes

Food-grade plastic posy pick

Fine-nose pliers

PREPARATION

1 Cover the cakes and cake drum as described on pages 16–17. Place the large cake on top of the coated cake drum and blend the join together using the straight-edged sugarpaste smoother. Place the small cake offset on top of the larger cake using a small amount of sugarpaste softened with clear alcohol to hold it in place. Once again use the straight-edged sugarpaste smoother to blend the joins together between the two cakes. Allow to dry overnight.

2 Attach a band of fine soft green satin ribbon around the base of each cake, using a small amount of softened sugarpaste at the back of the cakes to secure the ribbon in place. Secure the broad soft green satin ribbon to the cake drum's edge using non-toxic glue.

GINGKO SIDE DESIGN

3 Melt some grated cocoa butter onto a dish above a mug filled with just-boiled water. Add some vine petal dust to the melted cocoa butter and a touch of edelweiss to create an opaque painting medium. Use a fine paintbrush to paint the leaves freehand onto the sides of the cake. Allow the first layer of colour to set before adding a touch of moss and foliage petal dusts to the painting medium. Add depth and detail veining on top of the gingko leaves to complete the design.

4 Assemble the bouquet. Insert a food-grade plastic posy pick into the top tier and insert the handle of the bouquet into it. Curve and trail the length of the bouquet around the cake. Use fine-nose pliers to reposition any of the flowers or foliage that might need a tweak to make them fit in with the shape of the cake design.

Perfumed perfection

White perfume flowers form a stunning focal point to this beautiful cake design that would be wonderful as a small wedding or anniversary celebration cake. The delicate twisted petals of ylang-ylang flowers create lots of movement within the bouquet.

MATERIALS

25 cm (10 in) oval rich fruitcake placed on a thin cake board of the same size

35 cm (14 in) oval cake drum

1.25 kg (2 lb 12 oz) white almond paste

1.25 kg (2 lb 12 oz) white sugarpaste

Thin green and lemon striped ribbon

Clear alcohol (Cointreau or kirsch)

Broad pale lemon satin ribbon

Non-toxic glue stick

EQUIPMENT

Straight-edged and rounded-edged sugarpaste smoothers

Food-grade plastic posy pick

Fine-nose pliers

FLOWERS

Perfumed perfection bouquet (p 180)

1 Cover the cake and cake drum as described on pages 11–12. Allow to dry overnight. Transfer the cake centrally onto the drum and use the straight-edged sugarpaste smoother to blend the join between the base of the cake and the drum together. Next, polish the surface of the cake using a pad of sugarpaste pressed into your palm.

2 Attach a band of thin green and lemon striped ribbon around the base of the cake using a little sugarpaste softened with clear alcohol to hold it in place at the back of the cake. Secure the broad pale yellow satin ribbon to the cake drum's edge using non-toxic glue.

3 Insert the posy pick into the top of the cake and insert the handle of the bouquet into it. Use fine-nose pliers to gently reposition and curve any of the flower and leaf stems that require it.

Moon and sun

The blue moon-like qualities of the beak of this flower and the stark contrast of the sunray-like petals form a striking combination on this unusual and stunning celebration cake that would be suitable as a birthday cake or perhaps a sapphire wedding anniversary cake!

MATERIALS

20 cm (8 in) round rich fruitcake placed on a thin cake board of the same size

750 g (1 lb 10 oz) white almond paste

750 g (1 lb 10 oz) white sugarpaste

Light gold satin ribbon

Clear alcohol (Cointreau or kirsch)

Small amount of white flowerpaste

White bridal satin dust

Vine and foliage petal dusts

Silver cake stand

Food-grade plastic posy pick

EQUIPMENT

Non-stick rolling pin

Non-stick board

Tiny monstera leaf cutter (Ai-mizuke)

Foam pad

Small metal ball tool

Plain-edge cutting wheel

Small dusting brush

Fine paintbrush

Fine-nose pliers

FLOWERS

Moon and sun bouquet (p 50)

PREPARATION

1 Cover the cake as described on pages 11–12. Leave to dry overnight. Attach a band of light gold satin ribbon around the base of the cake using a small amount of sugarpaste softened with clear alcohol to hold it in place.

SIDE DESIGN

2 Roll out some well-kneaded white flowerpaste thinly onto the non-stick board. Use the tiny monstera leaf cutter to cut out several leaf shapes. Place the leaves onto the foam pad and soften the edges using the small metal ball tool.

3 Use the small end of the plain-edge cutting wheel to mark a central vein down each leaf and then add a single side vein to each of the leaf sections. Pick up each leaf and pinch it from the base through to the tip to accentuate the central vein.

4 Attach the leaves to the side and the top surface of the cake using clear alcohol to secure them in place. Leave to dry and then set in place.

5 Next, mix together some white bridal satin dust with a touch of vine petal dust. Use a small dusting brush to gently colour the cut-out leaves, taking care not to get the colour onto the surrounding areas of the cake. Add some detail veining using a fine paintbrush and a mixture of vine and foliage petal dusts diluted with clear alcohol.

ASSEMBLY

6 Place the cake onto the silver cake stand. Assemble the sprays as described on page 50. Insert a food-grade posy pick into the upper surface of the cake. Insert the handle of the larger spray into the posy pick. Use fine-nose pliers to rearrange the various elements of the spray to create a more balanced display on the cake. Create a second smaller spray using remaining flowers and foliage. Place the smaller spray at the base of the silver cake stand to complete the design.

Magical sensation

The intense striped markings of the scorpion orchids are a perfect match for this beautiful dark red rose. The pattern created by the umbrella tree stalks provided very simple inspiration for the painted design on this striking birthday or ruby anniversary cake.

MATERIALS

1 kg (2 lb 3 oz) white almond paste
1.5 kg (3 lb 5 oz) white sugarpaste
23 cm (9 in) heart-shaped rich fruitcake placed on a thin cake board of the same size
33 cm (13 in) heart-shaped cake drum
Vine green paste food colour
Fine and broad dark red satin ribbon
Clear alcohol (Cointreau or kirsch)
Non-toxic glue stick
Food-grade plastic posy pick
Aubergine, ruby and vine petal dusts

EQUIPMENT

Fine-nose pliers
Very fine and fine paintbrushes

FLOWERS

Magical sensation spray (p 72)
4 umbrella tree stalks (p 71)

PREPARATION

1 Colour the white sugarpaste with a little vine green paste food colour. Leave to rest a little before coating the cake and cake drum as described on pages 11–12. Attach a fine band of dark red satin ribbon around the base of the cake, using a small amount of sugarpaste softened with clear alcohol. Secure the broad dark red satin ribbon to the cake drum's edge using non-toxic glue.

2 Tape the flowers and foliage together as described on page 72. Insert the posy pick into the top of the cake and then insert the handle of the spray into it. Use fine-nose pliers to re-adjust any of the flowers that might need it to create a more pleasing effect once the flowers are on the cake.

SIDE DESIGN

3 Dilute a small amount of aubergine and ruby petal dusts with clear alcohol. Use a very fine paintbrush to create the spoke-like stems of the umbrella tree directly onto the cake and the cake drum. Next, dilute a small amount of vine petal dust and use a fine paintbrush to add a dot at the very centre of the spokes.

4 To complete the display, tuck a few extra umbrella tree stalks around the base of the cake.

Tranquil waters

The crystal-filled glass cake stand lends an almost floating, tranquil platform for this pretty celebration cake that would be suitable for a small birthday celebration or anniversary. A single blue water lily creates a very calm vibe to this design.

MATERIALS

15 cm (6 in) round fruitcake placed on a thin cake board of the same size

350 g (12 oz) white almond paste

350 g (12 oz) white sugarpaste

Crystal-filled glass cake stand (or similar)

Purple organza ribbon

Clear alcohol (Cointreau or kirsh)

Silver organza ribbon

Food-grade plastic posy pick

EQUIPMENT

Straight-sided sugarpaste smoother

Fine-nose pliers

FLOWERS

Tranquil waters spray (p 186)

PREPARATION

1 Coat the cake as described on pages 16–17. Position it on top of the glass cake stand and use the straight-sided sugarpaste smoother to blend and neaten the join between the cake and the stand.

2 Attach a band of purple organza ribbon around the base of the cake, using a small amount of sugarpaste softened with clear alcohol to hold it in place. Layer a length of silver organza ribbon over the top. Leave to dry.

3 Assemble the blue water lily spray as described on page 186. Insert the posy pick into the top surface of the cake and insert the handle of the spray into it. Use fine-nose pliers to reposition any of the flowers and leaves that require it to create a more pleasing connection between the cake and the floral display.

Chasing rainbows

The colourful braid around the base of the cake was the inspiration for this cute birthday cake. This design illustrates that you do not need to use many flowers on a cake to create a pretty design.

MATERIALS
15-cm (6-in) round rich fruitcake
Apricot glaze
Icing sugar
350 g (12 oz) white almond paste
Clear alcohol (Cointreau or Kirsch)
450 g (1 lb) white sugarpaste, to cover cake
   and board
White royal icing
Multicoloured daisy braid, to trim the cake
Broad silver satin ribbon, to trim the board
Non-toxic glue stick (Pritt) (or a couple
   of large corsage pins)
Nile green floristry tape
Pink, blue, orange, purple, green and yellow
   paper-covered wires

EQUIPMENT
15-cm (6-in) thin round cake card
Pastry brush
Non-stick large rolling pin
Make-up sponge
Sugarpaste smoothers
23-cm (9-in) round cake board
Sharp knife
Piping bag and no. 42 rope piping tube
Fine-nose pliers
Posy pick

FLOWERS
1 rangoon creeper (see pages 172–3)

PREPARATION

1 Place the cake on the cake card. Brush the cake with warmed apricot glaze and cover with almond paste. Allow to dry overnight if time allows. Use a make-up sponge to moisten the surface of the almond paste with clear alcohol and then cover with white sugarpaste. Use sugarpaste smoothers to create a smooth, neat finish. Allow to dry.

2 Cover the cake board with white sugarpaste. Trim off the excess using a sharp knife and then position the cake centrally on top. Use a straight-edged smoother to create a neat join between the cake and the board. Allow to dry.

DECORATION

3 Fit a piping bag with a no. 42 rope piping tube and fill with white royal icing. Pipe a shell border around the base of the cake. Allow to dry. Attach a band of colourful braid above the piped border using a small amount of royal icing at the back of the cake.

4 Secure a band of silver satin ribbon to the board edge using a non-toxic glue stick or a couple of large corsage pins.

FLOWERS

5 Take several lengths of multicoloured paper-covered wires and twist together at one end. Create an open loop and then start to plait the remaining length together to form a long tail. Add the large rose to form the focal point of the spray. Complete the display with the rangoon creeper flowers and foliage. Insert a posy pick into the cake and place the handle of the spray into it. Reshape the plaited wires if needed.

Silver trail

Using a large posy of flowers on top of a fairly small cake makes a very bold statement that requires plenty of space in the rest of the cake design. The silver cut-out leaves at the base of the cake and the trails of metallic crimped wires help to balance and also soften the design as a whole.

MATERIALS
18-cm (7-in) round fruitcake
Apricot glaze
750 g (1 lb 10 oz) white almond paste
Icing sugar
Clear alcohol (Cointreau or kirsch)
900 g (2 lb) white sugarpaste, to cover cake and larger board
White royal icing
White satin ribbon, to trim cake board
Non-toxic glue stick (Pritt) (or large corsage pins)
White flowerpaste
Edible silver leaf (SK)
Pale blue pearl dragées
Vine, foliage and white petal dusts

EQUIPMENT
18-cm (7-in) round thin cake board
Pastry brush
Large non-stick rolling pin
Sugarpaste smoothers
Make-up sponge
25-cm (10-in) round cake board
Piping bag and no. 42 piping tube
Non-stick board
Small non-stick rolling pin
Monstera leaf paper punch
Fine paintbrush
Posy pick

FLOWERS
Silver trail posy (see pages 174–5)

PREPARATION

1 Place the cake on to the cake board of the same size. Brush the cake with warmed apricot glaze and cover with almond paste. Leave to dry overnight. Moisten the surface of the almond paste with clear alcohol using a make-up sponge and cover with sugarpaste. Use the smoothers to create a neat result. Lightly moisten the second cake board with clear alcohol and cover with a layer of white sugarpaste. Transfer the coated cake to the covered board and blend the bottom edge of the cake to the board with the straight-edged smoother. Leave to dry overnight.

2 Using a piping bag fitted with a no. 42 tube and filled with white royal icing, pipe a small shell trail around the base of the cake. Leave to set for a few hours. Attach a band of white satin ribbon to the edge of the board using non-toxic glue stick or corsage pins.

SILVER LEAVES

3 Roll out a small amount of well-kneaded white flowerpaste very thinly on to a non-stick board. Peel back the paste to reveal the sticky side. Place the sticky side of the paste on top of a sheet of silver leaf. Rub over the paste to secure the two mediums together. Turn the paste over to reveal the silver side and trim away any excess paste from the edges. Allow the paste to rest for about 10 or 20 minutes before using it in the paper punch.

4 Cut out several monstera leaves using the paper punch. Cut out extras to use at a later stage as the silver is expensive, so you really should not waste any. Allow the leaves to dry.

5 Attach the silver leaves at intervals around the base of the cake using tiny amounts of royal icing. Place a single pale blue pearl dragée on each silver leaf and secure with a tiny dot of royal icing.

6 Mix a 'paint' using vine, foliage and white petal dusts diluted with clear alcohol. Paint a few dots on each leaf using a fine paintbrush.

ASSEMBLY

Insert a posy pick into the cake and place the posy handle into it to settle the flowers in place. Angle the posy slightly and reshape any of the flower or wire components as required.

Christmas celebration

A sugar-frosted white tree is the focal point of this festive cake. I have arranged the flowers and fruit next to the cake to complete the design – however, the tree design also works well by itself if you are short of time!

1 Cover the cake as described on p 16-17. Attach the cake to the decorative base using a small amount of sugarpaste softened with a little clear alcohol. Use the sugarpaste smoothers to apply pressure and also blend the paste down onto the base to create a good bond. Attach a band of green velvet ribbon around the base of the cake, using a dab of royal icing or softened sugarpaste to hold it in place. Leave to dry.

FROSTED TREE

2 Mix together equal proportions of white sugarpaste and white flowerpaste. Roll out the paste quite thickly and cut out a freehand tree shape using the plain-edge cutting wheel. Cut into the edges of the tree shape using the plain-edge cutting wheel to create a more feathered edge.

3 Moisten the back of the tree with clear alcohol and place it on top of the cake. Cut into the edges if needed and then cut into the body of the tree with fine scissors. Flick the snipped sections to give more curves to the shape. Use the plain-edge cutting wheel to create a bark texture to the trunk.

4 Dust the tree with bridal satin petal dust and the trunk with nutkin. Embed some gold dragées at intervals in the tree.

5 Cut out some baubles from gold leaf-covered flowerpaste (see p 19 for more information) using the circle cutter, and some stars using either star cutters or rose calyx cutters. Attach the largest star at the top of the tree and the baubles and smaller stars dotted around at intervals.

6 Finally sprinkle the whole tree with granulated sugar to give a frosted finish. Arrange the flowers and fruit into a cresent-shaped spray using half-width nile green floristry tape. Insert a posy pick into the side of the cake and insert the handle of the spray into it. Curve the stems of flowers and fruit to frame the side of the cake.

3

TEMPLATES

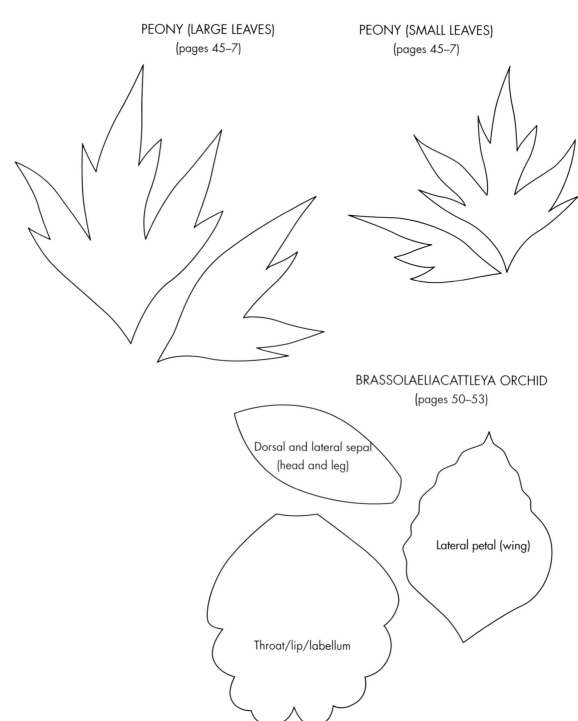

PEONY (LARGE LEAVES)
(pages 45–7)

PEONY (SMALL LEAVES)
(pages 45–7)

BRASSOLAELIACATTLEYA ORCHID
(pages 50–53)

Dorsal and lateral sepal
(head and leg)

Lateral petal (wing)

Throat/lip/labellum

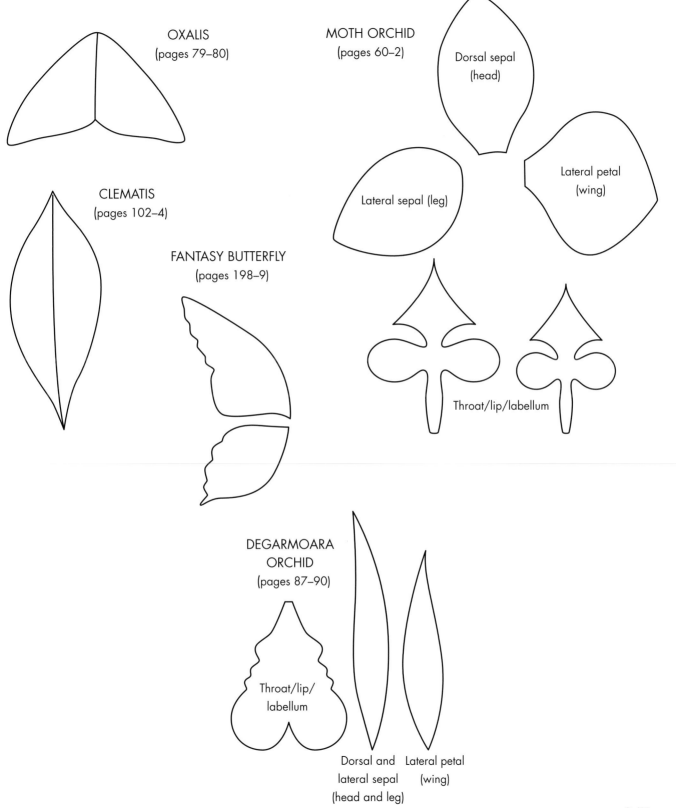

OXALIS
(pages 79–80)

MOTH ORCHID
(pages 60–2)

Dorsal sepal
(head)

Lateral petal
(wing)

Lateral sepal (leg)

CLEMATIS
(pages 102–4)

FANTASY BUTTERFLY
(pages 198–9)

Throat/lip/labellum

DEGARMOARA
ORCHID
(pages 87–90)

Throat/lip/
labellum

Dorsal and
lateral sepal
(head and leg)

Lateral petal
(wing)

ROSE AND ORCHID
WEDDING
(pages 222–3)

ENGAGEMENT
(pages 220–1)

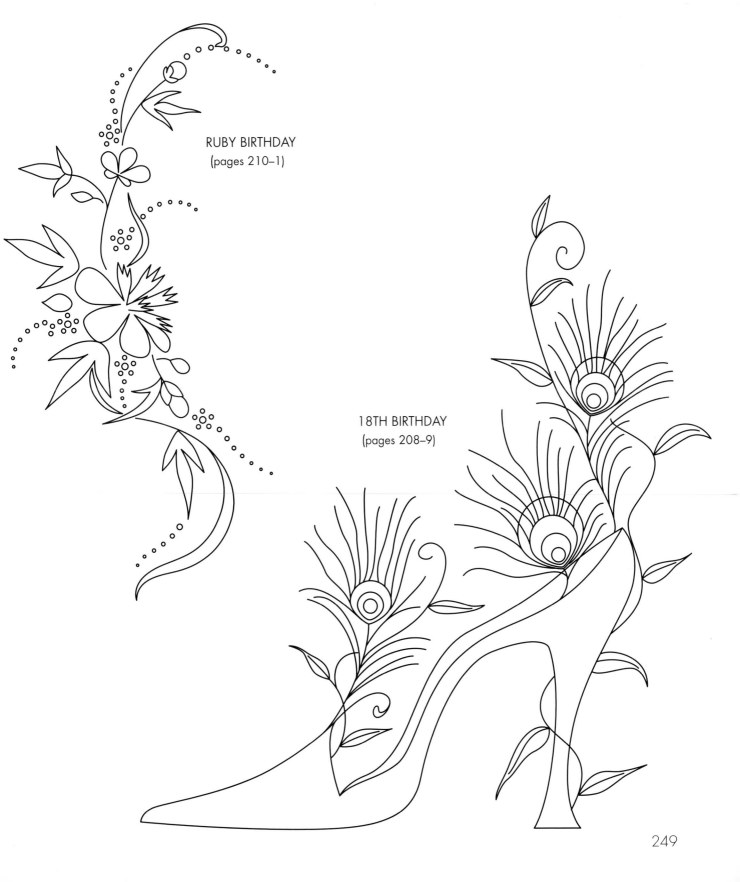

RUBY BIRTHDAY
(pages 210–1)

18TH BIRTHDAY
(pages 208–9)

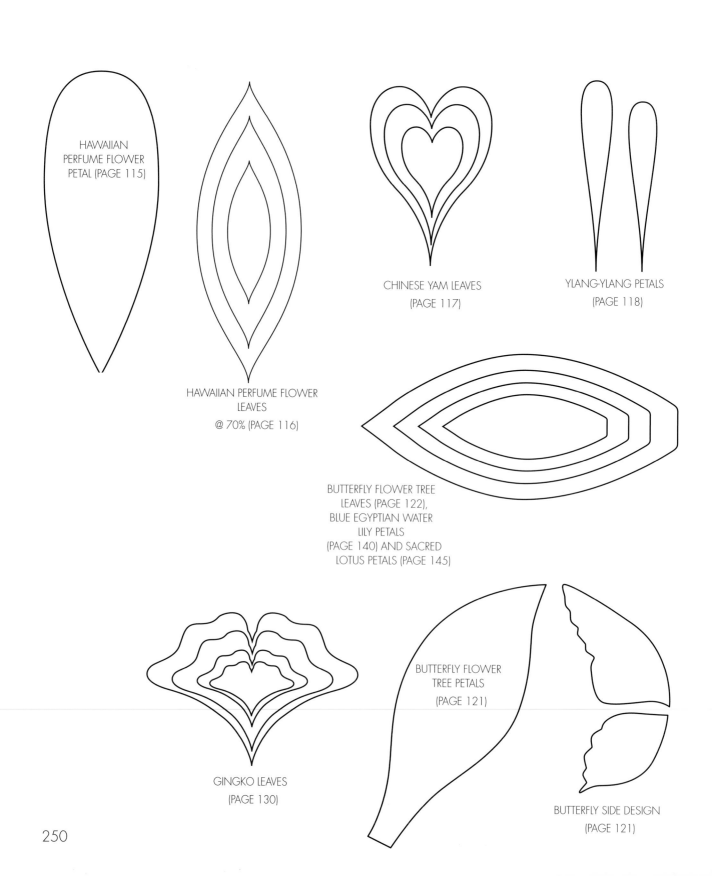

HAWAIIAN
PERFUME FLOWER
PETAL (PAGE 115)

HAWAIIAN PERFUME FLOWER
LEAVES
@ 70% (PAGE 116)

CHINESE YAM LEAVES
(PAGE 117)

YLANG-YLANG PETALS
(PAGE 118)

BUTTERFLY FLOWER TREE
LEAVES (PAGE 122),
BLUE EGYPTIAN WATER
LILY PETALS
(PAGE 140) AND SACRED
LOTUS PETALS (PAGE 145)

GINGKO LEAVES
(PAGE 130)

BUTTERFLY FLOWER
TREE PETALS
(PAGE 121)

BUTTERFLY SIDE DESIGN
(PAGE 121)

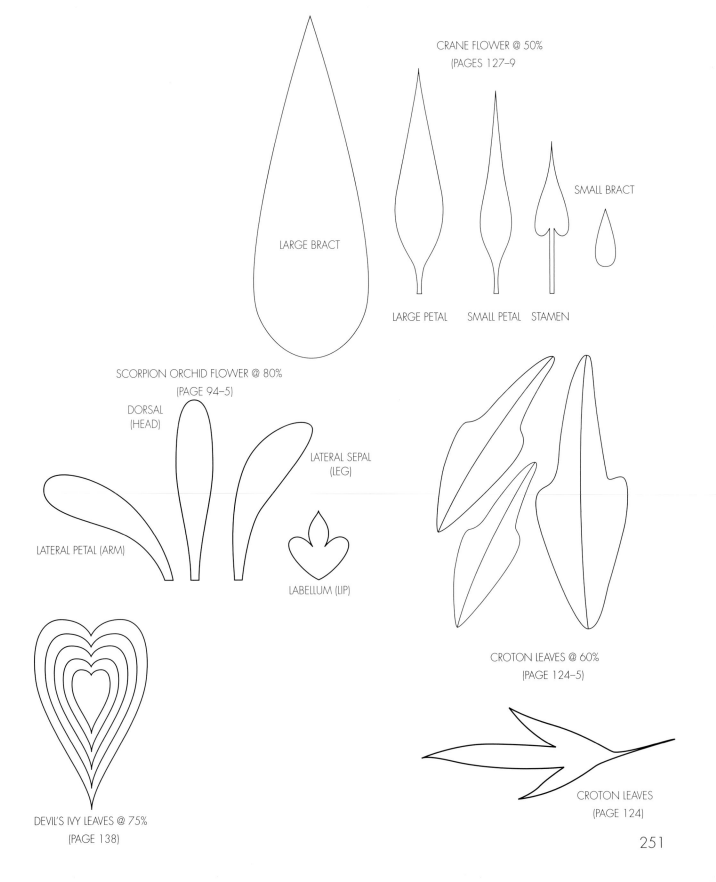

LARGE BRACT

CRANE FLOWER @ 50%
(PAGES 127–9

SMALL BRACT

LARGE PETAL   SMALL PETAL   STAMEN

SCORPION ORCHID FLOWER @ 80%
(PAGE 94–5)

DORSAL
(HEAD)

LATERAL SEPAL
(LEG)

LATERAL PETAL (ARM)

LABELLUM (LIP)

CROTON LEAVES @ 60%
(PAGE 124–5)

DEVIL'S IVY LEAVES @ 75%
(PAGE 138)

CROTON LEAVES
(PAGE 124)

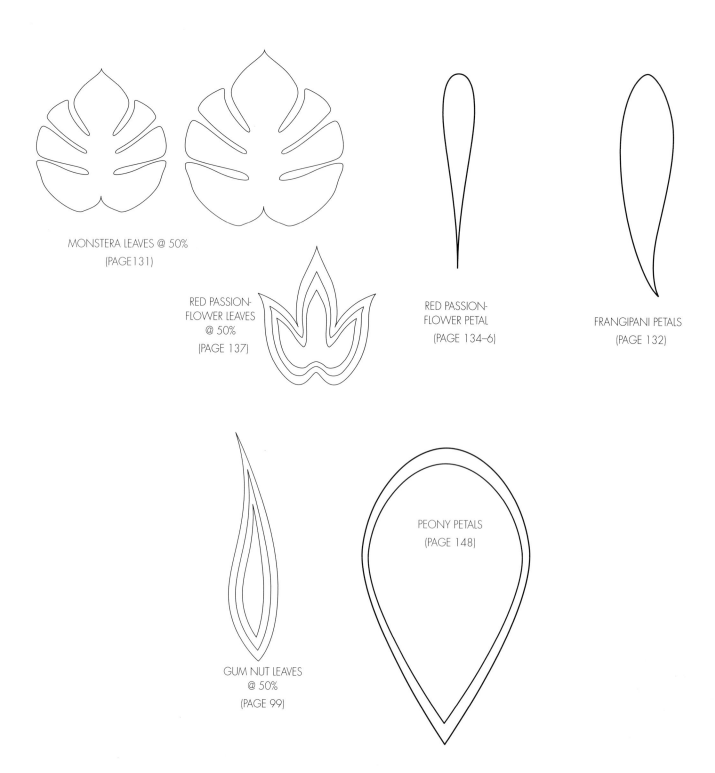

MONSTERA LEAVES @ 50%

(PAGE131)

RED PASSION-
FLOWER LEAVES
@ 50%

(PAGE 137)

RED PASSION-
FLOWER PETAL

(PAGE 134–6)

FRANGIPANI PETALS

(PAGE 132)

GUM NUT LEAVES
@ 50%

(PAGE 99)

PEONY PETALS
(PAGE 148)

ANEMONE PETALS,
LARGE AND SMALL
(PAGES 63–5)

BEETLEWEED LEAVES,
LARGE AND SMALL
(PAGE 169)

HEART'S DESIRE ORCHID (PAGES 151–2)

BEGONIA LEAVES,
LARGE AND SMALL
(PAGE 49)

ANEMONE LEAF
(PAGES 65)

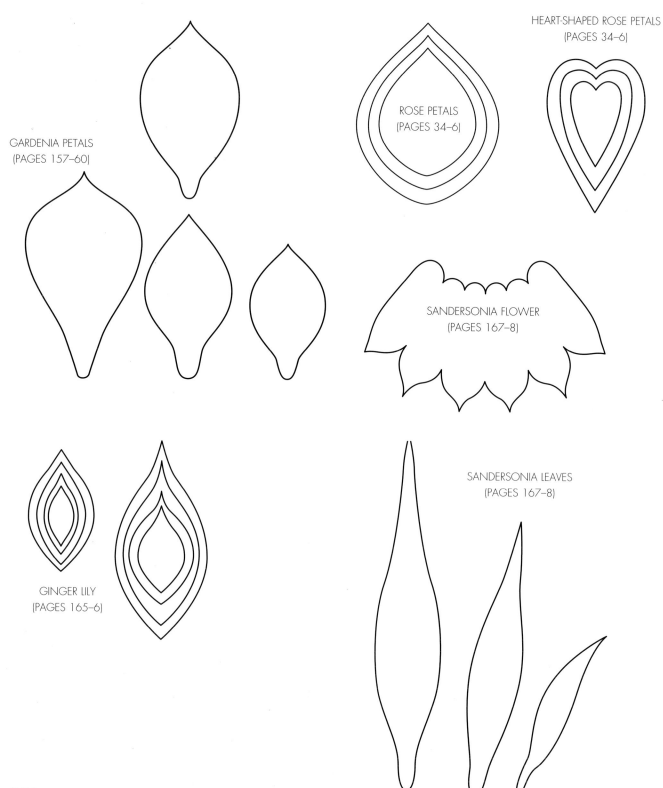

HEART-SHAPED ROSE PETALS
(PAGES 34–6)

GARDENIA PETALS
(PAGES 157–60)

ROSE PETALS
(PAGES 34–6)

SANDERSONIA FLOWER
(PAGES 167–8)

SANDERSONIA LEAVES
(PAGES 167–8)

GINGER LILY
(PAGES 165–6)

SUPPLIERS

A Piece of Cake
18 Upper High Street
Thame
Oxon OX9 3EX, England
www.sugaricing.com

Aldaval Veiners (ALDV)
16 Chibburn Court
Widdrington
Morpeth
Northumberland NE61 5QT
+44 (0)1670 790 995

Cakes, Classes & Cutters
23 Princes Road
Brunton Park
Gosforth
Newcastle-upon-Tyne NE3 5TT
wwwcakesclassesandcutters.co.uk

CelCakes & CelCrafts (CC)
Springfield House
Gate Helmsley
York YO41 1NF
www.celcrafts.co.uk

Celebrations
Unit 383 G
Jedburgh Court
Gateshead
Newcastle-upon-Tyne
NE11 0BQ
www.celebrations-teamvalley.co.uk

Culpitt
Jubilee Industrial Estate
Ashington
Northumberland NE63 8UQ
www.culpitt.com

Design-a-Cake
30–31 Phoenix Road
Crowther Industrial Estate
Washington
Tyne & Wear NE38 0AD
www.design-a-cake.co.uk

Guy, Paul & Co Ltd
 (UK distributor for Jem cutters)
Unit 10, The Business Centre
Corinium Industrial Estate
Raans Road
Amersham
Buckinghamshire HP6 6EB
www.guypaul.co.uk

Holly Products (HP)
Primrose Cottage
Church Walk
Norton in Hales
Shropshire TF9 4QX
www.hollyproductsco.uk

Items for Sugarcraft
72 Godstone Road
Kenley
Surrey CR8 AA
www.itemsforsugarcraft.co.uk

Orchard Cake Tools (OP)
www.orchardcaketools.com
(Note: Temporarily closed at time of print)

The British Sugarcraft Guild
for more information contact:
Wellington House
Messeter Place
Eltham
London SE9 5DP www.bsguk.org

The Old Bakery
Kingston St Mary
Taunton
Somerset TA2 8HW
www.oldbakery.co.uk

Tinkertech Two (TT)
27 Florence Road
Poole
Dorset BH14 9JF
+44 (0)1202 738 049

Squires Kitchen (SKGI)
Squires House
3 Waverley Lane
Farnham
Surrey GU9 8BB
www.squires-shop.com

PME
Knightsbridge Bakeware Centre
Unit 23, Riverwalk Road
Enfield
Essex EN3 7QN
www.cakedecoration.co.uk

AUSTRALIA
My Cake Delights
219 High Street
Preston
Victoria 3072
www.mycakedelights.com.au

Contact the author
www.alandunnsugarcraft.com

First published in 2012 by
New Holland Publishers
London • Sydney • Cape Town • Auckland
www.newhollandpublishers.com

Garfield House 86–88 Edgware Road London W2 2EA United Kingdom
1/66 Gibbes Street Chatswood NSW 2067 Australia
Wembley Square First Floor Solan Road Gardens Cape Town 8001 South Africa
218 Lake Road Northcote Auckland New Zealand

A catalogue record of this book is available at the British Library and the National Library
of Australia

ISBN: 9781780092553

Publisher: Fiona Schultz
Publishing director: Lliane Clarke
Design: Lucy Partissi
Photography: Sue Atkinson
Cover designer: Kimberley Pearce
Production director: Olga Dementiev
Printer: Toppan Leefung Printing Limited

10 9 8 7 6 5 4 3 2 1

Follow New Holland Publishers on
Facebook: www.facebook.com/NewHollandPublishers